PIMLICO

558

MASTER OF MIDDLE-EARTH

Paul H. Kocher was born in Trinidad in 1907, but became an American citizen after moving to New York with his family. He taught courses on the whole range of English literature and its background at a number of American colleges and universities, including the Universities of Washington, Nebraska and Stanford (California). After retiring from Stanford in 1970, his chief preoccupation was the research for his book on Tolkien's works, which he admired for many years. Professor Kocher's other books include *Christopher Marlowe* (1946) and *Science and Religion in Elizabethan England* (1955).

MASTER OF MIDDLE-EARTH

The Achievement of J.R.R. Tolkien

———

PAUL KOCHER

PIMLICO

Published by Pimlico 2002

2 4 6 8 10 9 7 5 3 1

First published in Great Britain by Thames & Hudson 1973
Pimlico edition 2002

Pimlico
Random House, 20 Vauxhall Bridge Road,
London SW1V 2SA

Random House Australia (Pty) Limited
20 Alfred Street, Milsons Point, Sydney,
New South Wales 2061, Australia

Random House New Zealand Limited
18 Poland Road, Glenfield,
Auckland 10, New Zealand

Random House South Africa (Pty) Limited
Endulini, 5A Jubilee Road, Parktown 2193, South Africa

The Random House Group Limited Reg. No. 954009
www.randomhouse.co.uk

A CIP catalogue record for this book
is available from the British Library

ISBN 0-7126-3697-8

Papers used by Random House UK Limited are natural,
recyclable products made from wood grown in sustainable forests;
the manufacturing processes conform to the environmental
regulations of the country of origin.

Printed and bound in Great Britain by
Mackays of Chatham PLC

Contents

Master of Middle-earth

CHAPTER I

Middle-earth:
An Imaginary World?

In 1938 when Tolkien was starting to write *The Lord of the Rings* he also delivered a lecture at the University of St. Andrews in which he offered his views on the types of world that it is the office of fantasy, including his own epic, to "sub-create," as he calls it. Unlike our primary world of daily fact, fantasy's "secondary worlds" of the imagination must possess, he said, not only "internal consistency" but also "strangeness and wonder" arising from their "freedom from the domination of observed fact." [1] If this were all, the secondary worlds of faery would often be connected only very tenuously with the primary world. But Tolkien knew, none better, that no audience can long feel sympathy or interest for persons or things in which they cannot recognize a good deal of themselves and the world of their everyday experience. He therefore added that a secondary world must be "credible, commanding Secondary Belief." And he manifestly expected that secondary worlds would combine the ordinary with the extraordinary, the fictitious with the actual: "*Faërie* contains many things besides elves and fays, and besides dwarfs, witches, trolls, giants or dragons: it holds the seas, the sun, the moon, the sky; and the earth and all things that are in it: tree and bird, water and stone, wine and bread, and ourselves, mortal men, when we are enchanted."

Tolkien followed his own prescription in composing *The Lord of the Rings*, or perhaps he formulated the prescription to justify what he was already intending to write. In either case the answer to the question posed by the title of this chapter is "Yes, but—." Yes, Middle-earth is a place of many marvels. But they are all carefully fitted into a framework of climate and geography, familiar skies by night, familiar shrubs and trees, beasts and birds on earth by day, men and manlike creatures with societies not too different from our own. Consequently the reader walks through any Middle-earth landscape with a security of recognition that woos him on to believe in everything that happens. Familiar but not too familiar, strange but not too strange. This is the master rubric that Tolkien bears always in mind when inventing the world of his epic. In applying the formula in just the right proportions in the right situations consists much of his preeminence as a writer of fantasy.

Fundamental to Tolkien's method in *The Lord of the Rings* is a standard literary pose which he assumes in the Prologue and never thereafter relinquishes even in the Appendices: that he did not himself invent the subject matter of the epic but is only a modern scholar who is compiling, editing, and eventually translating copies of very ancient records of Middle-earth which have come into his hands, he does not say how. To make this claim sound plausible he constructs an elaborate family tree for these records, tracing some back to personal narratives by the four hobbit heroes of the War of the Ring, others to manuscripts found in libraries at Rivendell and Minas Tirith, still others to oral tradition.[2] Then, in order to help give an air of credibility to his account of the War, Tolkien endorses it as true and calls it history, that is, an authentic narrative of events as they actually happened in the Third Age. This accolade of history and historical records he bestows frequently in both Prologue and Appen-

dices. With the Shire Calendar in the year 1601 of the Third
Age, states the Prologue, ". . . legend among the Hobbits
first becomes history with a reckoning of years." A few
pages farther on, Bilbo's 111th birthday is said to have occurred in Shire year 1401: "At this point this History begins." And in Appendix F Tolkien declares editorially, "The
language represented in this history by English was the *Westron* or 'Common Speech' of the West-lands of Middle-earth
in the Third Age."³

Many writers of fantasy would have stopped at this point.
But Tolkien has a constitutional aversion to leaving Middle-
earth afloat too insubstantially in empty time and place, or
perhaps his literary instincts warn him that it needs a local
habitation and a name. Consequently he takes the further
crucial step of identifying it as our own green and solid Earth
at some quite remote epoch in the past. He is able to accomplish this end most handily in the Prologue and Appendices,
where he can sometimes step out of the role of mere editor
and translator into the broader character of commentator on
the peoples and events in the manuscripts he is handling. And
he does it usually by comparing conditions in the Third Age
with what they have since become in our present.

About the hobbits, for instance, the Prologue informs the
reader that they are "relations of ours," closer than elves or
dwarves, though the exact nature of this blood kinship is lost
in the mists of time. We and they have somehow become
"estranged" since the Third Age, and they have dwindled in
physical size since then. Most striking, however, is the news
that "those days, the Third Age of Middle-earth, are now
long past, and the shape of all lands has been changed; but the
regions in which Hobbits then lived were doubtless the same
as those in which they still linger: the North-West of the Old
World, east of the Sea."

There is much to digest here. The Middle-earth on which

the hobbits lived is our Earth as it was long ago. Moreover, they are still here, and though they hide from us in their silent way, some of us have sometimes seen them and passed them on under other names into our folklore. Furthermore, the hobbits still live in the region they call the Shire, which turns out to be "the North-West of the Old World, east of the Sea." This description can only mean northwestern Europe, however much changed in topography by eons of wind and wave.

Of course, the maps of Europe in the Third Age drawn by Tolkien to illustrate his epic show a continent very different from that of today in its coastline, mountains, rivers, and other major geographical features. In explanation he points to the forces of erosion, which wear down mountains, and to advances and recessions of the sea that have inundated some lands and uncovered others. Singing of his ancestor Durin, Gimli voices dwarf tradition of a time when the earth was newly formed and fair, "the mountains tall" as yet unweathered, and the face of the moon as yet unstained by marks now visible on it. Gandalf objects to casting the One Ring into the ocean because "there are many things in the deep waters; and seas and lands may change." Treebeard can remember his youth when he wandered over the countries of Tasarinan, Ossiriand, Neldoreth, and Dorthonion, "And now all those lands lie under the wave." At their parting Galadriel guesses at some far distant future when "the lands that lie under the wave are lifted up again" and she and Treebeard may meet once more on the meadows of Tasarinan. Bombadil recalls a distant past, "before the seas were bent." By many such references Tolkien achieves for Middle-earth long perspectives backward and forward in geological time.

One episode in particular, the reign of Morgoth from his stronghold of Thangorodrim somewhere north of the Shire for the three thousand years of the First Age, produces great changes in Middle-earth geography. To bring about his over-throw the Guardian Valar release titanic natural forces, which cause the ocean to drown not only his fortress but a vast area around it, including the elf kingdoms of Beleriand, Nargothrond, Gondolin, Nogrod, and Belagost. Of that stretch of the northwestern coast only Lindon remains above the waves to appear on Tolkien's Third Age maps. The flooding of rebellious Númenor by the One at the end of the Second Age is a catastrophe of equal magnitude. But Tolkien gives the realm of Morgoth an extra level of allusiveness by describing it as so bitterly cold that after its destruction "those colds linger still in that region, though they lie hardly more than a hundred leagues north of the Shire." He goes on to describe the Forodwaith people living there as "Men of far-off days," who have snow houses, like igloos, and sleds and skis much like those of Eskimos. Add the fact that the Witch-king of Angmar (hereafter called simply Angmar), Morgoth's henchman, has powers that wane in summer and wax in winter and it becomes hard not to associate Morgoth in some way with a glacial epoch, as various commentators have already done. In his essay "On Fairy-stories" Tolkien refuses to interpret the Norse god Thórr as a mere personification of thunder.[4] Along the same lines, it is not his intention, I think, to portray Morgoth as a personification of an Ice Age. However, it would seem compatible with his meaning to consider Morgoth a spirit of evil whose powers have engendered the frozen destructiveness of such an age.

The possibility thus raised of fixing the three Ages of Middle-earth in some interglacial lull in the Pleistocene is tempting, and may be legitimate, provided that we do not start looking about for exact data to establish precise chronologies.[5] The data are not there, and Tolkien has no intention whatever of supplying them. The art of fantasy flourishes on reticence. To the question how far in Earth's past the Ages of

Middle-earth lie, Tolkien gives essentially the storyteller's answer: Once upon a time — and never ask what time. Choose some interglacial period if you must, he seems to say, but do not expect me to bind myself by an admission that you are right. Better for you not to be too sure.

Tolkien's technique of purposeful ambivalence is well shown too in the Mûmak of Harad, which Sam sees fighting on the side of the Southrons against Faramir's men in Ithilien: ". . . indeed a beast of vast bulk, and the like of him does not now walk in Middle-earth; his kin that live still in the latter days are but memories of his girth and majesty." As compared with its "kin," the elephant of today, the ancestral Mûmak was far more massive.[6] Is Tolkien hinting that it is a mammoth? Perhaps, but it is not shaggy, it is coming up from the warm south, and it is totally unknown to the hobbits farther north, where that sort of creature might be expected to abound. Tolkien is equally evasive about Angmar's huge winged steed, featherless and leathery: "A creature of an older world maybe it was, whose kind, lingering in forgotten mountains cold beneath the Moon, outstayed their day . . ." A pterodactyl? It certainly sounds like one, but Tolkien avoids naming it, and casts all in doubt with a maybe. If it is a pterodactyl, or a close relative, then the Age of Reptiles in which those species throve is "older" than the Third Age, apparently much older. Gwaihir is an eagle of prodigious size whose ancestor "built his eyries in the inaccessible peaks of the Encircling Mountains when Middle-earth was young." All these half-mythical creatures of Middle-earth are meant to subsist partly in our world, partly in another in which the imagination can make of them what it will.

Tolkien's lifelong interest in astronomy tempts him into observations which have a bearing on the distance of Middle-earth back in Earth's prehistory. Opening in Appendix D a discussion of the calendars devised by its various peoples he remarks, "The Calendar in the Shire differed in several features from ours. The year no doubt was of the same length, for long ago as those times are now reckoned in years and lives of men, they were not very remote according to the memory of the Earth." A footnote on the same page gives "365 days, 5 hours, 48 minutes, 46 seconds" as the period of Earth's annual revolution around the sun according to our best modern measurements. The year length for Middle-earth of the Third Age was the same, Tolkien says. In other words, Earth's orbit around the sun (or vice versa) was the same then as it is now. This bit of information is not as informative as it looks. In the absence of modern technology nobody before today could possibly have calculated the orbit with sufficient accuracy to tell at what epoch it began being different. But the implication is that at least the Third Age was not many millions of years ago. Tolkien wants for Middle-earth distance, not invisibility.

To strengthen visibility, and also to counterbalance the alien topography of Middle-earth's Europe, Tolkien lights its night skies with the planets and constellations we know, however different their names. Orion is seen by hobbits and elves meeting in the Shire woods: ". . . there leaned up, as he climbed over the rim of the world, the Swordsman of the Sky, Menelvagor with his shining belt." Unmistakably Orion. Looking out the window of the inn at Bree, "Frodo saw that the night was clear. The Sickle was swinging bright above the shoulders of Bree-hill." Tolkien takes the trouble to add a footnote on that page, that "the Sickle" is "the Hobbits' name for the Plough or Great Bear." Glowing like a jewel of fire "Red Borgil" would seem to be Mars. Eärendil's star is surely Venus, because Bilbo describes it as shining just after the setting sun ("behind the Sun and light of Moon") and just before the rising sun ("a distant flame before the Sun,/a wonder ere the waking dawn . . .").

The heavens of Middle-earth and Earth being not noticeably dissimilar, the lapse of time between the two epochs is short by planetary standards ("the memory of the Earth"), however long it may seem "in years and lives of men." Middle-earth has the same seasons we have in the same length of year, which means that it tilts its northern and southern hemispheres alternately toward and away from the sun as does Earth today. And apparently its days and nights are of the usual duration, which means that Middle-earth rotates on its axis in our twenty-four-hour period. All these are comfortable touches designed not only to show that Middle-earth could not possibly be another planet but also to reassure the reader that fundamentally he is on home territory. I have described the phenomena above in modern heliocentric terms, but they are equally valid for a geocentric view, which there is reason to think the peoples of the Third Age believed in, as will be discussed in a moment.

Strange but not too strange. Further to offset the alienness of the large-scale topography of Third Age Europe, Tolkien makes sure that on the small scale its local terrain, climate, and dominant flora and fauna are much as we know them today. We feel at ease with them at once. Spring in the Shire brings warm sun, a wind from the south, new green "shimmering in the fields" and Sam clipping the grass borders of Frodo's lawn. Tobacco grows in the more sheltered bottomland. The fox that sees the hobbits sleeping out overnight as they leave the Shire sniffs and marvels aloud in intelligent speech, but it is a fox, not a Jabberwock. The travelers are later spied upon by birds but they are crows, ordinary in everything except a heightened consciousness. When the Fellowship depart from Lórien they hear "the high distant song of larks." Fangorn Forest may be dire and mysterious but its trees are the same oaks, chestnuts, beeches, and rowans that make up our woods. As for the day-by-day scenery and climate through which his travelers move on their many journeys, no writer was ever more constantly aware than Tolkien of all the details of mountain, grassland, wood and swamp, of variations in temperature, wind or calm, rain or cloud, the quality of sunlight and starlight, the hues of each particular sunset. He keeps our senses wide awake. Picking out at random almost any one day during Frodo's tramp to Rivendell or Aragorn's pursuit of the orcs, a reader is likelier than not to be told exactly what the weather was and what their camping spot for the night looked like. Given this unbroken running account of familiar homely things, he is buoyed by a psychological reassurance that never fails him, and that allows him to absorb very large doses of the marvelous without disbelieving it. This is one of the hallmarks of Tolkien's personal style in fantasy.

As summarized in Appendices A and B the formal history of Middle-earth begins with the temptation and fall of the great elf leader Fëanor in Valinor and extends for about ten thousand years into the start of the Fourth Age. But into *The Lord of the Rings* Tolkien introduces the two oldest living beings on earth, Bombadil and Treebeard, whose memories stretch much farther back, to the first beginnings of life on the planet. Through them he is able to give his story full chronological depth by opening up the longest possible vistas into the past of its various races. Bombadil lived in unimaginable times before there was any vegetation, before even the rains began to fall. He saw the coming of men, "the Big People," and hobbits, "the little People." Before that the elves, earliest of intelligent peoples, passed him on their way westward from some unknown birthplace to the continent's edge, and thence across the sea to Valinor. All this "before the seas were bent" or Morgoth came to Middle-earth from Outside to breed his loathsome orcs.

For his part, Treebeard also antedated the elves, but ents did not know how to speak until the first wandering elves taught them. Treebeard has seen the day when the separate patches of forest surviving into the Third Age were joined in one unending woodland that covered the face of primeval Europe. And, along with the other ents, he has suffered the loss of the entwives, the females of his species, who in some prehistoric time left the woods to practice agriculture in the open fields and there taught their arts to primitive men. This is almost a parable of how Earth's originally nomadic tribes settled down in one place when they learned to till the soil.

All these are glimpses into Middle-earth's prehistoric past. At the end of his epic Tolkien inserts also some forebodings of its future which will make Earth what it is today. Apart from gigantic geological upheavals still to come, he shows the initial steps in a long process of retreat or disappearance by all other intelligent species, which will leave man effectually alone on earth. The greater elves are already going home to Eldamar, from which they will not return, while the lesser ones who remain sink into oblivion. Orcs shut themselves into their caverns under the mountains. After an estrangement from mankind, as remarked in the Prologue, hobbits will retire from all communication with us, reduced in size, numbers, and importance. The slow reproductive rate of the dwarves foreshadows their gradual extinction, leaving behind them imperishable monuments of stone. Ents may still be there in our forests, but what forests have we left? The process of extermination is already well under way in the Third Age, and in works outside the epic Tolkien bitterly deplores its climax today. The hunger men still feel to converse with birds and animals is a residual trace of the free intercourse between the species prevailing on Middle-earth, and since lost.[7]

Tolkien is sure that modern man's belief that he is the only intelligent species on Earth has not been good for him. Cut off from nature and its multitudes of living beings, mankind has developed a hard artificial industrialism stifling to that side of him which is sympathetic, imaginative, free. One symptom of our loss is the trivializing in contemporary folk-lore and fairy tales of the lordly elves and formidable dwarves traditional to them. In Appendix F of his epic Tolkien condemns with angry sadness the "fancies either pretty or silly" which now dishonor those and other great races of Middle-earth. "Smith of Wootton Major," written later, is a short story dealing in part with the scorn of our skeptics for a charming world of fancy that their imaginations are no longer flexible enough to enter. According to the essay "On Fairy-stories," creative fantasy has the power to heal this blindness by "recovery" of fresh knowledge of ourselves and the world about us, and of the kindly insight we once had into other species, other minds.

But to return to Middle-earth. One region of it is so far outside our experience that Tolkien can only ask us to take it completely on faith. This region contains the Undying Lands situated far out in the ocean west of the continental land mass, home of the Guardian Valar and their pupils, the immortal elves. Eldamar of the elves is definitely an island, but nearby Valinor seems to be attached to a "mighty Mountain Wall" encircling the whole of Middle-earth. Both places are therefore at World's End, the Uttermost West, beyond which living beings cannot go. Early in the First Age and before, access to the Undying Lands was by an arduous though otherwise ordinary sea voyage, but elves were the only race permitted to make it. After their rebellion and self-exile in that Age, Elbereth Star-kindler, Queen of the Valar, cast a deep belt of shadow across its ocean approaches, through which the exiles could return only when forgiven, as most of them were after Morgoth's defeat at the end of the Age.[8] When this barrier proved insufficient in the Second Age to keep out the armadas of Númenor sailing in to seize immortality by force, the One made the Undying Lands forever inaccessible to men.

Because of the integral place these lands have in the geography and spiritual history of Middle-earth they are not strictly an other-world. Their closest counterpart in literature is in those early medieval Celtic tales known as *imrama*, about voyages made by Irish explorers to the western Atlantic in search of the Land of Promise. That Tolkien knew these tales is clear, for he wrote a poem which he entitled "Imram" narrating such a voyage by St. Brendan, which takes him after seven years of adventure to an island of refuge set aside by God for his Saints. In the Latin prose version of the Brendan search, almost certainly read and used by Tolkien for his poem,[9] the Land of Promise has many elements in common with the Undying Lands of *The Lord of the Rings*, raising the possibility that it also provided Tolkien with ideas for his epic.

For instance, Brendan's Land of Promise is screened by a miraculous circle of darkness through which all comers must pass, as the Undying Lands are walled off by Elbereth's belt of shadow. The saint and his monks are allowed to walk only to a river where an angel in the form of a shining man forbids them to advance farther and sends them back to Ireland. Similarly, the Valar are demiurgic spirits in human or elfin form, radiant in appearance, and they not only exile the elves at one time but also impose the Ban against all mankind which precipitates so much tragedy in the epic. The angel tells Brendan that the Land of Promise is being reserved by God for a refuge at a future time when Christians will be persecuted. Likewise, the Valar have occupied the Undying Lands "because of their love and desire for the Children of God (*Erusén*) for whom they were to prepare the 'realm' " against the day when elves and men shall have attained "their future forms." [10] Most important for our present purposes, both lands are at the extreme western limit of the physical world but still a geographical part of it.

If the navigable sea has any such boundaries Middle-earth cannot be a rounded sphere as we now conceive Earth. In the *imrama* tales this point posed no difficulty to the wonder-oriented Celtic mind of the Dark Ages, which popularly accepted the world as bounded and flat anyway, or, when it did not, was quite willing to forget roundness under the spell of a good story. But is such a prescientific cosmology intended by Tolkien for Middle-earth? He never discusses the question explicitly one way or the other. He leaves us to survey the text of the epic and its Appendices for ourselves. Quite possibly he considers the question to be of no real importance to the story, and so is indifferent whether it is raised or not. Those who wish to raise it will find, I think, that none of the astronomical passages are incompatible with a geocentric view of a flat, saucerlike Middle-earth. Since such a view is implicit in the conception of Valinor as being at World's End, consistency would require its acceptance as representing the beliefs of the inhabitants of Middle-earth.

But does the divine act of the One in removing the Undying Lands "for ever from the circles of the world" at the end of the Second Age signal a change to a more advanced astronomy? Possibly so, if that cryptic phrase means that they were taken out of the physical continuum of Middle-earth, which then becomes free to be spherical. However, one difficulty is that the encircling mountains may still be there (the text is silent). Also, Tolkien continues to allow the elves still on Middle-earth during the Third Age to act as if the Undying Lands are visible and reachable. In the *palantír* at the Grey Havens Gildor and his company still can see Valinor, where the white figure of Elbereth stands gazing out and listening to their prayers. And, returning home when the Fourth Age begins, the great elves have only to take ships from the Havens, though these have been specially built by Círdan for the journey, to be sure. On the whole it seems wise not to inquire too curiously into a question that Tolkien himself chooses to ignore.

The Appendices are not mere barnacles on the epic as

some critical opinion would have them. For example, Appendix D on the Calendars of Middle-earth and Appendices E and F on its languages so orient their specialized topics as to become facets of the cultural history of all the major races. By this method the basic traits of each are revealed. Elvish empathy for the gradations of growth and dormancy in vegetation is reflected in their division of the year into six, rather than four, seasons, and of unequal length. The Númenoreans' insensitivity to such gradations, and preoccupation rather with practical affairs, lead to their abandonment of those divisions and substitution of twelve mathematically equal months. The hobbit love of holidays and feasting multiplies Lithedays in the summer and Yuledays in the winter, all given over to parties. That the elves are indeed "People of the Stars" and worshipers of the Valar could be known, if from no other source, from the objects and persons determining the names they give to the six days of their week: Stars, Sun, Moon, the Two Trees (of Valinor), the Heavens, and the Valar. They also have many special names for the hours of star-opening and star-fading. The experience of Númenoreans exclusively with the White Tree causes them to substitute its name for that of Two Trees and, being great mariners, they insert a Sea-day after Heavens' Day. Conservative by nature, the hobbits take over the Númenorean week but soon forget its meaning.

Nothing tells more about a people than the language it speaks and writes. This is bound to be a product of its psychological peculiarities, its traditions, its institutions, its whole outlook on life. Well aware of this truth, Tolkien as a professional philologist makes of his Appendices E and F on the languages he has invented for the several races of Middle-earth not only a tour de force of philological analytic imagination but also one more revelation of the races themselves from a new direction. These Appendices have the added interest of being the adult equivalent of Tolkien's boyhood games with invented tongues. Aimed first at demonstrating the written alphabets, oral pronunciation, and to some extent the grammar of the two inflected, superbly melodious Elvish dialects, Quenya and Sindarin, their material evidently comes straight out of that "history of Elvish tongues" which Tolkien prepared in the 1930s before he came to write *The Lord of the Rings*. When this history proved unpublishable he set it aside in order to proceed with a narrative about the races who spoke these languages. So the epic was born.

Nobody knows better than Tolkien that languages are not static but change continually. Hence part of the function of Appendix E is to trace some of the developments of the original Elvish spoken and written speech into Númenorean, and thence into Westron, the "Common Speech" of the West. Inevitably, I suppose, the laws of linguistic evolution which Tolkien sees at work on Middle-earth are the same as those discovered by modern philology to have governed the development of the Indo-European tongues in recent millennia on Earth. In this way another parallel is drawn, this time in the realm of philology, between events on ancient Middle-earth and those known to have taken place among us in our own era.

The linguistic history of Middle-earth corroborates and fleshes out other aspects of its history, with a corresponding gain in the credibility of all. In language, as in much else, the Noldor elves who have crossed the sea to Valinor are the fountainhead of culture. They carry back with them to Middle-earth the noble Quenya speech and the first written alphabet, invented by their most brilliant genius, Fëanor, who also made the *Silmarilli*. Cultural contact with the Sindar elves, who have remained behind on the continent, enriches both groups, modifies their speech and writing, and spreads their influence eastward among the Edain of the north and the dwarves of Moria to the south. Even the orcs are affected. When given the island of Númenor the Edain, too, abandon their former linguistic patterns in favor of the Elvish. It is a sign of the arrogance and rebellion to come that gradually they cast off all things Elvish and revert to a version of their former tongue. Out of this in later years after their destruction emerges in the Gondor lands they have settled the *lingua franca* of the west known as Westron, bearing the mark of influences of the more primitive human tribes already there as well as others from commerce with remaining colonies of elves. The rivalry between Westron and Sauron's Black Speech, spoken by all his servants, typifies the enmity of the two cultures, if Sauron's tyranny can be called a culture. This bald summary can give but a paltry idea of the profusion of detail poured in by Tolkien to show how the languages of Middle-earth both shape and reflect the destinies of those who use them.

Already noticed in the foregoing pages are many instances of Tolkien's art in gaining credence for his history of Middle-earth by introducing episodes of various sorts that tease us with their resemblance to episodes that we know have actually occurred in our not too distant past. A few more parallels, which designedly are never quite parallel, deserve mention too because they skirt the edges of large events in the history of western civilization.[11] Just as Earth has seen wave after wave of tribal migrations into Europe from east and north, so on Middle-earth the elves, the Edain, the Rohirrim, and the hobbits have drifted west at various periods from the same directions. Also, our Europe has warred from early times against Arabs from the south and Persians, Mongols, Turks from the near or far east. Similarly Gondor resists Easterlings and Southrons, who have pressed against its borders for millennia and have become natural allies of Sauron. The Haradrim of the south even recall Saracens in their swarthy hue, weapons, and armor, and suggest other non-European armies in their use of elephant ancestors, while the Wainriders from the east come in wagons rather like those of the Tartar hordes. The men of Gondor live and fight in a kind of legendary Arthurian, proto-medieval mode, and the Rohirrim differ from early Anglo-Saxons mainly in living by the horse, like Cossacks.

The Tolkien style in creating secondary worlds did not spring full-blown but developed out of his experience in writing *The Hobbit*, his first attempt at narrative. In that story Bilbo travels from Shire to Rivendell, as Frodo does, and meets Gandalf, Elrond, Gollum, and other characters who appear also in the epic. But the world of *The Hobbit* is not called Middle-earth, its vegetation and creatures are not visualized in patient detail, and it has no larger geographical or historical context whatever. Nor are the characters the same, although they bear the same names. Gandalf is merely a funny old wizard, for instance. And in a mistaken attempt to please an audience of children Tolkien trivializes and ridicules his elves and dwarves in precisely the manner he later comes to deplore. To call *The Lord of the Rings* a sequel to this childhood tale, as Tolkien does for the sake of continuity in the Ring plot, is to disguise the immense progress in technique evident in his epic fantasy.

Having once found his characteristic combination of the familiar with the unfamiliar, Tolkien never departed from it in any of the short verse and prose fiction he wrote after finishing the epic.[12] "The Homecoming of Beorhtnoth" is an imagined sequel to the battle of Maldon between Vikings and Saxons in Essex in A.D. 991. "Farmer Giles of Ham" is set in the valley of the Thames in pre-Arthurian Britain. "Smith of Wootton Major" takes place in an essentially medieval English village, slightly hobbitized, which is a point of departure and return for excursions into a country called Faery.

"Imram" tells of St. Brendan's sea voyage into the West in the sixth century. It starts and ends in Ireland. "The Lay of Aotrou and Itroun" is a Breton lay centering on the south coast of Britain in the chivalric age. "Leaf by Niggle" shows us a modern English village complete with neighbors, bicycles, housing regulations, a town council, and the rest, before taking off into a rather minutely pictured landscape where the soul after death goes through purgation.

In his unfinished *The Silmarillion* Tolkien faces the same problem in naturalizing the potentially fabulous happenings of Middle-earth's First Age.

CHAPTER II

The Hobbit

THIS EARLIEST of Tolkien's prose fictions, published in 1937, was so popular that when he started writing *The Lord of the Rings* soon afterward he called the latter a sequel. Such a designation of the two works as prologue and sequel respectively is a pity for a number of reasons. For one thing, many potential readers approaching Tolkien for the first time have inferred that they must tackle *The Hobbit* first. Unfortunately that work often puzzles, sometimes repels outright. Those who manage to get past it are likely to go on to the later epic with preconceptions which they find they must rapidly discard. The result can be equally disconcerting for those who move in reverse order from the heights and depths of the War of the Ring to the unilinear simplicities of Bilbo's "adventure." Not that *The Hobbit* is by any means a bad book. It is a misunderstood book, misunderstood in its purpose and its execution. Despite its surface connections with *The Lord of the Rings* the two works are so unlike fundamentally as to be different in kind. *The Hobbit* is a story for children about the stealing of a dragon's hoard by some dwarves with the reluctant aid of a little hobbit. *The Lord of the Rings*, on the other hand, stretches the adult imagination with its account of a world in peril. Each work has virtues proper to its kind, but they had better be read independently of each other as contrasting, if related, specimens of the fantasy writer's art.

The beginning of wisdom in understanding *The Hobbit* is to think of Tolkien, or another adult, in a chair by the fireside telling the story to a semicircle of children sitting on the floor facing him. From the opening paragraphs hardly a page goes by in which the narrator does not address the children directly in the first person singular. Since the breed of hobbits has just sprung freshly minted from his brain, he loses no time in telling his young listeners about how they look and behave, notably their shyness "when large stupid folk like you and me come blundering along," and he ends his description by, "Now you know enough to go on with. As I was saying . . ." [1] Sometimes he uses the direct address technique to create anticipation, as in introducing Gandalf: "Gandalf! If you had heard only a quarter of what I have heard about him, and I have only heard very little of all there is to hear, you would be prepared for any sort of remarkable tale." Sometimes his remarks to the child audience take on a genial, joking tone, as in pointing out the flaw in Bilbo's plan for freeing the captive dwarves by putting them into barrels (his inability to put himself into one): "Most likely you saw it some time ago and have been laughing at him; but I don't suppose you would have done half as well yourselves in his place." Then, there are jocular interjections of no special moment, but aimed at maintaining a playful intimacy: "If you want to know what *cram* is, I can only say that I don't know the recipe; but it is biscuitish . . ."

Tolkien also makes the technique work for him expositorily in making clear to the youngsters important shifts in the plot sequence. Normally he describes every scene from Bilbo's point of view, and describes none in which Bilbo himself is not present. But Chapter XIV diverges to report what happened at Lake-town, while Bilbo and the dwarves were shut inside Erebor, when Smaug the dragon attacked the town and was killed by Bard the archer. So Tolkien opens the chapter with the sentence: "Now if you wish, like the dwarves, to hear news of Smaug, you must go back again to the evening when he smashed the door and flew off in a rage, two days before." Incidentally, this careful score-keeping of days elapsed at every stage of his tale is typical of Tolkien. Having narrated events at Lake-town he steers his young audience back to their hero with the words, "Now we will return to Bilbo and the dwarves." And, on occasion, in order to remind them of an important fact, already explained some time before, which they may have forgotten, he repeats it. Thus when the Master in Lake-town judges Thorin's claim to the treasure by inheritance to be a fraud Tolkien reiterates what Gandalf and Elrond acknowledged earlier: "He was wrong. Thorin, of course, was really the grandson of the king under the Mountain . . ." This care in keeping the plot crystal clear is adapted to the possible squirmings and short attentiveness of the children he is speaking to.

Also for their benefit is Tolkien's method all through *The Hobbit* of prefacing the introduction into the story of each new race with a paragraph or so setting forth in plain words whatever needs to be known about its looks, its habits, its traits, and whether it is good or bad. He has started this practice off with the hobbits. He extends it to trolls, dwarves, goblins, eagles, elves, and lakemen as each of these makes its entry. These little capsules of racial qualities are enlivened usually with personal interjections: "Yes, I am afraid trolls do behave like that, even those with only one head each"; or "Eagles are not kindly birds," but they did come to the rescue of Bilbo's party, and "a very good thing too!" Goblins are wicked and bear a special grudge against dwarves "because of the war which you have heard

mentioned, but which does not come into this tale." Elves
are hunters by starlight at the edges of the wood and are
"Good People." After such set pieces no small auditor will
be in any doubt as to which people he should cheer for. The
whole tale gives him a very firm moral framework by which
to judge.[2]

Another minor but persistent device in the manner of its
telling likewise is meant to delight childish ears. The prose is
full of sound effects, which the eye of the reader might miss
but the hearing of the listener would not. Bilbo's doorbell
rings *ding-dong-a-ling-dang;* Gandalf's smoke rings go
pop!; the fire from his wand explodes with a *poof;* Bombur
falls out of a tree *plop* onto the ground; Bilbo falls *splash!*
into the water, and so on at every turn. Nor are these sound
effects limited to the prose. Many of the poems are designed
more for onomatopoeic purposes than for content. One
prime example is the song of the goblins underground after
their capture of Bilbo and the dwarves, with its *Clash, crash!*
Crush, smash! and *Swish, smack! Whip crack* and *Ho, ho,*
my lad. The elves' barrel-rolling song has all the appropriate
noises, from *roll-roll-rolling* to *splash plump!* and *down they*
bump! Tolkien knows that up to a certain age children like
their stories to be highly audible.[3]

But the question as to what age Tolkien is addressing cannot be long deferred. Probably he himself had no precise answer in mind, but the very nature of the tale and the methods
of its telling draw the principal parameters. The children listening to its recital must be young enough not to resent the
genial fatherliness of the I-You technique, the encapsulated
expositions, sound effects, and the rest, yet old enough to be
able to cope with the fairly stiff vocabulary used on many occasions and to make at least something of the maturer elements that keep cropping up in what they hear. For, although *The Hobbit* is predominantly juvenile fiction, it is not

all of a piece. Much of the confusion about it arises from the fact that it contains episodes more suited to the adult mind than the child's.

One such is Bard's claim to a share in Smaug's treasure after he has killed the dragon, a claim made not only on his own behalf but also on behalf of the elves and the people of Lake-town. Tolkien has built up here a very pretty conundrum in law, equity, and morals. The treasure consists of a hoard gathered by Thorin's ancestors, but Smaug has mingled with it unestimated valuables belonging to Bard's forebears in the city of Dale. So Bard has a clear legal claim to some unclear fraction. The Lake-town men have no title in law to any portion but rest their case on the argument that Thorin owes them an equitable share because the dwarves roused Smaug to destroy their town, leaving them now destitute; and besides they helped to outfit the dwarf expedition when it was penniless. Bard invokes for them, in fact, the general principle that the wealthy "may have pity beyond right on the needy that befriended them when they were in want." And what of the elves' contention that the dwarves stole the treasure from them in the first place, as against the dwarf reply that they took it in payment for goldsmith work for the elves under a contract which their king later refused to honor? A Solomon might well pick his way gingerly among these claims and counterclaims, especially when faced with Thorin's answer that he is not responsible for Smaug's devastations, and will not bargain under threat of siege by an army anyway. If so, what is even the wise child to make of it all?

Well, Tolkien does not leave his audience, young or old, without some guidance. He comes right out and says of Bard's claim when first uttered, "Now these were fair words and true, if proudly and grimly spoken; and Bilbo thought that Thorin would at once admit what justice was in them." Thorin's refusal is characterized as dwarfish "lust" for gold fevered by brooding on the dragon's hoard. The experienced reader of Tolkien's other writings recognizes here his usual condemnation of the cardinal sin of "possessiveness," which besets dwarves as a race and which indeed is at the core of all the evil underlying the War of the Ring, and much other ill in the world besides. But Bard is a little too eager to resort to arms, being himself somewhat afflicted by the same curse. He has to be rebuked by the elf king, who contrives to conquer the same inclination to greed in his own breast, "Long will I tarry, ere I begin this war for gold . . . Let us hope still for something that will bring reconciliation." Bilbo tries to break the deadlock by setting a moral example, but one which, oddly, requires an initial act of theft. After hiding in his pocket the great jewel Arkenstone he steals from the recovered treasure, on the theory that it represents the one-fourteenth share promised him by the dwarves, Bilbo carries it secretly to Bard's camp by night, gives it to him freely to use as a bargaining counter against Thorin, and returns to the dwarves inside the mountain to face the music. For all this he is highly praised by Gandalf, surely a spokesman for Tolkien. Bilbo's self-sacrifice does not work out as planned, however, and open war between the contestants for Smaug's gold is averted only by the unforeseen attack of an army of goblins, which unites them against the common enemy. Tolkien's solution of the complex problem of ownership is finally moral. It comes about through the dying Thorin's repentance for his greed, which leads his followers to a generous sharing of the hoard with their new friends. This strongly fortifies the moral tone of the adventure, which began sordidly enough from motives of profit and revenge. But a good deal of rather adult territory has to be traversed to reach this consummation. One wonders what most child auditors would get out of it beyond the general impression that it is wrong to fight over who owns what. In this climactic spot the story really operates at two separate levels of maturity.

A similar double track seems to run through that other critical episode of Bilbo's encounter with Gollum in the tunnels under the goblin mountain.[4] The riddle game the two play would be fun for audiences of any age, as its prototype was in Norse and Anglo-Saxon literature. But the case may well be otherwise when it comes to the portrayal of Gollum's character, with its mixture of cruelty, greed, and miserable loneliness, and Bilbo's response of horror, fear, and pity. Taken alone, any one of these emotions is as familiar to a child as to his parents, but their skillful blending as achieved by Tolkien requires some sophistication of understanding, which comes only with years. Particularly the pity that causes Bilbo to spare the life of a vile creature whom he hates and fears seems a high moral quality of which Tolkien writes, over the heads of all save a mature audience: "A sudden understanding, a pity mixed with horror, welled up in Bilbo's heart: a glimpse of endless unmarked days without light or hope of betterment . . ." Tolkien is already looking ahead to that scene of revelation in *The Lord of the Rings* in which Gandalf tells Frodo that Bilbo's compassion in sparing Gollum would later save the world. However that may be, in *The Hobbit* the whole episode is one more example of Tolkien's writing at the same time both for children and for the parents who will often be reading them the tale. A fair enough practice, provided it can be so managed as not to confuse or irritate both parties.

Plenty of other passages of the same double character come readily to mind, frequently in the form of sly hits by Tolkien at some favorite targets in modern life. He pokes fun, for instance, at the stodgy respectability of hobbit (or human) society which brands as "queer" any hobbit who travels to foreign parts or has even mildly unusual experiences. The family of such a black sheep always hastens to hush up the offense. Finding himself "no longer quite respectable" on his return from his adventure, Bilbo "took to writing poetry and visiting the elves." Whereupon his neighbors thought him mad. Tolkien laughs at this same rationalistic rejection of fantasy again in the Lake-town episode when he writes that "some young people in the town openly doubted the existence of any dragon in the mountain, and laughed at the greybeards and gammers who said that they had seen him flying in the sky in their younger days" — this despite the fact that Smaug is snoring on his hoard not many miles to the north. Or, another shaft at modern skeptical materialism: ". . . one morning long ago in the quiet of the world, when there was less noise and more green, and the hobbits were still numerous and prosperous . . ." Or, more plainly still, Tolkien's usual vendetta against our machine age showing through his remarks about goblins, that they love wheels and engines: "It is not unlikely that they invented some of the machines that have since troubled the world, especially the ingenious devices for killing large numbers of people at once," but in Bilbo's day "they had not advanced (as it is called) so far." Tolkien was ecologist, champion of the extraordinary, hater of "progress," lover of handicrafts, detester of war long before such attitudes became fashionable.

Besides the paramount interest *The Hobbit* can claim in its own right as the earliest specimen of Tolkien's fiction to be published and therefore as showing his art in its infancy, it has also great interest as the immediate precursor — and, to some extent, source — of the far more finished *Lord of the Rings*. In the Foreword to the latter work Tolkien describes *The Hobbit* as being drawn irresistibly toward the materials he had been assembling for several years past to tell the history of the earlier Ages of Middle-earth. So much so that glimpses crept into it "unbidden of things higher or deeper or darker than its surface: Durin, Moria, Gandalf, the Necromancer, the Ring." For the most part Tolkien manages to keep unobtrusive these "unbidden" incursions of serious historical matter not properly germane to a children's story, but they do color the tale and perhaps help to account for those graver, more adult touches we have been discussing. Contrariwise, the writing of *The Hobbit* may well have served to crystallize Tolkien's thoughts about the historical materials, and particularly seems to have supplied a number of ideas that found their way, transformed, into his epic.

The theme for *The Return of the King*, for instance, which has a major place in *The Lord of the Rings*, first appears in embryo toward the end of *The Hobbit*. Thorin is the rightful heir to Erebor by descent from his grandfather, King Thror, but he and his companions set out with no intention of killing Smaug and reclaiming the throne. Their purpose is simply to steal the treasure and abscond fast. Only when he arrives destitute in Lake-town and hears its people singing old legends about the golden age to ensue when a dwarf king comes back to the mountain does Thorin announce, "I return!" From this point his resolution to stay on as ruler develops naturally after he comes into possession of the treasure in the halls of his forefathers.

When Tolkien brought Strider into the plot of the epic at Bree without (by his own confession) having yet the least "notion . . . who Strider was," he could not have had in mind the possibility of revealing him later as heir to the throne of Gondor.[5] It looks very much as if Tolkien's first conception of the plot of *The Lord of the Rings* was solely of a dangerous journey by Frodo and his companions into Mordor, similar to Bilbo's mission to steal the dragon's treasure. Of this journey Strider was to be only a forester guide. The new role for him as future king was a master stroke, suggested by its prior use in *The Hobbit*, bringing in its train a far richer and more varied conception to the epic. Obviously Strider-Aragorn is no Thorin. Character is transmuted along with the role it serves, and his successive steps to the throne are planned with great skill to assist Frodo and Sam in their pilgrimage.

The eagles, too, have prominent parts in both works.

They save Bilbo and the dwarves from goblins and wargs when even Gandalf is powerless, and carry the whole party on their backs some distance eastward. At the Battle of the Five Armies their attack on the goblin host with beak and wing is the decisive blow which turns the tide against them. Tolkien remembered these eagles as he came to write the epic. When Gandalf needs rescuing from the prison of Orthanc or from the cliff on which his naked body lies after the fight with the Balrog, it is Gwaihir the Windlord who bears him away on his broad back. The eagles do no fighting in the final battle of Cormallen but they come flying to pluck Frodo and Sam off the slopes of Mount Doom just before it erupts. They are even welcomed by the beleaguered armies in both works with the identical cry, "The Eagles are coming!" [6] Yet the birds in the epic are dignified by the more stately context in which they operate. They no longer rend and tear, as in *The Hobbit*, but maintain an aloof lordliness as wings of rescue only.

Examples of this sort might be multiplied. But of special import is the use Tolkien makes of the Ring he first described in *The Hobbit* as a prize won by Bilbo from Gollum in the riddle contest. Judging by the text of that story as a whole, Tolkien originally thought of the Ring only as one of those rings of invisibility that abound in fairy tales, wonder-working but harmless. Bilbo puts it on his finger and takes it off frequently as a means of escape from dangers that threaten him from time to time in caves, forests, dungeons, and battles. Yet it does not enslave him or impair his moral outlook in the slightest. On the contrary, he has become a stronger and better hobbit by the time the story ends. After this first version had been completed Tolkien began writing *The Lord of the Rings* as a sequel and only then, it seems, conceived of the scheme of taking over Bilbo's Ring and turning it into the potent instrument of evil around which swirls all the action of the epic. Bilbo's finding of it, which in *The Hobbit* is merely a turning point in his personal "career," was to be magnified into a turning point in the history of Middle-earth. The Ring itself, which *The Hobbit* does not report as belonging to the Necromancer or anybody else, was to be attributed to Sauron as maker and master, in order to account for its malignant power over anyone wearing it.

The Ring, therefore, is the link that inseparably binds the later epic to the earlier children's story. But how to explain the glaring differences between Bilbo's harmless little gold band and Sauron's ruling Ring on which hung the fate of the world? Tolkien does not really try to explain them in any detail, but he does give some hints to pacify the curious reader. In the section of his Prologue to the second (1966) edition of the epic, titled "Of the Finding of the Ring," Tolkien remarks that Bilbo had not told his friends the true story of how he obtained the Ring and that Gandalf had long suspected the falsehood. Such a lapse on the part of a usually truthful hobbit struck Gandalf as very "strange and suspicious" and made him begin to doubt that the Ring was the innocent plaything it seemed on the surface. Of course, Gandalf knew the story of Sauron's Ring. He was starting to wonder what the cause of Bilbo's deceit could be and to connect it dimly with the Ring that had come so mysteriously into his possession.

By this new element prefacing *The Lord of the Rings*, as well as by some textual modifications in the later editions of *The Hobbit*, Tolkien provides for the necessary transition from the latter's mere ring of invisibility to the epic's great Ring of Power. Even so, of course, for the purposes of *The Hobbit* Bilbo's ring continues to be only a toy, useful for escapes and escapades, but having no deeper moral significance. No reader who had not previously read the epic would sense anything malefic about it. The story of *The Hobbit* has its own kind of logic quite different from that of the epic. To confuse them is to do a disservice to both tales. In sum, it is important to see *The Hobbit* as essentially independent of the epic, though serving as a quarry of important themes for the larger work.

To illustrate the latter point further, consider how similar the two pieces are in their basic structure. Both begin at Bilbo's home with a hobbit hero who is induced by Gandalf to set out on a long journey into enemy country to accomplish an apparently impossible quest. Each hobbit, with his companions, first finds refuge at Rivendell, where Elrond helps forward them on their mission. After overcoming many hostile creatures en route, varying much in the two cases but having in common such antagonists as trolls, wargs, orcs, and even spiders (those in Mirkwood are descendents of Shelob), both groups traverse desolate regions of terror. Bilbo's Desolation of Smaug parallels the Dead Marshes outside Mordor's north gate. *The Hobbit* of course lacks the great supporting scenes of *The Lord of the Rings* in Fangorn Forest, at Helm's Deep, Edoras, the Paths of the Dead, and so on, but despite their rich diversity that is all they are structurally, supporting scenes to the all-important struggle of Frodo and Sam toward Mount Doom. Finally, both plots crest in battles that pit against each other most of the persons and races prominent in previous actions of the story, and subside in the end with a return of the hobbits to the homes from which they set out.

All this is not to minimize the polarities in tone and scope between *The Hobbit* and its successor. If *The Hobbit* is a quarry it is one in which the blocks of stone lie scattered about in a much looser and less imposing pattern than that in which the epic assembles those which it chooses to borrow. For example, Bilbo's enemies are serial, not united under any paragon of evil, as is to happen in the epic. *The Hobbit*'s trolls, goblins (orcs), spiders, and dragon know nothing of one another and are all acting on their own. They are certainly not shown to be servants of the nameless and nebulous Necromancer, whose only function in the story is to cause Gandalf to leave Bilbo and company to confront exciting perils unaided for a time. Nor, as has been said, is that magician linked in any way with the Ring, which comes out of nowhere belonging to no one. Also, as there is no alliance on behalf of evil so there is none against it. Dwarves, elves, and men act mainly for their selfish interests, often at cross-purposes, until a coalition is forced upon them by a goblin army hostile to all at the very end. Even then the issue is relatively localized and not worldwide in its ramifications.

Some of the places later to be brilliantly visualized in the epic appear for the first time in *The Hobbit*, but its geography tends to be rudimentary and uncertain and it is not given a continental context. Bilbo's home is simply The Hill. No Shire and no hobbit society surround it. Rivendell is a valley where the Last Homely House stands, hardly described at all and not resembling the splendidly civilized palace it is to be. Bilbo's journey leads him northeastward to Erebor, without the slightest inkling that the broad cities of Gondor, capitals of the West, lie facing Mordor to the south. The existence of oceans and Undying Lands somewhere or other is mentioned only in passing. In fact, since Bilbo's world is never called Middle-earth until we run across a reference to the constellation of the Wain (stars in the Great Bear) in its northern sky, we may be pardoned for wondering whether it is any place in particular, assuming, of course, that we have not read the epic. Tolkien has not yet learned to take the pains he later takes to make us accept this world as our own planet Earth and the events of his story as a portion of Earth's distant prehistory.

The case is the same for the individual characters and the races in *The Hobbit* who will reappear in *The Lord of the Rings*. Tolkien's abrupt leap from a children's tale to an epic of heroic struggle requires a radical elevation of stature for all of them. As the Necromancer of *The Hobbit* is not yet Sauron, Gandalf is not yet Gandalf. The wizard of the child's story who "never minded explaining his cleverness more than once," who is "dreadfully afraid" of the wargs, who tricks Beorn into accepting thirteen unwanted dwarves into his house, and the like, needs nothing short of a total literary resurrection to become the messenger sent by the Valar to rally the West against Sauron. So, too, something drastic will have to be done to the petulant, cowardly dwarves who, to escape the wargs, sit "up in the trees with their beards dangling down, like old gentlemen gone cracked and playing at being boys," if their race is to be capable of producing a Gimli. Even Elrond the wise is a lesser digit who must be raised to a considerably higher power. And the elves of Rivendell and Mirkwood! No self-respecting elf in the epic would perpetrate the nonsense they sing in *The Hobbit*, or dance and carol on midsummer eve, do disappearing acts at the approach of travelers in the forest, and the like, as if they were the tiny nonentities of our debased folklore, as Tolkien everywhere else deplores it. Nor, happily, can trolls be allowed to go on speaking the bastard cockney of Tom, Bert, and Bill Huggins. That Tolkien was able to accomplish all such transmutations successfully bears witness to his possession of an almost incredible power of mind and art.

Much of this need for upgrading the characters and the plot of *The Hobbit* arises from Tolkien's treatment of them in many situations of that tale as seriocomic. He evidently believes that the children will enjoy laughing at them sometimes, as a relief from shivering in excitement sympathetically with them at others. In truth, *The Hobbit* is seldom far from comedy. Tolkien begins by making Bilbo the butt of Gandalf's joke in sending the dwarves unexpectedly to eat up all his food, proceeds on to the lamentable humor of the troll scene, hangs his dwarves up in trees, rolls them in barrels, touches the riddle scene with wit, makes the talk between Bilbo and Smaug triumphantly ridiculous, and tops it all off with Bilbo's return home to find his goods being auctioned off and his reputation for respectable stupidity in ruins. It must be acknowledged that the comedy is not invariably successful and that Tolkien's wry paternal manner of addressing his young listeners does not always avoid an air of talking down, which sets the teeth on edge. Nevertheless, *The Hobbit* was never meant to be a wholly serious tale, nor his young audience to listen without laughing often. In contradistinction, *The Lord of the Rings* does on occasion evoke smiles, but most of the time its issues go too deep for laughter. In the interval between the two stories the children are sent off to bed and their places taken by grownups, young or young in heart, to hear of a graver sort of quest in which every human life is secretly engaged.

CHAPTER III

Cosmic Order

TOLKIEN IS NOT A PHILOSOPHER or a theologian but a literary artist who thinks. Consequently he is not content merely to narrate a bare series of events but surrounds each high point of the action in *The Lord of the Rings* with convictions and opinions expressed by the participants as to its possible place in some larger plan under execution by greater hands than theirs. Their speculations on such a topic could easily lead to the familiar vexing, futile debates on predestination, foreknowledge, contingent futures, free will, and the rest of that thorny thicket. Tolkien, however, refuses to weigh down his story by letting his people think or talk like professionals in these areas. Virtually without exception the elves, men, hobbits, and their allies of the West come to believe in a moral dynamism in the universe to which each of them freely contributes, without exactly knowing how, and without being at all sure how it will eventually work out in the war against Sauron. But they eschew technical terms and discuss each crisis not as an intellectual problem but as a stern occasion demanding concrete choices and chances. Being thoughtful people, though, they say quite enough in the process to give a good idea of the kind of order in which they believe and the nature of the planner operating through it.

The first serious discussion about these matters takes place early in Part I, Book I, when Gandalf explains to Frodo what the Ring is and how Bilbo came to get it from Gollum in the caverns under the Misty Mountains: "Bilbo's arrival just at that time, and putting his hand on it, blindly, in the dark" was not the accident it seems but "the strangest event in the whole history of the Ring so far." At the call of Sauron's will his Ring was leaving Gollum to return to its maker, but Bilbo found it because "there was something else at work beyond any design of the Ring-maker. I can put it no plainer than by saying that Bilbo was *meant* to find the Ring, and *not* by its maker. In which case you also were *meant* to have it." Plainly Gandalf is saying that the "something else" which thwarted Sauron was stronger than he and used this recall of the Ring as a means of putting it, instead, into the possession of the Dark Lord's enemies through Bilbo. This intervention, coming just at this juncture, is crucial. Control of the Ring gives the West its one slim chance of defeating Sauron. Had the Ring remained with Gollum, or even stayed lost, Sauron's armies were strong enough to win easily without it, as everyone admits. The free peoples can overcome him only by destroying the Ring, and with it the vigor which he himself poured into it in the Second Age, and which is still necessary to his hold on life in Middle-earth. Bilbo's picking up the Ring in the dark is the first step on the long road to Mount Doom.

No conscious choice of Bilbo's led to his finding the Ring. He did not even know what it was at the time. But the incident did require of him a decision whether or not to kill Gollum. Out of pity he freely chose not to kill, a choice highly commended by Gandalf, which won Bilbo the personal "reward" of taking little hurt from the evil of the Ring. More importantly, Gandalf guesses, he knows not how, that Gollum is "bound up with the fate of the Ring," and that he "has some part to play yet, for good or ill, before the end." This can only be a piece of inspired foresight on Gandalf's part, however vague its content. He has no rational way of knowing that only Gollum, stumbling down into the Cracks of Doom with the Ring, will save it from Sauron at the last moment and accomplish his destruction.

Many of the wise on Middle-earth have such general glimpses of the future, but they are never more than vague and unspecific. The future is the property of the One who plans it. Yet is it fixed in the sense that every link in the chain of its events is foreordained? It cannot be, because in his encounter with Gollum Bilbo's choice to kill or not to kill is genuinely free, and only after it has been made is it woven into the guiding scheme. Tolkien leaves it at that. Human (or hobbitic or elvish or dwarfish or entish) free will coexists with a providential order and promotes this order, not frustrates it.

Gandalf has said that Bilbo was "meant" to find the Ring in order to pass it on to Frodo as his heir. Frodo was "meant" to bear it from then on. But Gandalf does not assume that Frodo will necessarily do what he was intended to, though he should. When Frodo, rebelling at first against the duty imposed on him, asks the natural question, "Why was I chosen?" the wizard can only reply that nobody knows why; Frodo can be sure only that it was not because of any surpassing merits he has: "But you have been chosen, and you must therefore use such strength and heart and wits as you have." The reasons why one instrument is "chosen" rather than another are not outwardly visible to any eyes on Middle-earth. Yet Gandalf carefully goes on to inform Frodo that he is free to accept or reject the choice: ". . . the decision lies with you." The option not to cooperate with the grand design is open to Frodo's will, as it is to that of all other intelligent creatures who are aware of the issues. Frodo groans but takes up his appointed burden. Sam later does the same on the trip to Rivendell when he tells Frodo: ". . . I have something to do before the end, and it lies ahead, not in the Shire. I must see it through . . ." It is no business of Tolkien's to tell us what would have happened had these choices been refused by the hobbits. We are left at liberty to presume that other persons would have taken their place. For it is becoming clear that the designer is working against Sauron and would, if necessary, have brought forward alternative means to confound him.

This impression is strongly fortified by a passage in Appendix B defining the mission of the five wizards, led by Gandalf and Saruman, to Middle-earth, as understood by later chroniclers: "It was afterwards said that they came out of the Far West and were messengers sent to contest the power of Sauron, and to unite all those who had the will to resist him; but they were forbidden to match his power with power, or to seek to dominate Elves or Men by force and fear . . . They came therefore in the shape of men . . ." Who "sent" them and who "forbad"? Surely it was either the Valar or the One who established them as guardians of Middle-earth and whose design they were charged to administer. It says a good deal about the character of that designer that he cared enough about the future of Middle-earthly peoples to send messengers to help them against evil and yet confined that help to education and persuasion, leaving their wills unforced. Stress is put on the moral side of the struggle against Sauron and on each person's right to select his own role, or lack of any role, in it. Being either one of the Valar himself or at least instructed by them, Gandalf knows as much as any creature can when he suggests a personal will that "means" and "chooses" as it works out its design. And no less so when he reminds all comers that they are the final masters of their own decisions, though what the consequences will be is not for them to know.

Gandalf had intended to escort the Ring-bearer to Rivendell to guard him from Sauron's agents along the way. Tolkien first strips Frodo of protection through Saruman's imprisonment of Gandalf and then restores it by Frodo's apparently accidental encounter with Gildor's elves just as he is about to be attacked by Black Riders. Gildor, knowing how rare the meetings of elves with other creatures in the woods are, suspects a hidden intention behind this one: "In this meeting there may be more than chance; but the purpose is not clear to me, and I fear to say too much." Being no more informed than anyone else on Middle-earth of the aims of this "purpose," the elf is reluctant to give any advice that may unduly influence Frodo's choices and so make them less free. What he can and does do is pass along to "those that have power to do good" the news that the hobbits are in peril. So warned, Bombadil, and later Aragorn, arrive at critical moments as substitutes for Gandalf to give them the aid which he cannot give.

Frodo himself raises the question whether his rescue by Bombadil from Old Man Willow was only happenstance: "Did you hear me calling, Master, or was it just chance that brought you at that moment?" Tom's answer is both yea and nay, but the yea is louder. He did not hear Frodo calling for help, and he was on an errand that afternoon which took him to that part of the Old Forest to gather waterlilies. On the other hand, he had been alerted by Gildor that the hobbits were in need and he was watching the danger spots. In sum, says Tom, "Just chance brought me then, if chance you call it. It was no plan of mine, though I was waiting for you." The incredulous "if chance you call it" tends to deny that the rescue was really chance, however mortals may commonly define the concept. "It was no plan of mine" invites the thought that there was a plan, though it was not his. Questions of this sort are meant to live on in the back of the reader's mind and to make him doubt that Aragorn's very opportune appearance later on at a time of maximum danger in the inn at Bree is as fortuitous as it seems.

Tolkien is here facing a joint literary-philosophical imperative. Literarily, he wants to keep an atmosphere of wonder at the mysterious hand which is guiding events, but he must not let this theme become so strong or definite as to persuade his readers that the hobbits are certain to reach Rivendell safely. To do so would be fatal to the suspense, and therefore to the story as story. Philosophically, if the guiding hand is really to guide effectively, it must have power to control events, yet not so much as to take away from the people acting them out the capacity for moral choice. The latter, being fundamental to Tolkien's conception of man (and other rational beings), must be preserved at all costs. So Tolkien cannot allow his cosmic order to be a fixed, mechanistic, unchangeable chain of causes and effects. The order must be built flexibly around creaturely free will and possible personal providential interventions from on high.

Tolkien uses several techniques to attain the desired balances. For one thing he never speaks about these matters as author, and thereby avoids authorial certitudes. His characters may be certain, or virtually so, that a providential order is at work but they are never sure of its final outcome, or exactly how it operates. Witness Gandalf, who is positive that the Ring was "meant" to fall into the hands of the West but not what its future is to be after that, and who guesses that Gollum has a part yet to play but knows not whether it is for good or ill. Witness also Gildor, who intuits a supervening purpose in his meeting with the hobbits but confesses his ignorance of its aims. And Bombadil, who, while intimating that his rescue of Frodo was not coincidence, regards himself as ultimately outside the contending forces in the War of the Ring.

Another technique Tolkien finds handy is to couple every

incident anyone calls foreordained with some notable exercise
of free will by one of the characters involved in it. For example, as noted, Bilbo and Frodo are said to be chosen as
Ring-bearers, but Bilbo is given the option to spare or kill
Gollum, and Frodo can always decline to serve. This duality
is repeated again and again straight through to the end of the
epic. Yet another device is to let most of the major characters voice premonitions or prophecies, seeming to entail a definite foreseeable future, yet to keep these either misty in content or tentative in tone, so loosening their fixity and hinting
that the routes are various by which they may come true.

All these devices Tolkien handles with persuasive tact. But
they are successful also because they create for life on Middle-earth a kind of atmosphere that our own existential experience of living accepts as genuine. Very common for us is
the sense that our lives are bound in with larger patterns that
we cannot change. Yet tomorrow seems never sure, and at
every new crossroads nothing is stronger than the feeling inside us that we are the masters of our alternatives.

Because Elrond's Council is a turning point in the history
of Middle-earth and because he himself, with Gandalf and
Galadriel, is the wisest of the assembled leaders of the West,
his solemn opening statement to them that some force greater
than themselves has brought them together at this crisis carries special weight. To decide what to do with the Ring, he
says, "That is the purpose for which you are called hither.
Called, I say, though I have not called you to me, strangers
from distant lands. You have come and are here met, in this
very nick of time, by chance as it may seem. Yet it is not so.
Believe rather that it is so ordered that we who sit here, and
none others, must now find counsel for the perils of the
world." Nothing could be plainer than Elrond's rejection
here of chance as the cause of the Council, however much on

the surface it may seem to be so. Almost as plain is his language pointing to the personal nature of the summoner. Words like *purpose*, *called* (thrice spoken), *ordered*, *believe* look to some living will and even have a distantly Christian aura. Moreover, whoever did the calling was concerned for the West's welfare in the struggle against Sauron. Yet the whole purpose of assembling its leaders was not to force any course of action upon them but to have them freely debate it for themselves. The conclusions of the Council are not predetermined in any way, though its summoning was. Noteworthy also is the care with which Elrond avoids giving the supreme being any of the traditional names for God.

The Council having agreed at length that the Ring must be carried back to Mordor to be destroyed, a silence ensues until Frodo, overcoming "a great dread," speaks up with an effort to offer himself as carrier. This is the vocabulary of free choice. Elrond accepts it as such while at the same time believing that the same power that convoked the Council has also appointed Frodo to undertake the task. He sees no clash between the two ideas: "If I understand aright all that I have heard . . . I think that this task is appointed for you, Frodo; and that if you do not find a way, no one will . . . But it is a heavy burden . . . I do not lay it on you. But if you take it freely, I will say that your choice is right . . ." Though Frodo is a chosen instrument most likely to succeed, it is not a foregone conclusion that he will succeed. Providence, for its own reasons which finite minds cannot understand, may perhaps intend Sauron to win this bout in the never-ceasing war between good and evil. Elrond leaves the end open. Frodo has the right to accept or refuse the office as he wills, and no other person should tell him what to do. Yet refusal may bring unspoken penalties, since all acts have their consequences. If Frodo's acceptance would be "right," would not refusal be, if not "wrong," at least an abdication of duty, diminishing him morally? Much is implicit here. Among the natural inferences also is that Frodo's appointment to carry the Ring is of like kind with the selection of Bilbo and Frodo to find and receive it earlier, and was made by the same all-seeing mind, in which Gandalf and Elrond, both pupils of the Valar, firmly believe.

Elrond here has ventured only a very generalized and conditional forecast of possible coming events. Gandalf's death in combat with the Balrog in Moria, however, is one of those main forks in the plot of which Aragorn as well as Gandalf has rather clear knowledge in advance. Aragorn is so sure beforehand of personal disaster to Gandalf that he insists on trying the alternate route over the Redhorn Gate first, and when they are forced by storm toward the old dwarf kingdom utters the strongest possible alarm to him: "I will follow your lead now — if this last warning does not move you . . . And I say to you: if you pass the doors of Moria, beware!" Aragorn does not say precisely what he fears, but the severity of his agitation can be for nothing less than Gandalf's death, and he accurately fears for no one else in the Company, since all the rest are saved by Gandalf's sacrifice of himself. Gandalf, too, knows what awaits him. Rebuking Gimli weeks later for saying that the wizard's "foresight failed him" in entering Moria, Aragorn implies that Gandalf foreknew and accepted the result: "The counsel of Gandalf was not founded on foreknowledge of safety, for himself or others . . . There are some things that it is better to begin than to refuse, even though the end may be dark." But the inference also is that Gandalf could have chosen not to accept death, as Frodo could have chosen not to accept the Ring. The foreseen event will occur only *if* a creaturely will freely consents first. In this way Tolkien keeps his providential plan personalized, nonmechanistic, and not rigidly determined yet quite potent enough, withholds advance details about the precise shape and manner of the event foreknown, and, not incidentally, enhances the suspense of his tale.

Arrived at Lórien without Gandalf, the Company seeks the advice of Queen Galadriel, "greatest of Elven women" in Tolkien's phrase, whose life span extends back to the start of the First Age and whose wisdom is unexcelled among her race. But she is unexpectedly chary of making any predictions for them, or for the success of the West in general. She knows what is to come only "in part," she insists, and her mirror reveals not what shall be but only what "may be." Indeed she warns Frodo and Sam that what they see in its waters "is dangerous as a guide to deeds." It mixes up past, present, and future so indistinguishably that the gazer cannot be sure which is which, and in striving to avert a danger he thinks he sees lying ahead he may take the very measures which are necessary to bring it about. All finite knowledge about the future is cursed by this Oedipean paradox. Necessarily so, because it is incomplete and therefore blind in its information about the means which must precede any given consequence. What then? Are all flashes of foreknowledge false? Galadriel does not say so. But it is noticeable that she prefers to rely mostly on rational inferences from what she already knows about the past and present: "I will not give you counsel, saying do this, or do that. For not in doing or contriving, nor in choosing between this course and another, can I avail; but only in knowing what was and is, and in part also what shall be . . . Your Quest stands upon the edge of a knife . . . Yet hope remains while the Company is true."

This insight, couched in the most general terms, amounts in essence only to a statement of belief that if the members of the Company remain faithful to their trust they still have a chance. As in all previous instances, even so mild a prediction is made to depend upon their free obedience to moral laws. Later, Galadriel explicitly refuses to forecast whether Sauron will be overthrown: "I do not foretell, for all foretelling is now vain: on the one hand lies darkness, and on the other only hope," but she is willing to assure Gimli that if he survives he will be rich, yet over him gold will not have the dominion it has over other dwarves. A likely enough conclusion from Gimli's stated preference for a strand of Galadriel's hair over all the gold and gems on earth. She is perhaps partly foreseeing, partly only comforting the Company when she urges them not to worry over their indecision about selection of a destination: "Maybe the paths that you each shall tread are already laid before your feet, though you do not see them." Nothing Galadriel says to them during their stay in Lórien shakes in any way the established doctrine of the epic that their future course is indeed laid out for them, provided they themselves choose to tread it. Her function in the story is to warn them, and herself, to tend to the duty in hand and not rashly to presume that finite minds can outguess the supreme architect who plans the whole.

Events bear out Galadriel's distrust of all creaturely foreknowledge, including her own. She proves to be only partly right in believing that the success of the Quest rests on the continued loyalty of everyone in the Company. At Parth Galen the evil desire for the Ring long growing in Boromir explodes into a physical attack on Frodo that splits the Company into groups, as it needs to be split, since each group has its own indispensable job to do in the complex compaigns that follow. Frodo, followed by Sam, is shocked into starting off by himself on the stealthy, inconspicuous course of slipping into Mordor in which lies his only possible chance of eluding Sauron's roving eye. Capture of Pippin and Merry by the orcs transports them to Fangorn Forest, where they escape just in time to rouse the ents to overwhelm Saruman at Isengard and Helm's Deep. Pursuing the captives, Aragorn meets Éomer, to begin the awakening of Rohan, and meets in the forest the reincarnated Gandalf, who completes the process by freeing Théoden from Wormtongue. In consequence, Saruman's threat to Rohan is wiped out, and the Rohirrim have just enough time to send the army that saves Minas Tirith from the first onset of Sauron's hosts. Even this would not have been enough had Aragorn not been released by Saruman's defeat to ride the Paths of the Dead and so bring the armies of southern Gondor to the aid of the city when the Rohirrim faltered. None of this would have happened had not Boromir succumbed for a time to the spell of the Ring. In retrospect that evil hour was necessary to defeat evil in the long run as nothing else could have.

The momentum built up by Tolkien earlier for the existence of an unseen design behind all the episodes of his story carries forward into this long sequence of hairbreadth successes stemming from Boromir's fall. Even if Tolkien never said a further word about it we would be inclined to see the finger of Providence in them. But through various spokesmen, especially Gandalf, he keeps up a running commentary to that effect. Hearing from Aragorn in Fangorn what happened at Parth Galen, Gandalf reflects on the unseen significance of the decision, made by Elrond only at the last moment, to include Merry and Pippin in the Company, which allowed Boromir to redeem himself by dying to protect them and which brought the ents into action: "It was not in vain that the young hobbits came with us, if only for Boromir's sake. But that is not the only part they have to play. They were brought to Fangorn, and their coming was like the falling of small stones that starts an avalanche in the mountains." He is using the same language he used to describe Gollum's "part" in the fate of the Ring. All are filling roles written for them by the same great playwright. And Gandalf has to laugh at the irony of the rival orc bands of Saruman and Sauron which captured the two hobbits, thereby serving to promote a good they never meant: "So between them our enemies have contrived only to bring Merry and Pippin with marvelous speed, and in the nick of time, to Fangorn, where otherwise they would never have come at all!" His own reincarnation he interprets as one more move in the plan, for he too has a role: "Naked I was sent back — for a brief time, until my task is done. And naked I lay upon the mountaintop," until an eagle sent by Galadriel brings him to Lórien for healing and consultation. The greater strength that the new White possesses as against the former Grey is needed for his coming labors, and he would never have had it, had not the Balrog first killed him down in the pit.

The irony of evil bringing forth good continues all through the epic. The flight of Wormtongue to his master Saruman seems at the time of no particular importance. But later, when Gandalf is parleying with Saruman at Orthanc, Wormtongue angrily tries to kill him by throwing down at him the precious *palantír* which Saruman would never willingly have parted with and which Gandalf could not have got by force from the impregnable tower, "Strange are the turns of fortune! Often does hatred hurt itself!" Gandalf is moved to exclaim. This is the *palantír* into which Pippin surreptitiously looks that night, to be saved partly by Sauron's sadistic urge to torture him in Mordor from having his mind read then and there by the telepathic Eye and all the strategy of the West ruinously exposed. "You have been saved, and all your friends too, mainly by good fortune, as it is called," remarks Gandalf, who does not believe in luck under any name. "As it is called" is reminiscent of Bombadil's "if chance you call it." Théoden expresses the awe of a more ordinary mortal: "Strange powers have our enemies, and strange weaknesses! . . . But it has long been said: *oft evil will shall evil mar*." He too sees how the very qualities of evil are being turned against themselves for other ends. The idea has achieved the wide circulation of a proverb.

The true importance of Wormtongue's murderous impulse in hurling the *palantír*, however, is seen only when Aragorn claims possession of it as Elendil's rightful heir and with it purposely reveals himself to Sauron in order to frighten him into attacking Minas Tirith before his preparations are complete. Aragorn hopes that Sauron will believe that he has assumed the powers of the Ring and that the West must be overrun immediately before he has learned to wield them. Sauron is duly deceived. In Aragorn's place he would have seized the Ring long ago. The ripples of Aragorn's open challenge spread far and wide through the remainder of the story. Sauron never thereafter even suspects that anyone else may have the Ring, least of all Frodo, whom he regards as a petty spy even after his presence in Mordor becomes known. He does launch his armies against the city prematurely. The darkness with which he enshrouds everything spreads despair, certainly, but it also conceals Frodo's movements into Mordor as well as the coming of the cavalry of Rohan. Hasty emergence of the army under Angmar from Cirith Ungol leaves the mountain pass badly and confusedly guarded. Aragorn is enabled to take the pirates of Umbar unprepared. And so the consequences roll on through multitudinous incidents too many to detail but all working to the disadvantage of a mistakenly preoccupied Sauron.

The direst need for every sort of providential aid and the most direct and unequivocal answers to it come during Frodo and Sam's long ordeal in the dark in Mordor. What finally routs Shelob is a prayer to Elbereth in the elfin tongue, which springs into Sam's mind though he does not know the language. A similar prayer uttered by Sam and Frodo breaks the "will of the Watchers . . . with a suddenness like the snapping of a cord" and lets them escape from the Tower of Cirith Ungol. Meantime, Sam, having to decide whether he should "put himself forward" by taking over the Ring and the mission from the master he thinks dead, realizes that, like Frodo before him, he has "been put forward" by a higher power, must make up his own mind whether to ratify the choice, and does so.

Then, during a rest from pursuit by orcs, while Frodo sleeps, Sam looks up to see far above the murk "a white star twinkle." Smitten by its beauty he understands that "in the end the Shadow was only a small and passing thing: there was light and high beauty for ever beyond its reach." This is far more than the sighting of the physical beaming of a star. It is a spiritual vision of beauty and permanence which Sauron and his passing vileness can never stain. It puts everything into right perspective for Sam and gives him peace: "Now, for a moment, his own fate, and even his master's, ceased to trouble him." The world is in abler hands than his. A less visionary kind of help is sent later on the very slopes of Mount Doom when Sam has to carry Frodo and finds the burden light, "whether because Frodo was so worn by his long pains . . . or because some gift of final strength was given . . ." Tolkien guards the secular alternative but his favor is pretty clearly for the religious one. Finally, of course, as Frodo succumbs to the ring at the Cracks of Doom, Gollum, playing out the role for which he has been preserved all through the epic, bites off Frodo's Ring-finger, overbalances (by no accident), and falls with the Ring into the flames below. The irony of evil is consummated by its doing the good which good could not do.

Providence, therefore, not only permits evil to exist but weaves it inextricably into its purposes for Middle-earth. In the short term it may even allow evil to triumph, and these short terms are often anything but short. Morgoth's tyranny defies the best efforts of elves and men throughout the thousands of years of the First Age until the Valar come against him. Sauron wins again and again in the Second Age until conquered by Númenor, and even then turns defeat into victory by seducing his conquerors into revolt against the Valar. His temporary overthrow in the drowning of Númenor is one which no doubt he would be delighted to repeat in the Third Age, since he then took down with him into the darkness the highest civilization yet achieved by man. Small wonder that with these terrible precedents behind them, the Western leaders in the Third Age almost despair of winning the War of the Ring. By its nature the cosmic order is directed toward good, and in the long run those who cooperate with it must overcome, but who knows how long the run is? Gandalf's retort to Denethor asserting that he too is a steward accepts the possibility that Sauron will overrun the West: ". . . all worthy things are in peril as the world now stands, those are my care. And for my part I shall not wholly fail of my task, though Gondor should perish, if anything passes through this night that can still grow fair or bear fruit and flower again in days to come." Morning will come again and good will flourish no matter how complete the devastation wrought by evil seems. This is Gandalf's equivalent of Sam's vision of the star riding high above Mordor.

Nevertheless, the cost of even a passing victory by Sauron is so dreadful as to call forth the united labors of the free peoples. He will not win if every player accepts the part assigned. Hence the attempts of Gandalf and the rest to educate every player in the importance of his role, freely enacted. Hence also another moral strand, not yet dwelt upon, running from end to end of the epic — the need of everyone in the West to resist the evil inherent in his own nature. Too many Gollums, Boromirs, Sarumans, Denethors, and so on would in effect turn the West into a second Númenor, corrupted and ripe for another flood. Though not the only one, the Ring of course is the chief instrument of temptation by its appeal to the evil within, an appeal made sometimes directly to the baser desires, sometimes more subtly through perversion of the loftiest instincts in the noblest minds.

As Tolkien writes his tale, he makes it one of the main objects of the providential order to test each of the major characters by putting the Ring within easy grasp if he will but reach out to seize it, or keep it, for himself. With Bilbo, who has the Ring to start with, the struggle is to give it up voluntarily to Frodo at Gandalf's urging. He barely succeeds. Isildur has failed before him. Then Frodo offers it to Gandalf, who vehemently refuses, well knowing that the Ring would turn to perverted ends the pity that is his most characteristic virtue. Aragorn's opportunity comes in the inn at Bree. The Ring is lawfully his, if anybody's, by inheritance from Isildur, and the hobbits are at his mercy. But he turns away and never turns back in all the weeks and months he spends in Frodo's company. This is his proof that he is worthy to be king. Elrond's rejection of the Ring took place ages before in the days of the Last Alliance, when he vainly urged Isildur under the walls of Barad-dûr to cast it into the nearby fires. Perhaps hardest of all is Galadriel's refusal to accept it when offered by Frodo in Lórien, because with it she could preserve the existence of that enchanted land which otherwise must pass away.[1] In one of the great scenes of the epic she dreams aloud of what might be, then shatters the dream herself: "I pass the test . . . I will diminish, and go into the West, and remain Galadriel." More than the others she is aware that they are all being put to the proof. So the testing goes on, with Boromir at Parth Galen, Faramir in Ithilien, Sam in Mordor. Frodo's trial, of course, is as long as the epic and he does not come out of it unscathed. Among Western captains only Théoden, Saruman, and Denethor are not directly exposed to the fascination of the Ring. For them other tests are set up. Théoden must overcome the hopeless lassitude of old age intensified by Wormtongue. *Palantíri* are the proximate occasions for the falls of the other two.

For most of the participants on both sides of the War of the Ring the rewards of virtue or vice are simply the normal consequences flowing from victory or defeat. The free peoples are united to live under the just rule of their rightful King. Sauron's human allies are sent back to their home territories under binding treaties. His orcs, those that survive the slaughter, pen themselves in their caves under the mountains. A general purging of evil goes on. Though Sauron cannot be killed, his spirit is driven off the face of Middle-earth, forever to languish impotently in outer darkness. It is not altogether clear whether the same fate befalls Saruman. Coming originally from Valinor, his spirit in the form of a gray mist yearns westward when his body dies, "but out of the West came a cold wind, and it bent away, and with a sigh dissolved into nothing." This sounds like final dissolution, or at least final exile. Consumed in the volcanic explosions of Mount Doom, the Nazgûl perish at last and their spirits presumably go to that abyss that Gandalf warned Angmar was prepared for him, an almost total loss of being in "the nothingness that waits you and your Master." Denethor's final fate as a man is left doubtful. He kills himself in despair, disregarding the warning of Gandalf that suicide is forbidden: "Authority is not given to you, Steward of Gondor, to order the hour of your death . . . And only the heathen kings, under the Domination of the Dark Power, did thus, slaying themselves in pride and despair, murdering their kin to ease their own death." The flavor of this prohibition is distinctly religious, condemning the practice as "heathen" and ascribing it to pride and despair, mortal offenses in the lexicon of Christianity and other religions. Nothing is added, however, about punishments in an afterlife for Denethor or any other among the free peoples. The epic tends to avoid eschatology.

The leaving of Middle-earth by the elves is a special case. It is not connected with anything they have done or not done in the War of the Ring, but rather with their disobedience to the command of the Guardian Valar not to pursue Morgoth to Middle-earth in the early years of the First Age. The exile then imposed upon them as a punishment has been expiated by long years of struggle and suffering, their banishment has therefore been revoked, and their deeply implanted longing for their former lands in the Uttermost West is calling them home. As a further spur they have been told, or they foresee, that if they stay on Middle-earth they are destined to undergo a deterioration, "to forget and to be forgotten." The Fourth Age is intended by the One who decides such things to be an Age of Men. So they are returning to live with the Valar as they were meant to do from the beginning. Galadriel is forgiven by the Valar for her former defiances and allowed to accompany her elves overseas "in reward" for what she has done to oppose Sauron, "but above all for her rejection of the Ring when it came within her power." [2] For their services involving the Ring, Bilbo and Frodo are the first hobbits to receive the unheard-of privilege of healing their wounds with the elves in the peace of the Undying Lands. Arwen, who has elected to become human by marrying Aragorn, is given the power to surrender to Frodo her seat in one of the boats sailing westward.

In all the foregoing arrangements of Peoples, and punishment or reward of individuals, the Valar are the immediate prime movers. But they are acting as executives of the will of the One, and their power of independent decision is limited. The Appendices tell of two pivotal events that reveal the outlines of these limits. When "as a reward for their sufferings in the cause against Morgoth, the Valar . . . granted to the Edain a land to dwell in . . ."—the island of Númenor, at the end of the First Age — they could triple the life spans of these men, but they could not make them undying as were the elves, because they "*were not permitted* to take from them the Gift of Men . . .": death (emphasis added). The Valar obeyed an edict coming down from above. On the other hand, they seem to have some discretion in applying this edict to the half-human, half-elven offspring of the two previous marriages between elves and men: "At the end of the First Age the Valar gave to the Half-elven an irrevocable choice to which kindred they would belong." Under the command to make this choice, Arwen abandons immortality in order to marry Aragorn.

The other occasion which the Valar clearly do not, perhaps cannot, manage by themselves is the invasion of Valinor by rebellious Númenoreans demanding immortality. Then ". . . the Valar laid down their Guardianship and called upon the One . . ." who sank Númenor under the waves. These incidents serve to show that while the Valar have what Tolkien calls incomprehensibly great "demiurgic" powers,[3] which they use in governing and guarding the affairs of Middle-earth and which justify the invocation of their help in prayer by many of its folk, they are only agents of "the One" and defer to his direct intervention in major emergencies. Beyond this point Tolkien does not choose to go in defining the relationship of the Valar to their superior. Why should he? He has told us all he needs to for the literary-philosophical framework of his tale.

As the Fourth Age begins, no successor of Sauron is in sight to rally the forces of evil against civilization. But signs are not lacking that sooner or later one will arise again on Middle-earth or out of the Undying Lands — another Morgoth, a more vicious Fëanor, a Denethor more wholly lost to good. Gandalf has said as much in the Last Debate: "Other evils there are that may come; for Sauron is himself but a servant or emissary. Yet it is not our part to master all the tides of the world, but to do what is in us for the succour of those years in which we are set, uprooting the evils in the fields that we know, so that those who live after may have clear earth to till. What weather they shall have is not ours to rule." [4] To judge by the history of the past three Ages evil will not be long in reviving. With brief respites Middle-earth has always been under siege by some Dark Lord or other. There seems to be something in the nature of things, or in the nature of the One who devises them,[5] that requires it. Sauron is Morgoth's servant, but whose emissary is Morgoth? In one sense, nobody's. Since like everybody else, he has a will free to choose, he is self-corrupted. In another sense, his master can only be the One, who, while not creating evil, permits it to exist and uses it in ruling his world — who, in truth, *needs* evil in order to bring on times of peril that test his creatures to the uttermost, morally and physically, as in Sauron's war.

If men and their colleagues of other races are to prove the stoutness of their fiber, such times must come again and again in the Fourth Age and future ages of whatever number. Evil has built-in weaknesses that make for self-defeat, and the One, with his smiling ironies, will sometimes manipulate it to that end. But the burden of *The Lord of the Rings* is that victory for the good is never automatic. It must be earned anew each time by every individual taking part. In this effort, says Aragorn to Éomer, man has the natural ability and the obligation to "discern" the difference between right and wrong. These are opposites, absolutes that do not vary from year to year or place to place or people to people. Those rational beings who would act well on Tolkien's Middle-earth do not have to stand on the shifting sands of historical relativism. The good is as unchanging above the tides of time as the beauty of Sam's star over Mordor, and derives ultimately from the character of the One who placed it there.

But does death end all for those who have not the unending lives of elves? The epic abounds with hints of some kind of afterlife for them, but these are faint. For example, the dying Aragorn, when taking leave of Arwen, encourages her to believe that they will meet again: "Behold! we are not bound for ever to the circles of the world, and beyond them is more than memory." But neither he nor anyone else speculates on the question of whether the rewards of virtue extend beyond death. There is plenty of natural religion in *The Lord of the Rings* but the epic tends to stand back from transcendence on this point, as some of Tolkien's shorter tales do not.

The farthest look into the future of mankind on earth is taken by Legolas and Gimli when they first enter Minas Tirith and see the marks of decay around them. The dwarf comments that all the works of men, however promising at first, "fail of their promise." Legolas counters that, even so, "seldom do they fail of their seed," which springs up afresh in unlooked-for times and places to outlast both elves and dwarves. Gimli is unconvinced. Human deeds, he still thinks, "come to naught in the end but might-have-beens." The elf takes refuge in a plea of ignorance: "To that the Elves know not the answer" — and presumably if not the elves, then nobody.

This sad little fugue about the outlook for humanity by representatives of two neighbor races is uncharacteristic in its sadness of the epic as a whole. *The Lord of the Rings* is at bottom a hopeful tale. The whole venture of the Ring always looks desperate. So does combat after combat against wildly superior armies. Yet against all persuasions to despair, Gandalf, Aragorn, Elrond, Faramir, and those who fight beside them hope on and keep on acting upon their hope. Without that, Sauron would have won a dozen times over. Tolkien himself is pessimistic about many aspects of our present age, but he is personally too robust to give up on man. I find the same stoutheartedness in the epic in the teeth of tragedy acknowledged and faced down. It strikes me rather as being a paean to hope.

CHAPTER IV

Sauron and
the Nature of Evil

LIKE GREEK DRAMA or Miltonic epic which begin late along
their plot lines, *The Lord of the Rings* begins just before
the climax of Sauron's efforts to subdue the West, which
have extended far back through the Second and Third Ages.
Indeed, when Tolkien comes to write his account of the
War of the Ring he has so much that is important to summa-
rize about the events leading up to it that he criticizes the
work in the Foreword, for all its three volumes, as "too
short."

To see Sauron in full stature we had best attend carefully
to the long tale of his past guile, ambition, and triumph told
in snatches by Gandalf, Elrond, and others, and by Tolkien
in the Appendices. All the more so because Sauron, never
personally appearing in any scene of the epic, is in some
danger of becoming a shadowy impersonality who does not
seem real in himself but fades into a symbol of evil. Yet his
was the seductive charm of body and mind that tempted the
Númenorean king Ar-Pharazôn to defy the Ban of the Valar
by arms, provoking the One to an anger that drowned all
Númenor under the sea at the end of the Second Age — a
signal victory. In the same Age he had already sown the first
seeds of the War of the Ring by deceiving the elven smiths of

Eregion into forging the rings of power, by which he designed to gain dominion over elves, dwarves, and men. This bold scheme of Sauron's, boundless in its ambitious reach, is the true beginning of Tolkien's epic.

Sauron perpetrated deception of the elven smiths by appealing to what he knew to be the ruling passion of the elves: "their eagerness for knowledge, by which Sauron ensnared them. For at that time he was not yet evil to behold, and they received his aid and grew mighty in craft, whereas he learned all their secrets, and betrayed them, and forged secretly in the Mountain of Fire the One Ring to be their master." As a result, the elves made three rings for themselves, seven that they gave to the dwarf leaders, and nine that they turned over to Sauron for the use of the chiefs of men. All were rings of power, but they reflected the characteristics peculiar to the races for which they were intended. The elf rings, for instance, increased "understanding, making, and healing, to preserve all things unstained." The dwarf rings, appealing to the treasure hunger that was the besetting sin of that race, served "to inflame their hearts with a greed of gold and precious things, so that if they lacked them all other good things seemed profitless, and they were filled with wrath and desire for vengeance on all who deprived them." The rings directed at men stimulated and implemented their ambition for power. Sauron gave these to chiefs of the Dúnedain, especially Angmar, who had not gone to Númenor: "Nine he gave to Mortal Men, proud and great, and so ensnared them. Long ago they fell under the dominion of the One, and they became Ringwraiths, shadows under his great Shadow, his most terrible servants."

But this plot of Sauron's demands a price. He can forge a ruling Ring strong enough to control all these subordinate rings only by pouring into it a large portion of his own native vigor, as Gandalf explains: ". . . he made that Ring himself, it is his, and he let a great part of his own former power pass into it, so that he could rule all the others." The price is greater than he realizes. As long as his vigor is undivided Sauron's spirit can survive death after death, living to fight another day by incarnating itself each time in a new body, as he has done twice before — after the drowning of Númenor and after his defeat by Elendil and Gil-galad, in both of which he perished. But once he infuses part of his strength into a Ring that can be lost he is weakened even while the lost Ring is intact, and he becomes vulnerable to permanent loss of the power to occupy any physical body if the Ring is ever destroyed. This, of course, is the one capital flaw that the West is finally able to exploit.

Why does Sauron ever embark on the forging of the rings in the first place under conditions of such peril? He need not have. The immediate answer must lie somewhere in his character. In his customary arrogance and blind contempt he never takes seriously, perhaps never sees at all, the possibility that he may one day lose the ruling Ring. Besides, he is an obsessed being, driven by his fever to dominate everything and everybody. He cannot rest. He is always on the offensive, always reaching out to draw all life to himself in order to subdue it. As W. H. Auden well remarks, this kind of lust of domination "is not satisfied if another does what it wants; he must be made to do it against his will." [1] It would be a mistake, moreover, to generalize Sauron into a conscious champion of the cause of abstract evil. He is quite simply a champion of Sauron, so far as his intent goes. That he is being used unwittingly by a higher power as one protagonist in a conflict between good and evil has been suggested in the previous chapter.

Setting aside its deadly risk to himself, Sauron's plot with the rings has only partial success. It works perfectly with the human ringwraiths, but with the dwarves it fails to do more than exacerbate their greed. By nature dwarves are not easily digestible. "Though they could be slain or broken, they could not be reduced to shadows enslaved to another will." From the beginning the dwarves "were made . . . of a kind to resist most steadfastly any domination." Since Sauron's whole appetite is for command of other wills, he is balked of his purpose here, though his ability to ruin the lives of individual leaders like Thráin and his partial perversion of general dwarf nature might count as success enough for a less exacting gourmet. One remembers the gloating message he sends after seeing Pippin in the *palantír:* "Tell Saruman that this dainty is not for him. I will send for it at once." Pippin, like every other living being, is to Sauron an impersonal "it" to be devoured.

Sauron's worst failure, however, is with the elf rings, and the manner of it tells much about him. After all the rings have been forged he stands triumphantly on Mount Doom, sets the ruling Ring on his finger, and repeats aloud in the Black Speech the spell by which it rules the others. He is arrogantly unaware that in Eregion across the long miles Celebrimbor, king of the elves, is "aware of him" and hides the elf rings so that no elf will wear one (until after the ruling Ring is lost). He then launches war against Sauron. Like Galadriel in Lórien he perceives the Dark Lord and knows his mind, though Sauron gropes for his thoughts in vain. This basic epistemological superiority of the good over the evil is symbolized by Lórien's light, which pierces to the heart of the darkness of Dol Guldur but cannot be pierced by it in return. Other instances of this blindness of Sauron will appear in due course. Lacking imaginative sympathy an evil intelligence cannot by understanding penetrate a good one, which does have that power in reverse. The former is too involved in self.

Sauron being what he is, that part of himself which he

pours into the ruling Ring makes of it a living will to devour utterly the wills of those who wear the lesser rings. As has been said in the previous chapter, for Tolkien every intelligent being is born with a will capable of free choice, and the exercise of it is the distinguishing mark of his individuality. Nothing can be more precious. So Gandalf, Elrond, Galadriel, Aragorn, and other leaders of the West are careful never to put pressure on another's choices, even to the point of reluctance to give him advice when he asks for it. By contrast, Sauron, who hates any freedom other than his own, focuses his attack in devising the rings against this ultimate bastion of freedom. His ruling Ring is at once a powerful instrument of coercion on all who come within its influence, particularly its wearers, and a carrier of temptation to them to coerce the wills of others. Its method is the subtle one of gradually capturing the mind by radiating an incessant inflationary spell over whatever desires are dearest to it, however harmless or even noble they may seem. So, wearing the ring, Sam sees himself "striding with a flaming sword" to make all Mordor into a garden, Gollum will become *the* Gollum, Isildur is to shine as the great winner of wergild for the deaths of his father and brother. Gandalf dares not wear it, knowing that "the way of the Ring to my heart is by pity, pity for weakness and the desire of strength to do good." Neither dares Galadriel to accept it, when offered the Ring by Frodo and urged by Sam to take it "to make some folk pay for their dirty work." "I would," she replies sadly. "That is how it would begin. But it would not stop with that, alas!" The Ring can work only by coercion of the will. Such is its nature. Anyone who uses coercion in even the best of causes is using an evil means to a good end and thereby corrupting the end — and himself. By definition, good objectives turn bad when achieved by the absolute power over others' wills which the Ring confers. "The very desire of it corrupts the heart," warns Elrond. That is why any gifted person who elects to make the Ring his permanent mode of action inevitably becomes another Dark Lord, and consequently why it cannot be allowed to go on existing.

In the Nazgûl, who are victims of the Ring's power carried to its last degree, the fullness of that power is most clearly visible. Not only are they its slaves, no longer having any wills of their own, but through it they have suffered far-reaching physical changes. The process of lengthening life which has kept Bilbo and Frodo young for some scores of years has prolonged theirs for tens of centuries since the rings were forged in the Second Age. They seem never to have died in the usual sense. They still inhabit their original bodies, but these have faded and thinned in their component matter until they can no longer be said to exist in the dimension of the living. Their flesh is not alive, not dead, but "undead." They have moved into a half-world of shadows, not lighted by our sun but not given over to complete darkness and nothingness either. In consequence their senses have altered so that normal perceptions have dulled or disappeared, while other nameless ones have sharpened. Aragorn describes them to the hobbits on Weathertop: "They themselves do not see the world of light as we do, but our shapes cast shadows in their minds, which only the noon sun destroys; and in the dark they perceive many signs and forms that are hidden from us . . . And at all times they smell the blood of living things, desiring and hating it. Senses, too, there are other than sight or smell." Just as men can feel their presence near, "they feel ours more keenly. Also . . . the Ring draws them."

By putting on the Ring when the ringwraiths attack the camp, Frodo foolishly throws himself into their world. He is able to see for the first time the bodies under their cloaks, and their eyes can see him. Aided by this vision, Angmar succeeds in wounding Frodo with the Morgul knife, and until he is healed at Rivendell Frodo drifts in and out of their land of shades. A shadow seems to him to lie between him and the faces of his friends. The woods and meadows recede as if into a mist. At the Ford the Black Riders look solid and he can suddenly hear their voices and dreadful laughter calling him to Mordor. Gandalf tells Frodo as he recovers in Rivendell what he has escaped: "If they had succeeded you would have become as they are, only weaker and under their command. You would have become a wraith in the dominion of the Dark Lord; and he would have tormented you for trying to keep his Ring . . ." Frodo's peril was gravest when he was wearing the Ring, moreover, "for then you were half in the wraith-world yourself, and they might have seized you." In the last stages of his journey across Mordor to Mount Doom Frodo is sinking rapidly into this world as his resistance to the Ring wanes and its strength waxes in the land where it was forged. "The Land of Mordor where the Shadows lie" blends imperceptibly into the wraith world of the Ring. Why should it not? The Ring, being only an extension of Sauron's personality and power, makes a world like its master's. Sauron is literally as well as figuratively the Dark Lord of a region which he has created (or uncreated) hospitably dark to house himself and those he has made like him. But, like Marlowe's Hell, Mordor has no geographical limits and is wherever its victims are.

These victims not only are morally debased and physically dematerialized but also drag out their days in torment. A mortal who keeps one of the rings of power lives longer, Gandalf tells Frodo at the start, "but he does not grow or obtain more life, he merely continues, until at last every minute is a weariness." One of the most dreadful, most pitiable things about the Nazgûl is their cry of lament: "A long-drawn wail came down the wind, like the cry of some evil and lonely creature." The despair in it is a weapon that Sauron uses to spread hopelessness among the people of Minas Tirith. Angmar especially, the leader of the Nine, is known as the Captain of Despair, who drives even his own troops mad with terror during the siege. He cannot induce it in others unless he first feels it in himself, and in the last analysis it may even come from some corner of Sauron's own withered conscience. When Angmar threatens Éowyn on the battlefield it is not with death: Sauron "will not slay thee in thy turn. He will bear thee away to the houses of lamentation, beyond all darkness, where thy flesh shall be devoured, and thy shrivelled mind left naked to the Lidless Eye." The Nazgûl chief is no stranger to these places of physical and spiritual torture, nor to Sauron's delight in them, somewhere at the heart of the darkness which cloaks him. Gollum too has become acquainted with them when captured in Mordor.

The Ring has rendered Gollum vile, but so miserable that he is pitied by all who encounter him in the long course of the Quest: Bilbo, Gandalf, Aragorn, the Mirkwood elves, Frodo, and eventually even Sam, who despises him most. Gollum's private torment actually stems from the fact that the Ring's conquest of his will is incomplete, leaving intact sufficient impulses toward good to breed an unending inner conflict. Out of this arise the two selves whom Frodo and Sam call Gollum and Sméagol, and whom they hear debating each other while he guides them south into Mordor. Critics generally agree that when Gollum uses the pronoun *I* in speaking about himself the better Sméagol-self is prevailing, whereas when he uses *we* he is submitting to Ring-Gollum. On the latter occasions he is sinking his own identity in the Ring, allowing his free personality to be swallowed up by it, as is the case with the Nazgûl. To quote Gandalf again, during the ages when Gollum hid the Ring under the mountains ". . . the thing was eating up his mind, of course, and the torment had become almost unbearable . . . He hated the dark, and he hated light more; he hated everything, and the Ring most of all." Frodo protests that Gollum could never have hated "his precious," the term by which Gollum always refers to the Ring, but the answer comes that "He hated it and loved it, as he hated and loved himself. He could not get rid of it." Without the inner war Gollum would never have hated the Ring or himself.

The reason why Gollum has not succumbed completely is that as a hobbit he originally has lacked the lust to dominate others, deriving from Sauron himself, which the Ring is specially potent to implant and amplify. This is the same hobbit trait that makes Bilbo and Frodo so toughly resistant to its lure. Nobody who handles the Ring, however, escapes the greed to possess it, which fastens upon him ever after. Tolkien indicates this avidity by the device of having each of its wearers describe it as "precious." Gollum, of course, does so in almost every other sentence he speaks. Significantly, by the word *precious* he means sometimes the Ring, sometimes himself, and sometimes both confusedly. This is Tolkien's brilliant literary method of showing that Gollum often is no longer thinking of the Ring as something separate from himself. He is the Ring; the Ring is Gollum. Apart from it he has no individuality of his own. Likewise, Isildur writes that although the heat of the Ring has burned him badly, "It is precious to me though I buy it with great pain." Bilbo alarms Gandalf greatly by insisting, "It is mine I tell you. My own. My precious. Yes, my precious." And in the last crucial moment when Frodo should be throwing the Ring into the fires of Mount Doom he refuses to do so, in almost the same language of ownership: "I will not do this deed. The Ring is mine!" The irony underlying this, of course, is that anyone who thinks he owns the Ring is in fact owned by it.

That the desire to reduce things and people to possessions

is all wrong is an article of Tolkien's personal creed. In his essay "On Fairy-stories" he holds it up as the cause of the triteness which our self-induced weariness too often makes us see in our world. Things look trite to us when we have "appropriated" them, legally or mentally, ". . . then locked them in our hoard, acquired them, and acquiring ceased to look at them." [2] The remedy is Recovery of a clear view, "seeing things as we are (or were) meant to see them — as things apart from ourselves . . . so that the things seen clearly may be freed from the drab blur of triteness or familiarity — from possessiveness." Here Tolkien is not speaking of the immorality of possessiveness, to be sure, but he is singling it out as the source of an overweening blindness in not seeing the world as we should — separate, free, and independent from ourselves — really the same blindness that underlies Sauron's lust for domination. The idea that "appropriation" is imprisonment of what is not ours is developed even more clearly in the essay's next paragraph, which describes how Recovery through creative fantasy "may open your hoard and let all the locked things fly away like cagebirds . . . and you will be warned that all you had (or knew) was dangerous and potent, not really effectively chained, free and wild; no more yours than they were you." [3]

These passages are packed with meaning for Tolkien's social philosophy in general, as well as specifically for his philosophy of evil in *The Lord of the Rings*. We are not to be like dragons hoarding in our dens as treasure whatever we can snatch from the living world around us. People and things are not meant to be our property; they belong to themselves. These are laws of our nature and theirs. The penalty for violation is a tormented exhaustion like Gollum's, a failure of perception like Sauron's, an exile from the healthy world of fact like the ringwraiths'. Urging Bilbo to give up the Ring, Gandalf pleads: "Let it go! And then you can go yourself, and be free . . . Stop possessing it." We are possessed, captured, by what we think we possess, says Tolkien. And if we believe we can wholly possess anything we delude ourselves. We, and Sauron, find our "precious" slipping out of our fingers. Under our jaded eyes it turns into something different, which we no longer want; our appetite burns for fresh treasures, which we will discard in their turn. The people we master become denatured of their humanity; and the process of enslaving them denatures us. In this way, as in others, evil is self-defeating. A Sauron who succeeded in making himself tyrant over all of Middle-earth would only be the slave of the slaves over whom he ruled.

Such are the main features of evil as they emerge so far in Tolkien's portrait of Sauron and of those influenced to greater or lesser degree by the spell of the ruling Ring. But his kingdom consists also of many others who come there voluntarily or under the direct compulsion of his will, without the Ring. These do not fade into the physical half-world to which the Ring reduces its victims. The Lieutenant of the Tower of Barad-dûr, for instance, is firmly material. But he hideously resembles those other followers of Sauron in the extent to which he has become absorbed into his master's aims and methods. Beginning long ago as a renegade Black Númenorian, he became a student of Sauron's from whom he "learned great sorcery and knew much of the mind of Sauron; and he was more cruel than any orc." He ends by being transformed into a replica of his teacher. "Mouth of Sauron" he calls himself, a man without any name of his own, "for he himself had forgotten it." Considering the high value placed in Tolkien's Middle-earth upon real names as indices of identity — Treebeard and the whole race of dwarves refuse to reveal their names to anybody, and virtually nobody will even pronounce Sauron's aloud in the Black Speech — such namelessness is the acme of total surrender. And this Mouth is the man who is Sauron's choice to be viceroy over Isengard and masticate the conquered folk after the West is won.

Saruman is more like Sauron than he realizes. They believe in the same thing, supremacy through absolute power, but since the supremacy Saruman works for is his own he is a rival, not an ally. Also, he is a pupil of Sauron's, but at a distance, through studying his crafts in the libraries of Gondor. Great and good at first, Saruman intended to learn them only in order to counteract them. But his fate bears out El-rond's warning: "It is perilous to study too deeply the arts of the enemy, for good or ill." Initiation graduates insensibly into imitation. Saruman's "deep and subtle" knowledge and "power over the minds of others" are appealed to and perverted by the similar qualities he finds in the mind of the enemy he studies. Before long he is trying to forge another ruling ring. After that come hypocrisy and treason. In Tolkien's estimate, the desire for knowledge can be a dangerous thing. Sauron seduces by this same Faustian thirst the elven smiths who forged the rings, and seeks unsuccessfully to corrupt all the Eldar. Knowledge is not a good in itself. It is not allowed to remain neutral on Middle-earth, but is good or ill depending on the use to which it is put.

Denethor is another wise man who is not quite wise enough. To start with, he understands that if he looks into the *palantír* which he secretly owns he may lose control of it to Sauron, who is the stronger. As danger closes in on Minas Tirith, however, he takes the plunge in order to spy out the enemy's plans. Even then, had he been a humbler man, he might have been saved, for Suaron cannot deal with humility. But he is one of these proud, superior mortals vain about his deep learning. With these qualities Sauron is quite at home. In the struggle of wills that ensues Denethor is overcome, but not openly, and is tricked into thinking he has won. Through editing the information he is allowed to gather,

Sauron leads him to overpessimistic conclusions, despair, and eventual suicide. Gandalf divines the technique: "The knowledge which he obtained was, doubtless, often of service to him; yet the vision of the great might of Mordor that was shown to him fed the despair of his heart until it overthrew his mind." False knowledge was worse for him than none. Moreover, it was unseasoned by love. Boromir he cherished only as an image of himself. A purer brand of devotion to Faramir and to his people might have been his salvation.

In an article written for the *Tolkien Journal* [4] W. H. Auden expresses discomfort at Tolkien's portrayal of orcs as by nature a wholly evil race. The objection is well worth raising. If true it imperils the doctrine that underpins the moral structure of the epic, that every intelligent being has a will capable of choosing between good and evil. At first sight Auden's point seems well taken. Tolkien shows us orcs as always cruel, quarrelsome, vile in thought and language, enemies of all the civilized races who live around them. More, he explicitly describes them as "being filled with malice, hating even their own kind" to such an extent that they developed no racial language of their own "but took what they could of other tongues and perverted it to their own liking; yet they made only brutal jargons" scarcely intelligible from one orc community to another. Nevertheless, in several places Tolkien makes it very clear that no orc, no individual of any species, and certainly no species as a whole is created evil.

"Nothing is evil in the beginning. Even Sauron was not so," affirms Gandalf at Elrond's Council. The opposite view would be Manichaean, accepting the existence of a creative force in evil equal in power to that of the good. Tolkien firmly rejects it. When Sauron turns to evil he does so by choice, and is diminished in consequence. Evil is a diminution. The ruling Ring cannot give its wearer "more life," merely a longer continuation of the life he already has, but without its vital zest. Orcs are not original creations by Morgoth. He bred them in the First Age "in mockery . . . of elves" by genetic experiments with existing creatures, says Treebeard. The creatures used are not specified. Frodo is sure that no act of genuine creation took place: "The Shadow that bred them can only mock, it cannot make: not real new things of its own. I don't think it gave life to the orcs, it only ruined them and twisted them . . ." Saruman is continuing these genetic experiments and has produced a new variation (not a new species), Orcs of the White Hand, larger, better fighters and able to bear the light of the sun as ordinary orcs are not. Treebeard wonders: "Are they Men he has ruined, or has he blended the races of Orcs and Men? That would be a black evil!" Gamling at Helm's Deep calls them "these half-orcs and goblin-men that the foul craft of Saruman has bred . . ." But genetics cannot breed innately evil wills, or good ones either — only wills which can develop into one or the other as they are employed.

The explanation of orc behavior, then, seems to be that Sauron (and Saruman) has carefully trained them to be what they are, continuing the training begun by Morgoth. Close under his thumb in Mordor, they have been educated to brutality and their social patterns set in a mold which will perpetuate it and its cognate qualities in the generations to come. They have acquired the same delight in torture that Sauron feels, and he has added a nice taste in cannibalism. Yet he seems also to have inculcated in these coarse combative creatures a firm loyalty to himself that they never question, a loyalty that would be reckoned a virtue if turned in a better direction. They have evidently been taught also that the elves are rebels — against Sauron as their rightful lord, of course. The Uruk-hai at Helm's Deep are courageous fighters, and even have achieved considerable esprit de corps. In short, there is an orc point of view about things which it is possible to understand, even to pity. The poor brutes are so plainly the toys of a mightier will than theirs. They have been conditioned to will whatever Sauron wills. "And for me," exclaims Gandalf, "I pity even his slaves." Aragorn at Helm's Deep includes them in his warning against the Fangorn huorns, which are marching to crush them, but the orcs do not listen. Never in Tolkien's tale are any orcs redeemed, but it would go against the grain of the whole to dismiss them as ultimately irredeemable.

Throughout the hierarchy of life on Middle-earth consciousness extends higher, deeper, broader than it does in our world today, and with consciousness goes the power to work for good or for evil. Eagles are allies of Gandalf, whereas crows spy for Sauron and wolves are as fierce as orcs on his behalf. The hearts of many trees in Mirkwood, as well as a few in Fangorn, have turned bad under his influence. Others remain healthy. Whether the malice of the Grey Willow who stupefies the hobbits in the Old Forest derives from Sauron or from natural hatred for destructive mankind is not certain, but it embraces all travelers, innocent and guilty alike. The mountain Caradhras has long been known to the dwarves as purposefully "cruel" in trying to kill wayfarers with storms and falling rocks. Aragorn comments that "many evil and unfriendly things in the world . . . yet are not in league with Sauron, but have purposes of their own. Some have been in the world longer than he." Similarly independent of the Dark Lord are the "nameless things" gnawing at the roots of the world, whom Gandalf meets far underground in his fight with the Balrog. Tolkien obviously wants to leave us with a vague sense, all the more potent because it remains vague, of the almost limitless penetration of evil into the farthest crevices of conscious life.

By and large, though, Sauron has been able to enlist most

of the evil consciousness of Middle-earth under his banner in one way or another. Tolkien's ability to invent such beings in new combinations of body and spirit seems endless. The Balrog, a "fiery shadow" sprung from the "flame of Udûn" (hell), is barely physical and can shift its shape at will. Inherited from Morgoth after the fall of Thangorodrim in the First Age, he has been used by Sauron to drive the dwarves out of Moria, and now is loosed upon Gandalf, his spiritual opposite. This Balrog (referred to by all as *a* Balrog) evidently is not the only one of his kind. He seems akin to Sauron himself, who, when forced out of his body by the destruction of the Ring, appears as "a vast soaring darkness . . . flickering with fire" before he is dissipated by the wind. By contrast, the Watchers of Cirith Ungol are well-nigh unliving statues of stone designed by Sauron to keep out enemies. He has given them, however, radarlike senses that detect Frodo and Sam, and powerful wills that the hobbits are able to break only by prayer to Elbereth before they can escape.

Still different is the great spider Shelob, who cares nothing about either party in the War of the Ring but only about getting enough food for her insatiable paunch, whether it consist of elves, men, orcs, hobbits, or her own innumerable brood. Grossly physical though she is, "alone, swollen till the mountains could no longer hold her up and the darkness could not contain her" she is more "an evil thing in spider form" than a mere spider. She hungers to devour the minds as well as the bodies of her prey. Gollum's worship she has accepted long ago and "the darkness of her evil will" accompanies him on all his journeys thereafter, "cutting him off from light and from regret." Tolkien's language about her often takes on a symbolic tone: ". . . weaving webs of shadow, for all living things were her food, and her vomit darkness." Though Shelob is a solitary hunter, her lust to feed on the whole world differs from Sauron's only in the manner of its accomplishment. So, like the other monsters of the tale, in her particular form of unchecked appetite she is one of the many variations on the theme of evil of which Sauron is the generic type.

Finally there are the barrow-wights. These are the spirits of dead men, unable to rest, who haunt the burial mounds of the kings and queens of the old North Kingdom. They entrap passersby and kill them. The reader may be excused for assuming that they are the ghosts of the people whose graves they trouble, but the evidence in the text is otherwise. While Merry lies senseless on the burial slab decked out in the clothes and jewels of the king entombed there, he dreams that he is that king, who was slain by "the men of Carn Dûm" in a night attack. Bombadil reveals after his rescue of the hobbits that this attack was led by "the evil king of Carn Dûm in the Land of Angmar" — that is, by the chief of the ringwraiths. Tom also takes for Goldberry a brooch belonging to the fair and good queen buried there whom he knew ages ago in life. Accordingly, the dead are innocent victims of treachery and are not the right ones to be barred from a place of rest or to do harm to chance travelers on the Downs. No, the wights must be the ghosts of the evil attackers from Carn Dûm — not Angmar himself, who is still alive and busy elsewhere as a ringwraith, but his followers. Their resemblance is to the dead oath-breakers whose spirits Aragorn summons at the stone of Erech to keep their broken promise of aid to Isildur and his heirs. In the latter case Tolkien is relying on the Norse warrior code, which branded an oath-breaker as the worst of criminals, foredoomed to wander after death. In the case of the barrow-wights Tolkien seems to be invoking the same punishment upon treachery under the same code.

Their connection with Sauron is hinted at first in Tom's description of their coming: "A shadow came out of dark places far away, and the bones were stirred in the mounds. Barrow-wights walked in the hollow places with a clink of rings on cold fingers . . ." among the hills. This shadow is Sauron sending the barrow-wights. The incantation chanted by the wight who is about to kill the hobbits specifically condemns them to death "till the dark lord lifts his hand/over dead sea and withered land," after the sun fails and the moon dies. Here a servant of Sauron (and maybe Sauron himself) is looking forward to a Black Resurrection at the end of the world, when the dead arise to face judgment not by Christ but by a triumphant Dark Lord who has taken His place. It is all nonsense, of course. Tom exorcizes the wight to a prison "darker than the darkness,/Where gates stand for ever shut, till the world is mended." This mending of the world seems to refer to a Resurrection quite different from that anticipated by Sauron and his servants. Meantime, Tom's song frees the minds of the hobbits from whatever limbo the wight's spell has consigned them to.

The whole episode is significant as showing the range of Sauron's powers and his hopes. From the remoteness of Mordor he is able to bend the ghosts of dead men to his purposes nearly as absolutely as he does the still-living Nazgûl enslaved by the Ring. And he aspires to be God. If he can rule the races of Middle-earth while Earth abides, why not the souls of the dead after the world ends? Tolkien springs upon the reader surprise after surprise in the inexhaustible variety of evil beings of whom Sauron can dispose. Their powers are many but their chief weapon is fear. Gimli points this up in retelling how Aragorn put to flight the southern wing of Sauron's armies with the shadow host of dead oath-breakers: "Strange and wonderful I thought it that the designs of Mordor should be overthrown by such wraiths of fear and darkness. With its own weapons was it worsted!"

Sauron himself is not exempt from the same feelings of

doubt and dread which he inspires in others. The finding of his Ring by his enemies rouses him to a fearful awareness of dangers he had never foreseen. Increasingly as the epic proceeds, that Eye of his, which needs no lids because it never sleeps, anxiously searches for the Ring and its bearers, while also surveying the preparations for war on both sides. With the logic of ambition he expects some one of the Western leaders to turn the power of the Ring against him. But with the lack of imagination [5] that characterizes the self-involved he cannot conceive that they may refuse power and decide to destroy the Ring instead. As time goes on and the Ring still eludes him, his alarm grows. "Indeed he is in great fear, not knowing what mighty one may suddenly appear, wielding the Ring, and assailing him with war," Gandalf guesses on meeting Aragorn in Fangorn. Sauron fumbles his chance to read Pippin's mind in the *palantír* because he is hurried into the mistake of being "too eager" to torture the truth out of Pippin in person.

Most drastically shocking to the Dark Lord is Aragorn's sudden revelation of himself in the *palantír* as the heir of Isildur. "To know that I lived and walked the earth was a blow to his heart, I deem; for he knew it not till now . . . Sauron has not forgotten Isildur and the sword of Elendil," says Aragorn grimly after a struggle of wills in which he tears control of the Orthanc-stone away from the enemy. And he is right. The knowledge that Aragorn survives and (as he thinks) will surely become Lord of the Ring against him creates temporary tumult in Sauron's hold over Mordor. The warnings that Angmar sends back to headquarters after meeting Frodo and Sam on the stairs at Cirith Ungol go unheeded for several days while Sauron broods. The confusion among the orc guards allows the hobbits to slip into Mordor despite the battle with Shelob. And, best of all, Sauron is bluffed into launching his attack on Gondor prematurely. Down in the city Gandalf senses this with joy: "I feel from afar his haste and fear. He has begun sooner than he would. Something has happened to stir him."

Thereafter until the end of the tale signs of the Dark Lord's "doubt" and strained watching multiply, alternating with times when the Eye is "turned inward, pondering tidings of doubt and danger," thinking of Aragorn and the sword of Elendil which once killed Sauron on the slopes of Barad-dûr. Finally when he glimpses Frodo near the Cracks of Doom Sauron at last sees the magnitude of his folly in one flash and blazes with wrath and fear. "Wise fool," Gandalf calls him. So he is. But his very folly, his misjudgments, his fears, his doubts, his memories of past defeat, his hatred of Gondor for humiliations of old are what keep him a living figure instead of an impersonal evil. One can almost sigh as well as shudder when at the moment of dissolution he still stretches out over the world "a vast threatening hand, terrible but impotent," before the wind blows him away.

The question remains how far Tolkien wishes his treatment of evil to be considered not only moral but metaphysical. As remarked in Chapter III, Tolkien does not write in the technical language of philosophy. In one passage of his essay "On Fairy-stories" he deliberately sidesteps the epistemological problem of whether and in what form a physical world exists apart from man's perceptions. *Recovery* he defines as "a regaining of a clear view" of things, and adds, "I do not say 'seeing things as they are' and involve myself with the philosophers, though I might venture to say 'seeing things as we are (or were) meant to see them' — as things apart from ourselves." [6] The philosophers with whom he prefers not to involve himself are probably those of the idealist school from Berkeley down to our modern phenomenologists who, each in his own way, echo Coleridge's dejection, ". . . we receive but what we give/And in our life alone does Nature live." Yet of course Tolkien cannot escape metaphysics. By introducing the word *meant* he implies intention, and only a person of some kind can have an intent for mankind. He is merely turning an epistemological problem into a theological one. Without using blatantly theological terms his ideas are often clearly theological nonetheless, and are best understood when viewed in the context of the natural theology of Thomas Aquinas, whom it is reasonable to suppose that Tolkien, as a medievalist and a Catholic, knows well. The same is true in the area of metaphysics. Some of Thomas' less specifically Christian propositions about the nature of evil seem highly congruent with those which Tolkien expresses or implies in laymen's terms in *The Lord of the Rings*. We must be very tentative, of course, and alert not to force a literary masterpiece into any tight philosophical mold, Thomistic or otherwise. Middle-earth is avowedly pre-Christian.

"Nothing is evil in the beginning. Even Sauron was not so." It is well to repeat often Tolkien's basic moral and ontological dictum. Before he succumbed to the promptings of Morgoth, Sauron had the excellence native to the species into which he was born, whatever that species was. So did Saruman; so did Gollum; so did the Nazgûl, and all the rest. Grima Wormtongue, even, did Théoden honest service before he sold himself to Saruman. Sauron may have been a Vala, as Auden suggests,[7] or he may have belonged to some other powerful race. It is not very important. What matters is that he had great gifts of mind, a full range of perceptions, a handsome body, and a sense of fellowship that made him welcome to everyone. After his fall, his moral vision narrowed down to what could serve his ambitions. This is a grievous loss of perceptive faculties, resulting in the blindness and lack of imaginative insight we have so often noted. It is also monomania. After a time his body became black and burning hot, so ugly that he had to hide himself away in Mirkwood and

Mordor. This process describes not merely an almost Platonic loss of personal beauty but a diminution of physical existence. It is also a loss of normal intercourse with others, a retreat into a loneliness cut off from equals. Literally and figuratively, light is exchanged for darkness. Sauron's every change is a deterioration from those good and healthy norms with which he began. Aquinas would call them all losses of Being. Evil is not a thing in itself but a lessening of the Being inherent in the created order.

Tolkien does not write in so many words about *Being*, any more than he does about *form, substance, essence, existence,* and other metaphysical concepts. But as his evildoers suffer loss after heartbreaking loss from origins which he holds up as admirable these losses cry out for ontological interpretation. One of the few detailed descriptions we get of Sauron's omnipresent Eye overtly pulls us along in that direction: "The Eye was rimmed with fire, but was itself glazed, yellow as a cat's, watchful and intent, and the black slit of its pupil opened on a pit, a window into nothing." To see into Sauron's Eye is to look into nothingness. Sauron is getting as close as a subsisting creature can get to absolute non-Being. His watchtower on Cirith Ungol is built in the same image. Its searchlight is "like a noisome exhalation of decay, a corpse-light, a light that illuminated nothing. In the walls and towers windows showed, like countless black holes looking inward into emptiness . . ." The emptiness, be it noted, is "inward." Resemblance to Sauron's restless Eye is enhanced by the revolving tower, "first one way and then another, a large ghostly head leering into the night." And here again (for the symbolism pursues us through the epic) the light of Mordor is no light but the flicker of darkness over the dead. Add Gandalf's stern command to Angmar when he confronts the Nazgûl at the gates of Gondor: "Go back to the abyss prepared for you! Go back! Fall into the nothingness that awaits you and your Master." Over and over Tolkien's own words connect Sauron and his servants with a nothingness that is the philosophical opposite of Being.

Add, finally, the outer and inner decay of Saruman who "was great once, of a noble kind that we should not dare to raise our hands against. He is fallen . . ." — to repeat what is virtually Frodo's epitaph over him. After the defeat of his armies he still has at least the spell of his wonderful voice left to him but he misuses that too and cheapens it by cursing as he rejects chance after chance to redeem himself to usefulness. In the end he trudges the roads in "rags of grey or dirty white," an object of sorrow to Gandalf: ". . . alas for Saruman! . . . He has withered altogether." His death finishes the downward plunge. The spirit rising from his shrunken body is dissipated by a wind from the West, "and with a sigh dissolved into nothing." That word *nothing* is a repeated knell for the passing of the lords of wickedness in *The Lord of the Rings*. Tolkien is careful never to say anything explicit about that nothingness to which they go, doubly careful never to call it hell, but it shares with hell the distinguishing feature of total estrangement from ultimate Being.

CHAPTER V

The Free Peoples

CRITICS LIKE EDMUND WILSON, who pontificates that "for the most part such characters as Dr. Tolkien is able to contrive are perfectly stereotyped," [1] or Mark Roberts, to whom *The Lord of the Rings* is "simply an adventure story" [2] are refuted on their own ground, I hope, by chapters prior and subsequent to this one. My concern here is to demonstrate that these critics, and others, are taking too narrow a view of what a Tolkien "character" is. As Tolkien conceives the matter, characters are not limited to the individuals who play parts in the war against Sauron. They include also, and perhaps even predominantly, the various races to which each person belongs. Tolkien is at least as interested in exploring the characteristic traits of elves, hobbits, dwarves, men, ents, and other intelligent species who swarm Middle-earth as he is in depicting, say, Frodo, Elrond, Aragorn, and Gimli, or in telling the events of the War of the Ring. The essay "On Fairy-stories," that indispensable handbook of Tolkien theory, should have warned the commentators to look at the epic in that light. The aim of *The Lord of the Rings* is certainly to tell a story of more than ordinary fascination, but it is also to satisfy our basic human hungers to hold communion with as wide a range as possible of creatures like and unlike ourselves.[3] In Tolkien's analysis, this is one of the imperatives of good fantasy.

The question has inevitably been raised whether Tolkien wants us to view each of his many intelligent species as having its niche in some sort of vertical Chain of Being in which some are "higher" than others.[4] If so, by what principle of classification? Today's spirit of egalitarianism predisposes us against any such interpretation. Moreover, Tolkien's own wide dissemination of consciousness, the power of speech, and especially moral freedom among nearly all the living creatures of his world may seem to blur the distinctions that we usually regard as existing between species in these particulars. Nevertheless there are cogent reasons for thinking that he means to set at least one major grouping of species above all the rest.

This grouping consists of those whom Treebeard, in reciting his catalogue of "living creatures" to Merry and Pippin in Fangorn Forest, calls "the free peoples":

> Learn now the lore of Living Creatures!
> First name the four, the free peoples:
> Eldest of all, the elf-children;
> Dwarf the delver, dark are his houses;
> Ent the earthborn, old as mountains;
> Man the mortal, master of horses:

Having listed elves, dwarves, ents, and men as free peoples, Treebeard clears his throat and proceeds to call off the names of a selection of beasts, birds, and reptiles:

> *Hm, hm, hm.*
> Beaver the builder, buck the leaper,
> Bear bee-hunter, boar the fighter;
> Hound is hungry, hare is fearful . . .
> *hm, hm.*

> Eagle in eyrie, ox in pasture,
> Hart horn-crownéd; hawk is swiftest,
> Swan the whitest, serpent coldest. . . .

Several observations stand out. Four species are "free peoples" whereas all the others are not. And these four are named "first," with the inference that they deserve priority. Hobbits and wizards do not appear on the list because it is one which Treebeard learned long ago as a young ent before the ents met either of those races. So far as hobbits are concerned, after inspecting Merry and Pippin, Treebeard makes a place for them in proper alphabetical order between ents and men:

> Ents the earthborn, old as mountains,
> the wide-walkers, water drinking;
> and hungry as hunters, the Hobbit children,
> the laughing-folk, the little people . . .

Wizards never do get into Treebeard's catalogue. By his standards, if the five of them can be called a race at all, they are rank newcomers who did not turn up until the middle of the Third Age. "I do not know the history of wizards," he remarks with some disdain.

Elrond also has a concept of "free peoples" as distinct from other living creatures, and in choosing members of the Fellowship of the Ring he is politic enough to include at least one representative of each. In his mind the category embraces men, wizards, dwarves, elves, and of course hobbits. He omits ents not because he does not know of them or does not rate them among free peoples but because of obvious disparities in size, habits, location, and so forth, which would make their membership in the Company impracticable.

In the phrase *free peoples* both the adjective and the noun are operative words. Orcs, trolls, dragons, and their like do not qualify for the designation because they are not free any longer. According to Tolkien's basic maxim that "Nothing is evil in the beginning" they were free once, but they have surrendered their wills to Sauron and become his slaves. On the other hand the normal creatures of the wild whom Treebeard classes as "living" but not as "free peoples" have not attained the level of social organization that would earn them the title of "peoples." This defect implies also a lower order of both intelligence and moral perception than that which characterizes the five or six races to which Elrond and Treebeard assign primacy among the living beings of Middle-earth. Within these half-dozen, however, neither the elf nor the ent proposes any ranking of superiority. Elrond makes his selections in no particular order. Treebeard's roll call is a mnemonic device and therefore strictly alphabetical and alliterative, with the single exception of the elves to whom ents historically give the place of honor as the one race which taught them language. Consequently, the only vestige of a Chain of Being which Tolkien, through Treebeard and Elrond, is accepting is the dominance of the free peoples. The gulf between them and all other creatures alive can be bridged by conscious communication of many kinds, including speech, but never completely erased.

The Christian root of this type of dualistic thinking by Tolkien stands revealed in his essay "On Fairy-stories," in which he formulates the relations between human and subhuman life in terms of the doctrine of Creation and Fall. Tolkien accepts the doctrine that at his creation Man was given dominion over all other creatures. In order that he might rule them justly both he and they were endowed with understanding of each other's speech. The Fall did not take away Man's ordained superiority but it did sever the tie of communion through language. Ever since, "a strange fate and guilt lies on us. Other creatures are like other realms with which Man has broken off relations, and sees now only from the outside at a distance . . ." Fantasy tries to satisfy our hunger for reconciliation by creating many varieties of living creatures with which we can once more converse. But it does not try to pretend that the breach can ever really be healed this side of Paradise; it does not gloss over the "sense of separation" from the subhuman, which must continue to haunt us all our lives as a result of the Fall.

In Appendix G of the same essay Tolkien is moved to lay upon modern dogmas of evolution the blame for improperly blurring this sense of separation "by the hypotheses (or dogmatic guesses) of scientific writers who classed Man not only as 'an animal' — that correct classification is ancient — but as 'only an animal.' " In this view of man as possessing a rational soul, which other creatures do not have, Tolkien is again, of course, Christian. He is not opposing evolutionary theories but he is definitely objecting to any interpretation of them that dogmatically denies that at some point the human being has been given faculties which transcend the evolutionary process.

There is nothing at all in *The Lord of the Rings* to hint that any of the free peoples has evolved from other creatures or from one another. On the contrary, allusions keep cropping up to their special creation by some nebulous divine act or to some kind of life they are to enjoy after death, or to both. What Tolkien does in the epic is to broaden the traditional concepts of Man's primacy into the primacy of a group of free peoples who are more or less on a par with Man. But having made the times pre-Christian, he has freed himself from the need to deal with them in a Christian context, which would be awkward if applied to elves, ents, dwarves, and the rest. He can and does retain, however, a general foundation of natural theology in the areas of moral norms and the working out of a providential cosmic order. Combining these with intimations of divine origins and destinations, Tolkien achieves for his free peoples a status on Middle-earth which if not precisely Christian is still very much like it in overall tone.

So much is true of them as a group. Tolkien's real mastery as a writer, though, consists in his power to establish for each individual race a personality that is unmistakably its own.[5] A dwarf is as different from an elf as an ent from a hobbit, and all from a man and from one another. Further, each race has not only its gifts but also its private tragedy, which it must try to overcome as best it can. And it must work out its own often difficult way of living with its peers. All this imparts great variety and drama to the epic within the broader movement of events. It is worth watching in each race in turn.

Since Treebeard awards the elves pride of place, we shall make no mistake in doing the same. Besides, Tolkien has given them his heart.

1. *Elves: The People of the Stars*

As if challenging those modern sophisticates who scorn all tales about elves as childish fancies, Tolkien takes delight in drawing them as the most superlatively gifted race ever to walk Middle-earth. They are "eldest of all, the elf-children," in Treebeard's catalogue of free peoples. According to *The Hobbit* they came out of "the twilight before the raising of the Sun and Moon" to wander in the forests. Their desire "always . . . to talk to everything," as Treebeard recalls, is a sign of their curiosity and keen original sympathy for other living beings. In order to speak with ents, elves taught them the "great gift" of language, the first act in their long career as teachers of the other peoples of Middle-earth. It was an elf who, deeply sensing the tragedy of the ents, composed the sad dialogue ballad between them and their departing mates which Treebeard sings to Merry and Pippin. As compared with men, he ruminates, elves are "less interested in themselves . . . and better at getting inside other things." Some of these remarkable people stayed on in the forests of the continent to become Silvan elves, but three of their tribes became "the People of the Great Journey" by sailing far westward across the sea to find the Valar in Valinor. There they "lived for ages, and grew fairer and wiser and more learned, and invented their magic and their cunning craft in the making of beautiful and marvellous things before they came back into the Wide World." [6]

Why the demiurgic Valar should choose the elves alone from all the other intelligent species on Middle-earth Tolkien does not explain in so many words. But it is a fair inference that the choice was connected with the one salient characteristic that sets them apart from other beings — their immortality of body. Not that they are altogether invulnerable. They can be wounded and killed, as are Gil-galad and many of his elfin warriors in the joint assault with Elendil on Sauron's tower of Barad-dûr at the end of the Second Age. Short of violent death, however, elves live forever, aging slowly but never growing old, knowing no sickness or other ills of the flesh. In a world where everything else is always dying such deathlessness can prove to be a fatal privilege. Endless life can turn into endless boredom and stagnation, or assert itself in cruel domination over other species, who do not live long enough to acquire equal power and knowledge. Tolkien is setting up some interesting dilemmas here. The Valar being aware of these, it would seem, undertake to teach the elves how to endure their immortality. They are given a home in the Undying Lands, an environment suited to their case because in it nothing ever grows old or dies. Their intellects and artistic sensibilities are afforded every stimulation so that they may always have inexhaustible fields for the highest sorts of mental activity. Religious longings are assuaged by their love for Elbereth, who kindled the stars. And surely, as wards of the Valar appointed by the One as guardians of all Middle-earth, they come to apprehend those differences between good and evil that are written into the cosmic order. For, as we know, the laws of morality bind elves as much as they bind all the other free peoples, and do not vary with place or time.

These laws the elves, like all other intelligent races, retain free will to obey or disobey. Fëanor's feat of imprisoning in three jewels, the *Silmarilli*, the light of the Two Trees that illuminates Valinor, requires genius, but it is criminal. It is a theft of beauty, an act of selfish "possessiveness" which makes the jewels "precious" to him and his followers in the same bad sense that the one Ring is "precious" to Gollum, to Bilbo, to Isildur, and its other victims. Unhappily, they also become precious to Morgoth — a renegade Vala? — who steals them in his turn and escapes with them to his fortress on Middle-earth. So the history of the First Age begins. Pursuit of him by the elves is expressly forbidden by the Valar as being motivated not by a desire to undo a wrong but to recover the baubles for themselves. For their "pride" in violating this edict the Noldor elves are exiled from Valinor and allowed for centuries to wage hopeless wars against Morgoth in which "they were at last utterly defeated." [7] In one sense only are their fall and subsequent misery in a world of miseries a *felix culpa*, a fortunate fall. They at least civilize the first primitive tribes of mankind whom they enlist as allies. But all have to be rescued from disaster together at the end of the First Age by the armies of the relenting Valar.

Although many elves then return to the Undying Lands, many others have become too interested in the affairs of Middle-earth to leave it. They spread their culture among neighboring races. Halfway through the Second Age, however, the elven smiths of Eregion, tricked by Sauron, commit a second grievous error, this time with the noblest intentions but nonetheless fraught with doom for Middle-earth and for their own future on it. The three rings of power which they forge to enlarge the powers of elves are all meant for good uses, as Elrond explains at the Council in Rivendell. They were not made as weapons of war or conquest. "Those who made them did not desire strength or domination or hoarded wealth, but understanding, making, and healing, to preserve all things unstained." No purposes could be loftier. In part they are attained. Through one of the three Elrond becomes "a master of healing," and through a second Galadriel "makes" the lovely light of Lothlórien, which opposes Sauron's darkness. But the trouble is that the elf rings, like the others forged for dwarves and men, are ultimately dependent on the master Ring secretly manufactured by Sauron. So, says Elrond, ". . . all that has been wrought by those who wield the Three will turn to their undoing, and their minds and hearts will become revealed to Sauron, if he regains the One." Well may he add grimly, "It would be better if the Three had never been."

More, and worse, about the predicament into which the elves have stumbled is disclosed to Frodo and Sam by Galadriel during their stay in Lórien: ". . . if you fail, then we are laid bare to the Enemy. Yet if you succeed, then our power is diminished, and Lothlórien will fade . . . We must depart into the West, or dwindle to a rustic folk of dell and cave, slowly to forget and be forgotten." That is, the destruction of Sauron's one Ring, which is Frodo's mission, will also annul the power of the elf ring she wears, through which she created Lórien and sustains it in existence. That power gone, Lórien must fade, as Barad-dûr immediately dissolves when

Gollum falls into the fire of the Cracks of Doom wearing the one Ring that built it. So must go all other works performed by the other two elf rings.

But why must the elves dwindle if they do not then forthwith return to Valinor? The answer can only be guessed at. Yet in the very nature of a ring of power it may possibly be found. A ring can have only such power as its maker gives it, and that power must come from somewhere. In the case of the one Ring Sauron had to instill much of his own native vigor into it to produce the awesome thing it was, thereby weakening what was left in himself. The legitimate inference is that the elven smiths of Eregion likewise had to infuse a large portion of elf vitality into the three. These smiths were, after all, descendants of Fëanor, who knew how to entomb the supernal light of the Two Trees in his *Silmarilli*. Though enfeebled in themselves by the making of their three rings, the elves suffered no loss in the total sum of their vigor while the three remained active. Yet when these went dead upon the melting of the one Ring their stored energy was dissipated, never to be regained. The loss of energy in Sauron's Ring renders his will too weak to hold his body together. He is deprived of his grasp on physical existence on Middle-earth, though not of spiritual existence elsewhere. By analogy the elves lose vital energy which can be replenished only in Valinor.

Galadriel foresees all this long in advance. Her age and wisdom are extraordinary even for her race, however. It does not follow that all elves recognize the full ramifications of their predicament as the epic opens. Before Frodo left the Shire, elves could be seen passing westward on their way out of Middle-earth, but their reason for leaving was simply that they "were no longer concerned with its troubles." They are obeying the homing impulse for Valinor deeply implanted in all their race.

Gildor and his band, too, are feeling this homesickness when they meet the hobbits in the Shire woods. "We are Exiles," he tells them, "and most of our kindred have long ago departed, and we too are now only tarrying here a while, ere we return over the Great Sea." The lovely hymn these elves chant to Elbereth is full of nostalgia for the Undying Lands. They have lost interest in earthly affairs. Sauron is not in their thoughts. They seem surprised when Frodo asks them about the Black Riders tracking him, but respond by safeguarding the hobbits with their company for that one night. Asked by Frodo for advice how to proceed, Gildor complies reluctantly and not very helpfully: "Now you should be grateful, for I do not give this counsel gladly. The Elves have their own labours and their own sorrows, and they are little concerned with the ways of hobbits or of any other creatures on earth. Our paths cross theirs seldom, by chance or purpose." [8] Gildor cares enough for the hobbits to send word of their danger ahead to the Wandering Companies, to Bombadil, Aragorn, and Elrond. But he does not offer to escort them to Rivendell, nor does he turn up there to take part in Elrond's Council. Whether he even helps in the actual fighting against Sauron is doubtful. This withdrawal inward, coupled with a strong sense of isolation from all other creatures, is not characteristic of all elves, naturally, or the Ring-bearer would have found no help at Rivendell or Lórien. Yet it can be met with even in Elrond's household, when Lindir laughingly tells Bilbo it is not easy for him to tell the difference between a hobbit and a man because "Mortals have not been our study. We have other business."

There lies the key to that body of elf opinion represented by Gildor and Lindir and latent even in those others who help to rally the West against Sauron. Hobbits and such are "mortals," very different from the immortals who watch their brief generations blurring by. Mortals are "creatures on earth"; at heart elves are of the Undying Lands. Gone in most elves is the childlike curiosity of the firstborn who wanted to talk to everything alive. Well, the elves are older now by many Ages and have acquired "their own labours and sorrows." Sam has noticed this in Gildor's elves: ". . . so old and young, and so gay and sad, as it were." When asked by Frodo how he likes them, he replies wistfully, "They seem a bit above my likes and dislikes, so to speak." He feels the distance between the species too.

Tolkien keeps probing into various facets of the differences between elf and mortal as the epic runs its course. But he knows he must keep showing the resemblances, too, if we are to believe in elves. Besides, Tolkien has a bone to pick with the view now current among us that elves are tiny and quaint, either in appearance or behavior. Physically the elves of Middle-earth look much like men: "They were tall, fair of skin and grey-eyed, though their locks were dark, save in the golden house of Finrod; and their voices had more melodies than any mortal voice that now is heard." Their clothes are not in any way peculiar, except the elven cloaks designed for camouflage. Elves have a particularly sustaining kind of bread and drink for wayfarers traveling far and light, but otherwise they eat the common foods. The banquet Elrond serves at Rivendell is eaten by elves, dwarves, hobbits, and men alike. Legolas needs no special diet while traveling with the Company. Gildor and his band may walk the dark woods in "a shimmer, like the light of the moon," but there is nothing ethereally unphysical about them. "Now is the time for speech and merriment!" he calls out, as bread, fruits, and liquor are passed around to elves and hobbits.

Jokes and laughter are often on elves' lips, and their singing wrings the heart with mingled joy and sadness. They have the vitality of everlasting youth and the melancholy of their centuries. Legolas enjoys an endurance that never tires in the long chase after the orcs, as well as a lightness of body that allows him to skim along on the crust of the snow of Caradhras when even the smaller hobbits break through the surface. He can always see farther than anybody else, and can hear the very stones of Eregion lamenting the passing of their elven masters many years before: " '. . . *deep they delved us, fair they forged us, high they builded us; but they are gone . . . They sought the Havens long ago.*' " Elf senses are keener, bodies more perfectly composed, than ours, as befits immortals, but they are still physical senses and bodies raised only a notch above the human, and not beyond the reach of our understanding. Elves are not immaterial spirits. They are not supernatural but "natural, far more natural" than man, Tolkien insists in the essay "On Fairy-stories."

Over against the many elves who have abandoned Middle-earth, or who linger on uncaring, Tolkien sets the many others, past and present, who assume the burdens of its history. On Weathertop, where Elendil and his host once awaited his elfin allies led by Gil-galad in the Last Alliance, Sam chants the ballad of that last of the elvenkings, "whose realm was fair and free/between the Mountains and the Sea." Those were the days of elfin power and leadership. Gil-galad cared enough for the fate of Middle-earth to give up his otherwise immortal life for it in battle. The elves are far weaker in the Third Age and cannot take the offensive to oppose the reincarnated Sauron, but their tradition of concern is carried on by Elrond, who makes Rivendell a rallying point for all the races of Middle-earth endangered by the impending war. Born half-man, half-elf from the union of Eärendil the man with the elfin princess Elwing, and subsequently made all elf by the Valar, a veteran also of past battles against the Enemy, Elrond is the logical chairman, his house the inevitable place, for the Council of Free Peoples, which debates what to do with the Ring Frodo has just brought there. Yet the sorrow is that, whether Sauron wins or loses, Elrond and his elves will lose. If Sauron wins, they must flee Middle-earth or become his slaves. If Sauron loses, by the destruction of his Ring and theirs they must still flee, or diminish from their elf natures to a lesser breed. What holds Elrond to his task is what holds Galadriel, a moral choice that "what should be, shall be." It is enough.

The Council at Rivendell is guided by "the long wisdom of Elrond." It is clear from the start that in his opinion the Ring should be melted down in the fires of Mount Doom, into which he long ago vainly urged Isildur to throw it. But with Gandalf's help, and Aragorn's, he skillfully nudges the discussion of the various speakers along in directions that will lead them to reach that decision for themselves. He is adamant that he himself will not handle the Ring in any way: "I fear to take the Ring to hide it. I will not take the Ring to wield it." If nothing else, this self-distrust of one of the noblest among the elves should prove that elves are not incapable of evil.[9] Elrond's assent to Frodo's offer to take the Ring to Mordor arises from his faith that a higher providence is guiding the deliberations of the Council. Accordingly, in the search for a Ring-bearer he is not inclined to rely on the more obvious selection of candidates who are wise and strong. The task may well be one for the weak, aided by the strength that is not of earth, for "such is the course of deeds that move the wheels of the world: small hands do them because they must . . ."

The same principle, together with a wise political expediency, seems to govern his choice of members of the Company that will go south with Frodo. Sauron has sowed distrust among the free peoples. Therefore each of these (save the ents, who are forestbound) must have a representative who, by living daily with the others, will help to constitute a community of mutual trust. Moreover, each will serve as an ambas-

sador of good will to the different species he will meet along
the road. No less than Gimli for the dwarves is Legolas an
emissary for the elves, both races being now suspected by
each other and by other races, especially men. Elrond might
have picked a mighty elf lord like Glorfindel or an older, more
experienced dwarf. Instead he prefers young and adaptable
unknowns. Tolkien's point about Legolas, for instance, surely
is that he is a rather typical young elf in whom the essential
qualities of his people shine out most visibly. The close friendship that develops between Legolas and Gimli is exactly what
Elrond hopes for.

Rivendell stands for the horizontal capacities of elf society
to reach out, touch, and influence the other intelligent peoples of Middle-earth. Everybody is welcome there, everybody feels at home, everybody talks to everybody else freely
as he would in no other place. Very different is Lórien, "the
heart of Elvendom on earth," as Aragorn calls it. That is all
perpendicular, all elvish. Strangers are not welcome there.
The population consists wholly of Silvan elves living not in
houses but on platforms in the tops of huge mallorn trees,
which grow nowhere else on Middle-earth. Indeed, all its
vegetation, from the flowers of *elanor* and *niphredil* in the
grass to the tree walls enclosing the city of the Galadrim is
unique. So, especially, is "the power and the light that held
all the land in its sway," perceived by Frodo. Later he comes
to understand that the whole enchanted region is created by
the power of Galadriel focused through the elf ring Nenya,
which she is wearing: "The power of the Lady is on it . . .
where Galadriel wields the Elven-ring."

No such light shines over cosmopolitan Rivendell. In
Lórien is the purest essence of faery, resembling the light of
the Two Trees in Valinor, whereby Galadriel has made for
herself and her people a region and a life as close to that of
the Undying Lands as she can contrive on Middle-earth. In

keeping with the nature of the elf ring from which it springs, Lórien the fair is a land of peace and healing where the Company recovers from weariness and grief for the loss of Gandalf, and where the reborn Gandalf himself comes after his fight with the Balrog, naked, to be clothed in white and nursed by Galadriel. Just across the river Sauron's stronghold of Dol Guldur broods on its stony heights above twisted, rotting trees. But the darkness it generates can make no headway against its opposite, the light of Lórien. Tolkien has arranged the confrontation with a purpose, of course. The elf Haldir speaks for him in seeing in the combat between light and darkness large implications for the theme underlying the whole War of the Ring: "In this high place you may see," he points out to Frodo standing on a tree platform, "the two powers that are opposed to one another; and ever they strive in thought, but whereas the light perceives the very heart of the darkness, its own secret has not been discovered. Not yet." But Tolkien also wants to bring the struggle being waged in Lórien right down to a personal one between Galadriel and Sauron. He manages this in a subsequent garden scene in which she demonstrates to Frodo and Sam how her mirror works. What defends Lórien, she tells them, is not so much the singing or even the arrows of her elves as her ability to read the Enemy's thoughts in its waters: ". . . I perceive the Dark Lord and know his mind, or all of it that concerns the Elves. And he gropes ever to see me and my thought. But still the door is closed!" Matched against the sight which the inherent sympathies of goodness give it, the selfishness of evil is blind.[10]

Nevertheless this advantage cannot save Lórien in the end. It was doomed an Age ago at the first forging of the rings. Haldir, speaking for his fellows, knows and laments it. Even if Sauron is beaten, "For the Elves, I fear, it will prove at best a truce, in which they may pass to the Sea unhindered and leave the Middle-earth for ever. Alas for Lothlórien that I love! It would be a poor life in a land where no mallorn grew. But if there are mallorn-trees beyond the Great Sea, none have reported it." A homebody himself, Sam recognizes that the elves "belong here" in Lórien, more even than hobbits do in the Shire. From this love of the elves for Lórien, which Galadriel tells Frodo is deeper than the deeps of the sea so that their regret for it will be undying and never wholly assuaged, arises most acutely her temptation to accept the Ring when Frodo freely offers it to her. For this would be the one forbidden way to save her land. For centuries she and her husband, Celeborn, have loved it and "fought the long defeat" (superb phrase!) which is to be their lot. Now if she accepted the one Ring she could not only conquer Sauron with it but preserve the elf ring on which hangs the very existence of her country. She has even thought of taking it by force from her guest. In the final temptation scene, one of the finest Tolkien ever wrote, she dreams aloud of all the good she might do as Queen of Middle-earth, building up to the explosive recognition, "All shall love me and despair!" This settles the issue for her. Rather, she will "remain Galadriel," fight the good fight against Sauron for the sake of Middle-earth, and return with all her people to Valinor across the sea.

Tolkien's characterization of this greatest of elf women is remarkable throughout. One of the original Noldor leaders who left the Undying Lands with Fëanor in the First Age, she proudly declared, when exiled, that she had no wish to return. Consequently the approaching loss of Lórien is made more poignant for her by the possibility that she will be obliged to remain on Middle-earth, and sink to a rustic state in which she will "forget" all her high knowledge.[11] Her temptation to accept the one Ring is increased correspondingly. Her intuitive understanding of Gandalf's motives for risking the Moria passage is keener than her husband's. So is her ability to absorb at a glance the inmost thoughts of each of her guests, especially Gimli, whose adoration she wins by a single unexpected glance of love. She has sternness, too. Apart from its meaning for Lórien, Frodo's mission is too crucial for all Middle-earth for her not to test the integrity of his companions by an unspoken offer to each of whatever he most desires. Boromir's knowledge that he has failed her scrutiny makes him hate her and drives him to looks and actions that warn Frodo of his danger. "There is in her and in this land no evil, unless a man bring it hither himself," Aragorn has assured the Company. Boromir has brought his in his own heart — the intention to seize the Ring.

As the Company prepares to leave Lórien, Galadriel has the fortitude to encourage her sad lord though "already our evening draweth nigh." She and her women with their own hands weave cloaks for all the travelers into which they embroider the hues of the land they cherish, "for we put the thought of all that we love into all that we make." Much better than the anonymous products of our machines today, Tolkien implies. She also bestows on Frodo and his companions parting gifts carefully selected to meet the needs of each. Aragorn's brooch of elfstone is both the fulfillment of a prophecy and a "token of hope" for his kingship; Frodo's phial of water infused with the light of Eärendil's star will take him safely through dark places in Mordor, and so on. The strands of her golden hair that Galadriel gives Gimli bind them together in affection and signify the passing of the old feud between elves and dwarves. All her gifts come from a generous, wise, and tactful heart. She appears briefly once more at the end of the epic, pardoned by the Valar and ready for the journey overseas. Her true farewell, though, is at her last meal with the Company in Lórien, where to Frodo "already she seemed . . . as by men of later days Elves still at times are seen: present and yet remote, a living vision of that time which has already been left far behind by the flowing streams of Time."

But we do not understand her yet, not until we understand better the slow pace of time in Lórien, and why she made it so. Through this we shall learn something fundamental about the inner life of all elves. As they float down the river, Anduin, the members of the Fellowship debate why their stay in Lórien seemed to them subjectively to last only a few days, whereas the shape of the moon they now see overhead indicates that by objective time they were there about a month. Frodo remembers that on first stepping over its borders he felt "that he had stepped over a bridge of time into a corner of the Elder Days, and was now walking in a world that was no more. In Rivendell there was a memory of ancient things; in Lórien the ancient things still lived on in the waking world." He thought himself in a timeless country exempt from change, and actually heard the cries of seabirds whose race had perished when the world was young. Accordingly he now suggests that in Lórien "we were in a time that has elsewhere long gone by." It must have been before any moon existed, for he saw none there. Time had been stopped.

Legolas, out of his personal experience, corrects him by saying that time never stops, though it may flow more slowly in some places than in others. He then goes to the heart of elf psychology: "For the Elves the world moves, and it moves both very swift and very slow. Swift, because they themselves change little and all else fleets by: it is a grief to them. Slow, because they do not count the running years, not for themselves. The passing seasons are but ripples ever repeated in the long long stream." This analysis tells why the deathlessness of the elves makes them forever sad. Undying themselves, they watch all mortal things around them, which they love, always growing old and dying. "It is a grief to them."

This is the swiftness of time. Then they turn inward to contemplate their own hardly changing natures. This is the slowness of time.

Frodo immediately divines that Galadriel has slowed time, and with it the processes of growth and decay, inside the boundaries of Lórien: things still wear out there, "but the wearing is slow in Lórien . . . The power of the Lady is on it. Rich are the hours, though short they seem, in Caras Galadon, where Galadriel wields the Elven-ring." Correspondingly lessened, then, is the grief of Lórien's elves in being surrounded by the processes of decay. They can be happy there, as they were only in the yet more perfect peace of the Undying Lands, where nothing ever grows old, and as they can be nowhere else on Middle-earth. They love the place passionately. Losing it will be an intolerable return to sorrow, which must drive them back eventually across the sea.

So in elves the difference between subjective and objective time produces tensions that tend to split their lives into two streams, inner and outer. Men feel this difference, too, in lesser degree, but the greater reach of elvish minds and the deeper ache they feel from the transiency of things around them sharpens the split and turns them more inward. Treebeard's comments to the hobbits on the innate empathy of elves for all living and dying creatures points up their pain. Far more than men or dwarves, for instance, elves have built up out of their memories of the past an independent world, parallel to the present, into which they can retreat. In Gimli's words, for elves "memory is more like to the waking world than to a dream. Not so for Dwarves." This in response to Legolas' attempt to comfort Gimli for his loss of Galadriel by reminding him that his memory of Lórien will never fade or grow stale. During their pursuit of the orcs Legolas' sleep is quite unlike that of his companions, and his dreams are a reality apart to which he consciously turns for rest: ". . . he could sleep, if sleep it could be called by Men, resting his mind in the strange paths of elvish dreams, even as he walked open-eyed in the light of this world."

Elves have learned to penetrate also into that ambiguous region where life verges upon death. The Valar have taught them how. That, as Gandalf tells Frodo, is why Glorfindel and other lords of the Eldar are able to stand against the Nazgûl: "They do not fear the Ringwraiths, for those who have dwelt in the Blessed Realm live at once in both worlds, and against both the Seen and the Unseen they have great power." To live at the same time in the worlds of the seen and the unseen is perhaps only the ultimate extension of those powers of intellect, memory, imagination with which the elves have learned to occupy their immortality. Legolas may not be able to stand against the Nazgûl, or against the spirit of the Balrog risen from its dungeons underground, but he is the only one of Aragorn's followers able to walk in the dark among the wraiths of the dead oath-breakers unafraid as in a familiar country.

In all the traits just discussed elves have departed in spirit far from the ways of other creatures on Middle-earth, including men. But one further difference, even more radical, remains. All the mortal races look forward to some sort of life after death in some unspecified somewhere, but not the deathless elves. The latter never seem to expect more than endless life in Valinor. Will they never meet the other races again after the resurrection? Apparently not. This is why the elf princesses Lúthien, Elwing, and Arwen choose to become mortal, in order not to be separated after death from the mortal men they love. Speaking of Lúthien, the first to accept this Doom of Men, Aragorn tells the hobbits in the camp on Weathertop: "But she chose mortality, and to die from the world, so that she might follow him . . . they passed, long ago, beyond the confines of this world." For this reason the parting between Arwen and her father Elrond is so poignant, because it is forever: ". . . and yet grievous among the sorrows of that Age was the parting of Elrond and Arwen, for they were sundered by the Sea, and by a doom beyond the end of the world." [12] Even beyond the ending of Middle-earth. Grievous indeed the parting, not only for the individuals concerned but also for the races whose destinies decree so final a separation. The knowledge of it deepens the sadness of the elves' departure as the epic closes.

They leave Middle-earth with reluctance. Tolkien pictures them sitting together under the stars far into the night, looking to the chance wanderer like gray figures carved in stone, unspeaking, but in thought "recalling the ages that were gone and all their joys and labours in the world, or holding council, concerning the days to come." One wonders how content they will be in the Undying Lands. These are not Paradise. No beatific vision or new celestial life awaits the returning elves. In the endless tranquillity will Haldir and the others of Galadrim cease to long for the mallorn trees of Lórien of the Blossom, or Elrond for some struggle or other which he can lead? Enough — perhaps — that they will always be free to explore the boundless horizons of the mind, and need no longer die vicariously, as on Earth, with the constantly dying life around them.

2. *Dwarves: Durin's Folk*

The band of dwarves in *The Hobbit*, animated by a lust for treasure and for revenge, are a bumptious lot whom Bilbo often finds annoying. Beorn is "not over fond of dwarves," and the Silvan elves of Mirkwood, having gone to war with them some time before in a dispute over the ownership of gold, "did not love dwarves" either. At the end of the tale Thorin, the dwarf leader, is so adamant against sharing

Smaug's hoard with those who have helped him recover it that his people are saved from battle with both elves and the men of Long Lake only by the descent of an army of orcs, which unites the three races temporarily. Evidently dwarf character has in it a strong vein of "possessiveness," never a virtue in Tolkien's lexicon, and a quickness to quarrel that does not endear it to other races. Thorin himself, repenting as he dies, admits as much to Bilbo: "Since I leave now all gold and silver, and go where it is of little worth, I wish to part in friendship from you . . . If more of us valued food and cheer and song above hoarded gold, it would be a merrier world." His successor Dáin establishes a lasting friendship with the men of Dale and Esgaroth by dividing the treasure with them on generous terms.

At the start of *The Lord of the Rings* many years later, however, Dáin's community of dwarves is the only one that has close relations with its neighbors. Glóin confesses to Frodo at Rivendell that Beorn's descendants still "are not over fond of dwarves." A dwarf community in the Blue Mountains, northwest of the Shire, seems never to be visited by anybody, and though its members travel freely through the Shire on business and put up overnight in the inn at Bree, they remain virtual strangers to the folk there. The embassy of Glóin to the Council of Elrond is a first notable move toward a working alliance with the other free peoples against Sauron, and allows the shrewd elf lord to carry it a step further by introducing Gimli, son of Glóin, into the Fellowship of the Ring, where he can come to know, and be known by, the representatives of hobbits, elves, wizards, and men. Gimli's subsequent troubles at Lórien, Fangorn, Rohan, and elsewhere along the line of action bear witness to the hard initial suspicion with which his race is almost universally regarded.

This isolation of the dwarves has not been caused solely by

the fact that they are "calculating folk with a great idea of the value of money" or that "there is no knowing what a dwarf will not dare and do for revenge or the recovery of his own," as *The Hobbit* puts it. Behind these traits lies the broader truth stated in *The Lord of the Rings* that "the Dwarves are a race apart," created in a way (of which Tolkien gives only the barest hints) unlike the origin of other species.[13] Durin, their forefather, "slept alone, until in the deeps of time and the awakening of that people he came to Azanulbizar." As the Fellowship passes through Moria, Gimli sings an ancient ballad of his folk which expands the account somewhat:

> The world was young. the mountains green,
> No stain yet on the Moon was seen,
> No words were laid on stream or stone,
> When Durin woke and walked alone.
> He named the nameless hills and dells;
> He drank from yet untasted wells;
> He stooped and looked in Mirrormere,
> And saw a crown of stars appear . . .

The ideas that Durin was first born without a companion and went about giving names recalls Adam in Eden. After recounting the glories of dwarf civilization in Moria under Durin's descendants, the ballad ends with what looks like a prophecy of his resurrection:

> There lies the crown in water deep,
> Till Durin wakes again from sleep.

The prospect of a reawakening after death is traditional among dwarves. In *The Hobbit* Thorin, dying, expects it: "Farewell, good thief . . . I go now to the halls of waiting to sit beside my fathers until the world is renewed." In Appendix A Tolkien adds that dwarves believed Durin's spirit to have been reincarnated in the bodies of five later kings of Moria, "for they have many strange tales and beliefs concerning themselves and their fate in the world."

The uniqueness of dwarf origins and endings is accepted also by the *Eddas*, from which Tolkien may have derived it as well as Durin's name and function. In the Norse account the race is fashioned by the gods from the dead body of the giant Ymir:

> Then went the rulers there   Modsognir, chief
> All gods most holy   Of the dwarfish race,
> To their seat aloft   And Durin too
> And counsel together took   Were then created.
> Who should of dwarfs   And like to men
> The race then fashion,   Dwarfs in the earth
> From the livid bones   Were formed in numbers
> And blood of the giant.   As Durin ordered.[14]

Dwarves are the only folk fashioned in this way. Tolkien keeps the idea of their uniqueness but not the particular method of it recounted in the *Eddas*.

Another racial peculiarity which he fastens upon dwarves is the small number of their women. Only one third of all dwarves are female, Tolkien says, and not all of these choose to marry. In consequence most dwarf males never marry, and children are few. Those males who do get wives keep them for life "and are jealous, as in all matters of their rights." The devastating effects of these statistics upon dwarf character in general can be imagined, and are certainly more than enough in themselves to produce the inbred clannishness and surly tenacity that drive away other races.

The sexual imbalance is the probable cause also of the intense secretiveness of Durin's folk. They have a language of their own which they guard so jealously that "few of other race have succeeded in learning it." Each dwarf, moreover, has his own "secret and inner" name, his "true" name, never revealed to any one of alien race. "Not even on their tombs do they inscribe them." What Gimli's true name is we never find out, nor does Legolas, intimately though the two come to know each other. Gandalf refers to this instinct for privacy in describing the rare silver mined in Moria, which elves call mithril: "The Dwarves have a name which they do not tell . . . The Dwarves tell no tale." Galadriel in Lórien knows how to make secrecy an element in her test of Gimli's loyalty to the Fellowship: "And it seemed to me too," he reports to his companions afterward, "that my choice would remain secret and known only to myself."

The artistic sensibilities of male dwarves, which make them master craftsmen in metals and stone, seem to be a sublimation of their sexual frustration. Being unable to have marriage, "very many" males come not to desire it, "being engrossed in their crafts." Even their love of beauty, however, is usually colored (or tainted) with the jealous possessiveness that runs through so many facets of their nature. Listening to Thorin's crew sing praise of the smithy work of their ancestors, Bilbo "felt the love of beautiful things made by hands and by cunning and by magic moving through him, a fierce and a jealous love, the desire of the hearts of dwarves." [15] We have Gimli's word for it, though, that when confronted by the supreme loveliness of the caves of Aglarond in Helm's Deep his people would rise above all thoughts of gain, as he does. "There would be an endless pilgrimage of Dwarves, merely to gaze at them . . . None of Durin's race would mine those caves for stones or ore, not if diamonds and gold could be got there . . . We would tend these glades of flowering stone, not quarry them." Caught up above his usual dour self, Gimli proceeds to give a superbly lyrical picture of the echoing domes and chambers underground, the glint of polished walls, marble columns of white and saffron and dawn-rose springing "from many-coloured floors to meet the glistening pendants of the roof: wings, ropes, curtains fine as frozen clouds; spears, banners, pinnacles of suspended palaces!" Here he is a true spokesman for the finer qualities of his race.

As suggested above, Gimli's membership in the Fellowship of the Ring enables him to become an ambassador for the dwarves to other members of the band and to the other peoples whom they meet on their journey. In Moria he opens the eyes of the hobbits, of Legolas, the elf, and Boromir, the man, to the past glories of Durin's civilization. To the Lórien elves he exhibits dwarf pride and obstinacy in preferring to fight rather than be treated as a spy. Galadriel welcomes him, after setting aside the law which excludes strangers, as an ambassador of good will for his race: ". . . today we have broken our long law. May it be a sign that though the world is now dark better days are at hand, and that friendship shall be renewed between our peoples." He learns in Lórien to accept the love and understanding that she offers him and, so learning, he outgrows the parochialism of his kind. In asking as a parting gift only a strand of her hair "which surpasses the gold of the earth as the stars surpass the gems of the mine" he transcends dwarf obsession for both gold and gems and frees the longing for beauty, the love of love, from the alloy of earthly price. Galadriel can then foretell of him that "your hands will flow with gold, and yet over you gold shall have no dominion." Gimli also accepts the role as peacemaker between elves and dwarves that she has proposed for him. When he returns home he will set her hair in imperishable crystal as "a pledge of good will between the Mountain and the Wood until the end of days."

This new admiration for Galadriel opens Gimli to a new understanding and liking for Legolas. Thereafter elf and dwarf become inseparable, to the wonder of all who see together these members of two inveterately hostile races. The friendship affords Tolkien countless opportunities for comparing elf and dwarf nature. Although both are sad when leaving Lórien, Gimli is the sadder because he is leaving Galadriel, whose memory will always be torturingly sweet to him. In his own memorable words: "Torment in the dark was the danger I feared, and it did not hold me back. But I would not have come, had I known the danger of light and joy." Legolas tries to comfort him with the thought that his memories will remain always clear, and never fade or grow stale. This is precisely the trouble, Gimli answers. Elves may enjoy memory as a reliving of past experience, but dwarves need the reality of the experience itself. "Memory is not what the heart desires. That is only a mirror . . . Elves may see things otherwise. Indeed I have heard that for them memory is more like to the waking world than to a dream. Not so for Dwarves." Inherent in the fabric of the two races is a difference in the operation and effect of memory.

Although Legolas and Gimli are standing together on the plains of Rohan when Éomer belittles Galadriel as a perilous enchantress, it is the dwarf, not the elf, who almost precipitates a hopeless battle by bluntly rebuking him, regardless of consequences. Gimli's renewal of the challenge to single combat in her defense on several later occasions takes on a comic aspect and is humorously avoided by Éomer, but Gimli never thinks it funny. In truth, the dwarf temper is not much given to humor. I can think of only one occasion when Gimli jokes about anything, and that comes when Pippin and Merry are reunited with their comrades outside Isengard and Gimli joshes them over and over as "truants" who had to be rescued from the orcs — not a notably hilarious subject. Legolas, by contrast, is high-spirited by nature, except when he longs for the sea. The two make a striking contrast as they walk into Minas Tirith for the first time, Legolas fair of face and singing, "but Gimli stalked beside him, stroking his beard and staring about him" at the city's masonry: "There is some good stone-work here . . . but also some that is less good, and the streets could be better contrived." In their ensuing argument about the durability of the works of men against change Gimli takes the pessimistic view against Legolas' more hopeful one. From the plurals they use they seem to be speaking as representatives of their respective races, as well as individuals.

At the start of *The Lord of the Rings* Durin's offspring, by nature, by circumstance, and by the machinations of Sauron, are largely outcasts and self-outcasts (the one follows hard upon the other) from the society of Western peoples. By the end of the tale the breach has been healed as well as it can be among races so disparate. Dwarves under Dáin have done their share in battle against the northern wing of Sauron's armies. Their leaders permit Gimli to take dwarf masons and other artisans to help rebuild and strengthen Minas Tirith, capital city of the new ruling race of men. As a trusted companion of Aragorn he will be a major link between the human race and his own. As the friend of Legolas, who visits Gimli's new dwarf colony in the caves of Aglarond, he is a link with the Silvan elves of Mirkwood, to whose kingship Legolas is heir. As a visitor to Fangorn Forest with Legolas he will become better known to the ents. And to every hobbit who reads Frodo's manuscript tale in the Red Book he will be as familiar as their own heroes of the Shire.

3. *Ents*

Tolkien's imperial success in his invention of the ent folk, the great tree herders of Fangorn Forest, owes not a little to a deep personal love for trees, which began early in life. Even as a very young boy his greatest enthusiasm was for stories about Indians "and above all, forests in such stories." [16] When he wrote of fantasy's power to tell tales of men conversing with birds and beasts, he always added "and trees," which he conceived of as speaking a language peculiar to themselves.[17] By his own account the primary inspiration for his autobiographical story, "Leaf by Niggle," was a poplar tree outside his bedroom window, which "was suddenly lopped off and mutilated by its owner, I do not know why. It is cut down now, a less barbarous punishment for any crimes it may have been accused of, such as being large and alive. I do not think it had any friends, or any mourners, except myself and a pair of owls." [18] Tolkien's sense of the aliveness of this poplar, and consequently of the cruelty done to it, is so strong as to arouse in him the indignation one might feel at the murder of a man.

Ents are the oldest of all living races, older even than the elf-sires of the First Age, but "asleep" at first in silent awareness of themselves alone. Then elves came along and "waked" them. This is the same metaphor of awakening from sleep which was used earlier to describe Durin's creation and birth. For the ents Treebeard recalls it in this way: "Elves began it, of course, waking trees up and teaching them to speak and learning their tree-talk. They always wished to talk to everything, the old Elves did." Appendix F, in analyzing the ent language, says that it is "unlike all others: slow, sonorous, agglomerated, repetitive . . ." and that to the elves the ents "ascribed not their own language but the desire for speech." In other words, before elves stirred them up ents had an undeveloped potentiality for speech. From the elves they got the elf tongues, which they used in talking to others, and the stimulus to articulate their own language, which they used only among themselves. "They had no need to keep it secret, for no others could learn it." Yet, purposely or not, ents now resembled dwarves in having a secret language and, possibly as a consequence, the same suspicious reluctance to divulge their "true" names, for fear of putting themselves in the power of their enemies. Treebeard will not reveal his to Merry and Pippin or anybody else, and reproaches them as rashly "hasty" in trusting him with theirs without knowing more about him. After all, there are plenty of wicked ents in the depths of Fangorn Forest who contracted evil from Morgoth during the Great Darkness in the north.

With these kinsmen Treebeard has no traffic, and keeps strangers out of their way; for the ents are subject to the same moral principles as are other fully conscious peoples. Aragorn's universal maxim, "Good and ill have not changed since yesteryear; nor are they one thing among Elves and Dwarves and another among Men," applies to the ents equally. Treebeard is practicing it when he assures Merry and Pippin that he has no intention of restricting their liberty: "I am not going to do anything *with* you: not if you mean by that 'do something to you', without your leave. We might do some things together." Like Elrond, Aragorn, Gandalf, and other principals he has a most tender regard for freedom of choice. Though the oldest and most respected leader of his tribe, he orders none of its members to attack Isengard but puts the question up for open discussion by the Entmoot. Noteworthy also is his care in ascribing "bad hearts" to trees only *after* they have turned into ents, when they have achieved full consciousness. "Some are quite wide awake, and a few are, well, ah, well getting *Entish* . . . When that happens to a tree, you find that some have *bad* hearts." Before then they may be somewhat contaminated ("That sort of thing seems to spread") but they are still essentially "asleep" and therefore not altogether responsible.

This slow awakening of some trees to ent status is going on all the time and forms one part of a remarkable cycle fundamental to the life of ents. Ents are like elves in that they never die unless killed by injuries inflicted by others from the outside. Nevertheless a number have died in this fashion down through the years. In the beginnings of their race these were replaced by the normal method of sexual reproduction through the entwives. At the time when Merry and Pippin enter Fangorn, however, these females have entirely disappeared from the ken of the males. They have not died out. Long ago, even in the First Age, the ents and entwives slowly developed such incompatibilities of interest that they grew apart entirely, and the entwives left the forests in which they were born. The ents remained there because they loved the trees in their wild state, "and ate only of such fruit as the trees let fall in their path; and they learned of the Elves and spoke with the Trees." But the entwives became interested in the shrubs, fruit trees, herbs, and grains growing in the meadows outside the woods. They were not content merely to speak to these plants and leave them as they were but they "wished them to hear and obey what was said to them" and made them grow as they were ordered, ". . . for the Entwives desired order, and plenty, and peace (by which they meant that things should remain where they had set them). So the Entwives made gardens to live in." By this route they became the inventors of the arts of agriculture, which men learned from them.

At first the male ents used to leave their forests periodically to visit the females, begging them to return, but in looking for better agricultural lands the latter moved so far away that the males lost sight of them entirely. When last seen they were being so changed in appearance by their work — "bent and browned by their labour," their hair bleached and cheeks reddened by the sun — that Treebeard is not sure he knows what they look like now. For a long while the ents searched Middle-earth for them in vain, but "the wild wood called and we returned to it" and now the memory of the entwives is

only a perpetual sorrow, still strong enough to keep Treebeard wistfully asking everybody he meets whether they
have been sighted anywhere. Like other races ents have a vision of a hereafter of happiness. For them it takes the form of
a reunion with the entwives in "a land where we can live together and both be content." According to the beautiful ballad dialogue which Treebeard hums for the hobbits, this land
lies in "the West" but can be reached only after a bitter winter
during which the two separated sexes lose all they have.

This separation is the abiding tragedy of the ents. It has
come about because the male propensity to wildness and free
wandering and the female desire for a settled, orderly home
have not been reconciled by a strong enough sexual instinct
for reproduction, as in other races. Consequently, in order to
insure the continuance of the species, nature has had to substitute a different method. Treebeard cannot explain it altogether to the hobbits because "I do not understand all that
goes on myself." He knows enough, however, to observe
that a cycle has been inaugurated by which some (not all)
trees grow into enthood while some (not all) ents decline into
treehood. His contemporary, Leaflock, for example, "has
grown sleepy, almost tree-ish . . . he has taken to standing
by himself half-asleep all through the summer with the deep
grass of the meadows round his knees." Of late even in winter he has been too drowsy to walk far. Leaflock and others
like him make up the class of huorns, half-tree, half-ent, who
tear down the walls of Isengard and smother to death the orc
army besieging Helm's Deep. Their ferocity terrifies the
hobbits. Relapsing back toward raw nature the passions of
the huorns are no longer bridled by rationality.

Ents share with dwarves an abnormality of sexual life and
with elves an endless longevity. But they react to these
problems in quite contrasting ways. Unlike dwarves they have
not let the loss of their mates drive them into either a surly pos-

sessiveness in some cases or a love of art in others. Ents have no art. They are friendly enough creatures, and they maintain a strong sense of responsibility for their work as guardians of the forest. Unlike elves they seem to have solved satisfactorily the puzzle of how to live undying in a world where everything else dies. The heart of their solution lies in their handling of memory. In Gimli's view elves' memory of the past can be as vivid as life in the present — a very mixed blessing for them, perhaps even a curse — whereas dwarves remember the past as irrecoverable past. Ents, on the other hand, have eyes in which Pippin sees "an enormous well . . . filled up with ages of memory and long, slow, steady thinking; but their surface was sparkling with the present: like sun shimmering on the outer leaves of a vast tree . . ." For them life is a history in which the past grows into the present, all in due order, and they remember every part of it sequentially and calmly. In fact their language is such as to incorporate into the names of persons and places all the events which have made them what they are, adding new events as they occur. Treebeard's true name "is growing all the time," and the name of Lórien is changing to match its fortunes.

In any comparison of ents with the other races of Middle-earth Treebeard's analysis of their similarities and dissimilarities with men and elves must be preeminent. The feeling of ents for trees is much closer than that of shepherds for sheep, he says, because ents are good at "getting inside other things." In this they resemble elves more than men, who are more interested in themselves than in other beings. On the other hand, ents are closer to men and farther from elves in taking on the color of any new environment they enter. Elves always remain the same. Finally, ents excel both elves and men in being able to "keep their minds on things longer" and more steadily. Treebeard's central interest here is the relative sensitivity of the three races to other "things," meaning living beings. Men seem to come off rather the worst of the three, as perhaps we should. Still, the analysis may not be altogether objective, since Treebeard confesses later, "I take more kindly to Elves than to others: it was the Elves that cured us of dumbness long ago . . . though our ways have parted since."

"Our ways have parted since." These are words which might have come from the lips of any one of the free peoples of Middle-earth in speaking of any or all of the others. Through natural preoccupation with its own needs or through discord sown by Sauron each has become an island unto itself. Treebeard tells Merry and Pippin that he has not troubled himself about wars heretofore. They mostly concern elves and men. Let wizards, whose business it is, worry about the future. "I am not altogether on anybody's *side*, because nobody is altogether on my *side* . . . nobody cares for the woods as I care for them, not even Elves nowadays." But as Aragorn brings to Rohan the doom of choice, so do the hobbits bring it to Fangorn with their news of the crisis in the outside world. "Young Saruman" has been irritating Treebeard for some time by cutting down trees for his factories. The understanding that the wizard is on one side of the coming struggle finally pushes the ent leader into action on the other.

His destruction of Isengard saves Rohan so that it in turn may help save Gondor. Aragorn's gratitude after he ascends the throne leads him to open wide areas west of the Misty Mountains to reforestation, and grants Isengard to the ents in fee. The king encourages new search for the entwives in the eastern lands, but we know they will never be found, and had better never be, since the sexes have become unsexed. Repeatedly there come ominous hints that the wildwood will not prosper in the expanding Age of Man.

4. *Hobbits*

Treebeard hits the mark when he describes the distinguishing traits of hobbits as a race: "hungry as hunters, the Hobbit children,/the laughing-folk, the little people." Created first for a child audience, they are a combination, on the one hand, of human children living in a society where the desires of children are ideally institutionalized because there are no grownups and, on the other hand, of some of the qualities traditionally ascribed to the "little people" of folklore. To fill out the child side of the combination they are about half the size of an adult, they eat six meals a day with snacks at will in between, life is one long round of birthday parties at which presents are given and received, games are played, no serious work seems to need doing, no living need be earned, nobody gets sick or dies, people may fight and quarrel but nobody bleeds, chatter is endlessly gay and trivial if sometimes a bit cruel, and tobacco does not have to be smoked in secret behind the barn. Perhaps even the living in comfortable holes in the ground appeals to the child's love of hiding in small enclosed spaces. Of course the hobbit is also a furry creature who does not have to wear shoes, rather like a rabbit, which likewise lives in burrows. An eagle in *The Hobbit*, who has never seen a hobbit, thinks Bilbo looks like a frightened rabbit, and Beorn in like case says of him, "Little bunny is getting nice and fat again on bread and honey." Children easily identify with small animals, especially bunnies.

Perhaps Edmund Wilson was half-right when he suggested in his now notorious book review that *rabbit* was one component of the name *hobbit*.[19] *Hobbs*, however, was a bad guess at the other component. If we are to disregard Tolkien's own etymology, *holbytla* ("hole-dweller"), as an afterthought appearing only late in *The Lord of the Rings*, the more likely candidate for the other component is Middle English *Hob*, for which the *Oxford English Dictionary* offers two pertinent meanings: (1) "rustic, clown"; (2) "Robin Goodfellow, hobgoblin." Robin is the English version of the "little people" of Celtic tradition. These were often thought of as silent, unseen little beings sometimes good-naturedly helping, sometimes mischievously hindering, the work of the house. The disappearance of household articles, the souring of cream, and other sorts of unexpected tricks could be traced back to them. This body of lore supplies to hobbits their silent tread and ability to disappear in an instant without being seen by other races. It also seems to give Bilbo his job with Thorin's expedition as an "expert burglar" and spy to help recover the treasure from Smaug. At first he is home-oriented and reluctant to go, but once started he uses a considerable bag of tricks and thieving skill on Gollum, on the Silvan elves, on the spiders, on Smaug, and on his own employer, Thorin, in stealing the Arkenstone.

Of course Bilbo changes as the story unfolds; he acquires constancy, courage, and above all a sense of moral responsibility. These are adult human traits which Tolkien adds because the increasing depth of his tale demands them. In short, Bilbo grows up before our eyes and returns home so matured that Gandalf wryly congratulates him: "Something is the matter with you! You are not the hobbit that you were."

Tolkien's Prologue to *The Lord of the Rings* elaborates the political, historical, and linguistic dimensions of hobbit society in preparation for the greater role it is to play, no longer in a child's tale but in an epic on the grandest scale. Yet at the start of the epic that society is still essentially the same utopia of childhood wish fulfillment from which Bilbo long ago set out to steal treasure. Other races have their sorrows. But before the War of the Ring the whole problem of the hobbits is that they have no problems. Protected by the Dúnedain rangers from winds of the outside world, they live their tight little lives in their tight little Shire, unknowing and unknown. Scarcely anyone on Middle-earth has any idea what a hobbit is except as a figment in old songs. So far as the hobbit race is concerned, the main theme of *The Lord of the Rings* is to tell how the unknowing come to know, and the unknown become known and honored by other races.

Those readers who find the hobbit atmosphere of the opening episodes tedious do so, I suspect, because they look at these child-men with purely adult eyes. So regarded, they do indeed become as tiresome as too many hours spent exclusively among the antics of the young. But Tolkien manages to see them both with the eyes of the child, and so to find them charming, and with the eyes of the man, and so to see what they lack in the larger canvas of the life of Middle-earth. Frodo is his spokesman on both counts, Frodo who can look at the Shire partly from the outside because he has been Bilbo's pupil and has talked with elves and dwarves: ". . . there have been times when I thought the inhabitants too stupid and dull for words, and have felt that an earthquake or an invasion of dragons might be good for them. But I don't feel like that now. I feel that as long as the Shire lies behind, safe and comfortable, I shall find wandering more bearable . . ." So Frodo is fully aware of its stifling stagnation, but values too its warm safety. He can see it both ways. Likewise nobody is a stauncher champion of hobbits than Gandalf. He knows they are "amazing creatures" whose toughness of moral fiber suits them uniquely to resist the temptation of the Ring. But their mixture of follies and virtues inevitably strikes him as seriocomic: "Ever since Bilbo left I have been deeply concerned . . . about all these charming, absurd, helpless hobbits. It would be a grievous blow to the world if the Dark Power overcame the Shire; if all your kind, jolly, stupid Bolgers,

Hornblowers, Boffins, Brace-girdles, and the rest, not to mention the ridiculous Bagginses, became enslaved." That is the right way for us to look at the hobbits as a race, if we can.

Indeed they are very like us. "It is plain," to repeat what Tolkien says in the Prologue, "that in spite of later estrangements Hobbits are relatives of ours: far nearer to us than Elves, or even than Dwarves. Of old they spoke the languages of Men, after their own fashion, and liked and disliked much the same things as Men did." If, in their original gay innocence, they resemble human children, hobbits suffering under the tyranny of Sauron and his agents intensify their resemblance to our sadder and wiser selves as grown men. Particularly, Frodo, Sam, Merry, and Pippin, who together represent most of the qualities of their race, grow increasingly human as the epic progresses. Tolkien's literary method requires them to. His decision to describe from their point of view every scene in which they are present (very few scenes are without at least one hobbit) makes it imperative that their point of view become quite like ours. Otherwise we as readers would not understand what is happening, or share in the grave trials which the hobbits are singled out to undergo, especially in Mordor. Consequently, with a few vestigial exceptions, the differences between hobbit and man are for all practical purposes extinguished once the pressures on the Fellowship turn severe. And Frodo and Sam especially are in effect human during the long physical and moral struggle toward Mount Doom. In conclusion, the Shire after the War is so much like any other devastated land that even there the actions of the four protagonists on their return, the responses of the population to their leadership, and the final cleansing of the place are all too familiar to twentieth-century experience.

So much has been written about Frodo, and much of it so

well, that here I shall zero in on only one strangely revealing aspect of his character, his dreams. No one else in the whole epic dreams so constantly and so diversely. Faramir is indeed visited several times by a dream, once shared by Boromir, warning him to seek in Rivendell the sword that was broken, now that Gondor is in desperate straits. Faramir also dreams of the drowning of Númenor. But that is all. Frodo's visions in sleep set him apart as unusual even before he leaves the Shire, and begin to affect his conduct and personality: ". . . strange visions of mountains that he had never seen came into his dreams." These would seem to be the Misty Mountains, for he is influenced to undertake his journey toward them. About to enter the Old Forest, he hears in a dream the sound of the sea and catches sight of the white tower at the Grey Havens where departing elves take ship for the West. He has never in his life been near either but he will be embarking there himself one day when the mission to Mordor is over. This dream, then, is a prevision of the future. The elf lords, Aragorn, and others sometimes have true hunches about coming events but not in dreams. For better or worse Frodo seems gifted with a power possessed only by the greatest among other races. While asleep in the house of Tom Bombadil he witnesses from afar Gandalf's rescue from Saruman's stronghold of Orthanc by the eagle Gwaihir, a feat which is taking place at about that same time, so far as we can tell from the chronology of the tale. Frodo has the same sort of vision of a present event occurring somewhere else when a dream in the inn at Bree shows him the Black Riders attacking his house at Crickhollow in a vain attempt to seize him. It is almost as if he were looking into a *palantír* or viewing Galadriel's mirror. Both these latter dreams are informative and monitory.

Alone among the hobbits in Rivendell, Frodo is given visions of Elvenhome in the Uttermost West: ". . . seas of

foam that sighed upon the margins of the world." Alone
among the Fellowship in Lórien, he receives from Galadriel a
gift that puts him under the protection of Elbereth, the phial
of water from her mirror in which is caught the light of Eärendil's star, a gift most precious to elves. Although Frodo
cannot actually turn into an elf, his innate spiritual kinship to
them is revealed by his physical state after recovery from the
wound inflicted by Angmar on Weathertop. Gandalf sees a
transparency about him and speculates to himself that Frodo
"may become like a glass filled with a clear light for eyes to
see that can." Sam had perceived this light "shining faintly"
within his beloved master in Elrond's house, but on their
journey to Mordor when Frodo slept "the light was even
clearer and stronger." His face is "old, old and beautiful." In
the extremity of his travail as they near Mount Doom Frodo
casts aside all weapons and armor. He prefers possible capture to the use of arms, a preference which he holds to later
in refusing to fight in the battle to free the Shire or to strike
back at Saruman when attacked. For him struggles for the
right must hereafter be waged only on the moral plane.

Yet even while he is taking this lofty moral stance he tells
Sam that he is falling more and more under the evil domination of the Ring and that he has lost the power to give it away
or remain sane if it is taken from him. Evidently he is being
torn by stronger and stronger forces of good and evil pulling
his mind in opposite directions. It is necessary to stress that
Frodo does not win his battle against evil in the climactic moment of choice at the Cracks of Doom. When he announces
there, "I do not choose now to do what I came to do . . .
The Ring is mine!" and sets it on his finger he becomes the
slave of the Ring. Only its providential destruction by Gollum saves him, and the West, from utter defeat. He can be
hailed by the host in Ithilien afterward not for final victory,
which was not his doing, but only for his heroic stamina in

getting the Ring to the one place where it could be destroyed. During the rest of his days on Middle-earth Frodo remains torn between the newly contending elements of his nature. Had he clearly mastered the Ring he would be whole and at peace. But since it came close to mastering him, he is still in the power of its memory. He still loathes it and longs for it after the fashion of Gollum. Here Frodo's propensity to dream is a curse because he cannot forget the "precious" even in sleep. In the midst of a Shire restored to happiness Farmer Cotton finds him one day "half in a dream," desperately clutching the white gem Arwen gave him and pining for the Ring. "It is gone forever," Frodo tells him, "and now all is dark and empty." [20]

Waking or asleep, Frodo is afflicted by a second life of memory, much as elves are. As an elfin princess married to a mortal, Arwen will have to endure a double life of the past superimposed upon the present all the rest of her days. Since her tragedy parallels Frodo's, she alone understands his case and tries to help him with the gift of a jewel conferring hope, "when the memory of the fear and the darkness troubles you . . ." Foreseeing also that there will be no cure for him on Middle-earth, she presents him with the place in the Undying Lands which she forfeits by wedding Aragorn. She could hardly make such a transfer unless Frodo has grown enough like an elf to be capable of the impress of immortality.

5. Men

In our world Man is without rival in intelligence and general culture. On Tolkien's Middle-earth he is only one of half a dozen highly developed species, each with its own genius, which are at least his equals and in some respects perhaps his superiors. How would we behave under similar circumstances? Tolkien does not, of course, try to answer that question. But he does set himself the fascinating task of imagining human reaction to the kinds of other intelligent beings who live side by side with man under the kinds of conditions he chooses to visualize for his epic and its historical backgrounds.

Man is not the earliest civilized creature to arise on Middle-earth. He is preceded by elves and ents. We cannot be sure where dwarves and hobbits stand in the order of chronological succession, but they seem later than man; wizards, orcs, and trolls, are definitely later. At some time early in the First Age the three tribes of the Edain drift westward from somewhere in the east and encounter the elves, some of whom have never left the mainland while others, having sailed to the Uttermost West to be tutored by the Valar, have already sailed back in pursuit of Morgoth. These latter, especially, have been educated to a state of wisdom and achievement far above that of barbaric man. Moreover, all elves are immortal, whereas man is mortal. He does not realize how mortal he is until he meets others who are not so. There is nothing in our experience to parallel the shock of such a meeting. Its effects never cease throughout the three Ages in which elves and men inhabit the same Middle-earth.

The first fruits are an alliance in which the human tribes array themselves unreservedly on the side of these apparently superior beings in their war against Morgoth. The fact that both species are soon soundly beaten is not enough to break Man's loyalty. The difference between mortal and immortal is a natural barrier to intermarriage between the two races which neither seems anxious to breach. Besides, the barrier is strengthened by an edict of the Valar, who manage such matters, that any elf who marries a human being must become mortal. In all the long centuries of the First and Second Ages only two elf maidens, Lúthien and Idril, are willing to make the sacrifice for love, and no male elves. The appearance of several generations of their offspring, part-elf, part-human, poses a new difficulty that the Valar resolve with another ruling, that each of these offspring must choose categorically between mortality and immortality. Elrond chooses to be elf but his brother Elros elects to be Man.

That there is something to be said on each side Tolkien has observed before in his essay "On Fairy-stories." Human tales about elves, he says, often depict the tedium of escape from mortality: "Few lessons are taught more clearly in them than the burden of that kind of immortality, or rather endless serial living, to which the fugitive would fly." And if elves tell corresponding stories about men they "are doubtless full of the Escape from Deathlessness." Each species yearns to have the gift of the other, but would not like it if once achieved. *The Lord of the Rings* has moments of hesitation in deciding whether death may not be a greater boon than "endless serial living." For example, the Edain, who are given the island of Númenor as a reward for their fight against Morgoth, are granted life spans thrice that of ordinary men, but "they must remain mortal, since the Valar were not permitted to take from them the Gift of Men (or the Doom of Men, as it was afterwards called)." Here death can be called a gift or a doom depending on who you are. Arwen, for one, comes to look upon it as a bitter doom. The higher authority of God forbids even the Valar to change the ordained composition of the races. Men must be men and die; elves must be elves and live on and on. There is no ambiguity about the preferences of either men or elves in the epic, however. The "Ban of the Valar" operates only in one direction. It prevents the Númenoreans from sailing to the Undying Lands of the elves, where presumably they might try to steal undying life, but does not prohibit elves from sailing to Númenor, for no danger exists of their trying to seize death.

The elves did come to Númenor with their advanced teachings, to the high profit of the Edain there, but the denial of immortality rankled the Edain. Their discontent festered, and finally they organized a naval expedition to seize the Uttermost West. Man's hunger for more and more life gave Sauron a fatal argument with which to drive Númenor into disobedience, but its people were obviously ripe for rebellion anyway. Even the drowning of the island and all its rebels did not still the same hunger among Númenoreans settled on mainland shores. The dwellings of the elves and the Valar, removed from "the circles of the world," were now beyond their reach. But "many" of these shore-dwellers looked for an alternative in the Black Arts and so "fell into evils and follies," as Faramir tells Frodo. In Gondor itself the frantic search for more life took varying forms, all morbid: old men compounded elixirs to lengthen their years, or cast horoscopes to calculate how many years of life remained to them; kings built tombs more splendid than the palaces they lived in; men mused about their ancestors instead of having children. The thought of death "was ever present" to the exclusion of the life that was legitimately theirs. So, immersed in death, they forgot that Sauron might come alive again.

This is the situation in Gondor during the early centuries of the Third Age. The Stewards alleviate the decay by mixing their Númenorean stock with that of sturdy sailors and mountaineers who, having had no dealings with elves, are not consumed by the contrasts of deathlessness. Nevertheless, a grievous aftermath remains. The people of Gondor now deeply distrust and fear elves. The attitude held toward them by even so wise and tolerant a man as Faramir is curiously ambivalent. He regrets that "Men now fear and misdoubt the Elves, and yet know little of them. And we of Gondor grow like other Men, like the men of Rohan; for even they, who are foes of the Dark Lord, shun the Elves . . . "; yet he censures those few men who visit Lórien, "For I deem it perilous now for mortal man wilfully to seek out the Elder People." But in the next breath he adds, "Yet I envy you that have spoken with the White Lady." Boromir, Denethor, and others in Minas Tirith hold the same prejudice. The Rohirrim feel it in virulent form. The desire for immortality by Man goes underground during the latter part of the Third Age, when the elves become fewer and more withdrawn. But the problem in another guise is painfully resurrected in Aragorn's wooing of Arwen, and in their eventual parting at his death. "If this is indeed, as the Eldar say, the gift of the One to Men, it is bitter to receive," she says, she who has known what it is to be immortal. She never really reconciles herself to death. From varying angles Tolkien keeps studying the probable consequences to both immortal elves and mortal men of living together on the same planet.

Faramir, one of the most high-souled and thoughtful men in the whole epic, divides the civilizations of men into three classes: the High, or pure Númenorean; the Middle, the Men of the Twilight, like the Rohirrim and their kin the Bardings; the Wild, the Men of Darkness, such as the woses of Druadan Forest, and perhaps the more primitive of the hill tribes. No doubt several factors enter into the classification, but the primary one for Faramir is the "love of war and valour as things good in themselves, both a sport and an end," which has lowered Gondor from the High, where it used to be, to the level of the Rohirrim, a young people whose values all reflect a zest for battle. Gondor, too, now esteems a warrior above men of other crafts. "Such is the need of our days." It was otherwise in happier times when Minas Tirith cherished the original Númenorean virtues of "gentleness and arts." These were the teachings of the elves. To them Faramir remains nostalgically loyal, though the safety of his city has forced him to take up the sword in defense against Sauron: "I do not love the bright sword for its sharpness, nor the arrow for its swiftness, nor the warrior for his glory. I love only that which they defend: the city of the Men of Númenor; and I would have her loved for her memory, her ancientry, her beauty, and her present wisdom." Herein lies the real breach between him and his elder brother Boromir, whom he laments. Boromir was totally the "man of prowess," a great captain, ambitious to be king. Faramir, by contrast, has no personal ambitions and would be glad to see the line of Elendil restored. Knowing his brother only too well, he is completely able to understand why the trial of the Ring was too sore for Boromir, while he himself would not pick it up even if he found it lying in the highway.

Faramir, however, is no pacifist. Unlike Frodo he has not renounced the sword, though he detests having to use it. Once faced with the dire needs of his city against invading armies, he becomes a brave and resourceful war leader. Only the entreaties of Frodo induce him to spare Gollum, whom he is quite ready to kill as a potential danger. On the other hand his grim performance of duty is at the opposite pole from the pomp with which Théoden, for instance, invests war. Nor is he like Aragorn, who neither loves nor hates fighting but accepts it as a fact of his times, a duty which he must perform in the recovery of his throne and, later, its protection. Through these figures, and others in *The Lord of the Rings*, Tolkien is exploring several possible positions toward war and peace. He speaks for himself more openly in "The Homecoming of Beorhtnoth" (see Chapter VII).

Middle-earth at the end of the Third Age is so embattled a world that few opportunities exist in the epic for picturing societies wholly at peace. The agriculture of the Shire and the commerce of Bree are brief exceptions. In the quieter landscape of *The Hobbit*, though, Tolkien has time to imag-

ine the town of the men of Esgaroth built out over the waters
of Long Lake on wooden pilings for greater safety. The idea
of it may come from his recollection of the lakeside dwellings of our primitive ancestors which some archeologists postu-
late. In any case, Lake-town is pictured as a merchant community trading with the Silvan elves and with men farther
south along the River. But even trade corrupts. The Master is
a merchant prince whose mind is given altogether "to trade
and tolls, to cargoes and gold, to which habit he owed his position." War, here too, is inescapable. The town has been
wrecked before by Smaug and is presently burned again. But
once the dragon is killed and the orc army driven off in the
Battle of the Five Armies, new dwarf and human settlers
crowd in, the valley blossoms, "and much wealth went up
and down the Running River; and there was friendship in
those parts between elves and dwarves and men."

Such a restoration of peace and friendly commerce between all the free peoples is Tolkien's idea of what constitutes
a happy ending. The whole struggle of the War of the Ring
has this as its ultimate goal. Tolkien, however, does not de-
siderate any such mingling of species as will erode the special
identity of each. They are not to inhabit the same towns and
adopt the same modes of life. Dwarves and elves may help to
rebuild Minas Tirith but, after the work is done, dwarves will
return to their smithies in the caves of Aglarond, Erebor, and
the Iron Mountains, elves to their hunting and song in Mirkwood. Hobbits may come as visitors, but the Shire will remain their home. Ents must herd their trees in Fangorn Forest. Hobbits and men will continue to live together in Bree,
but mark the conditions: ". . . on friendly terms, minding
their own affairs in their own ways, but both rightly regard-
ing themselves as necessary parts of the Bree-folk. Nowhere
else in the world was this peculiar (but excellent) arrangement to be found." Bree's arrangement is unique, made possi-

ble only by the fact that hobbit and Man are very close kin. Even there the two species pretty much go their separate ways, without intermarriage.

The general rule is that the free peoples do not interbreed. In most cases it is physically impossible anyway, but where possible it seldom happens. The three lonely unions between elf maidens and men, with their historic but largely tragic results, only prove the rule. Sexual matings between free and unfree peoples are disastrously wrong. The original breeding of orcs and trolls by Morgoth, followed later by the crossing of orcs with men by Sauron and Saruman, is regarded with horror by everyone in the West. Such unions produce not only the Uruk-hai but "squint-eyed" half-men. Bill Ferny's accomplice in Bree is one of these.

On quite a different footing, of course, is intermarriage between members of different tribes or clans within the same species. The three branches of hobbit folk freely intermarry, as do the various families of elves. Faramir praises the Stewards' success in strengthening the failing stock of Númenorean Gondor by unions with more primitive peoples of mountain and seashore; Faramir himself happily weds Éowyn of Rohan, and so on.

The coexistence of the free peoples of Middle-earth with one another is founded on mutual respect and appreciation. Radically incompatible with these is the kind of contempt Boromir expresses for all halflings, elves and wizards, not to mention Aragorn, in the scene when he tries to take the Ring from Frodo at Parth Galen. In this context his saying, "Each to his own kind," is in effect a proclamation of the superiority of men over other species, of Gondoreans over other men, and eventually of Boromir over other Gondoreans. In some degree some members of all the other species are smirched by this sense of the alienness of other peoples and the peculiar excellence of their own. Summed up in Boromir's words, which might have come straight from the brain of Sauron, the principle is at the root of all division on Middle-earth: "Each to his own kind." The business of *The Lord of the Rings* is to eradicate it inside the civilization of the West. Aragorn the statesman makes a beginning by reaching out to the men of the South and the East through treaty and alliance. But for the most part the bringing of Southrons and Easterlings into full reconciliation with the West is left as unfinished business.

CHAPTER VI
Aragorn

In his essay "On Fairy-stories" Tolkien takes pains to make the point that most good fairy stories are not "stories about fairies" but about "the adventures of men in the Perilous Realm." Aragorn is unquestionably the leading man in *The Lord of the Rings*, which is a fairy tale within Tolkien's broad definition of the genre, yet he is probably the least written about, least valued, and most misunderstood of all its major characters. By some critics, like Roger Sale,[1] he is completely neglected in favor of Frodo as central hero; by others, like William Ready, he is dismissed as "almost too good to be human; he has some of the qualities of a noble horse."[2] Mr. Ready wants him to display "a sharp taste for sin."

It is not clear why this demand, more appropriate to a realistic novel than to heroic fantasy, should be made, on penalty of being horsy, of Aragorn alone among the foes of Sauron. What is clear is that if it were made of all alike it would blur the clear dichotomy between good and evil on which Tolkien has chosen to build his epic. Of course, Mr. Ready may mean only that Aragorn has no weaknesses, suffers no limitations. If so, he is demonstrably wrong. But merely to dwell on Aragorn's faults in order to refute Mr. Ready's school of criticism would be too negative a stance for a fair-minded reader to adopt. Our understanding of this complex man will be better served by showing how his varied qualities complement or contend with one another, and how he struggles to keep uppermost those that are best. This is the same struggle that has to be waged under different guises by all the leaders and many of the followers of the West. Without it they would not be good. One of Tolkien's major achievements in these degenerate days is to win our sympathy for their triumph over the evil from within.

Admittedly, Aragorn is rather more difficult to know truly than any other important person in the story. The fault is partly Tolkien's. As noted elsewhere, in the Introductory Note to *Tree and Leaf* he confessed that during the period 1938–1939 when he first brought Aragorn (disguised as Strider) and the hobbits together at Bree he "had then no more notion than they had of . . . who Strider was; and I had begun to despair of surviving to find out." Consequently, Tolkien had not put into the narrative before then any preparatory allusions to Strider's real identity, his present reasons for interest in the Ring, and his many past years of travel and labor connected with it in the Wild. We do not begin to get most of this essential information about Isildur's heir until the Council of Elrond several chapters later, and only in retrospect can understand his actions and feeling at Bree. Even at Rivendell we may well miss the bare hints which are all that Tolkien finds space for about Aragorn's love for Arwen since youth. Yet this, along with his concurrent planning to recover the throne of Gondor, is basic motivation without a knowledge of which Aragorn remains a mystery. Unless the reader is very alert to the few obscure references to Arwen scattered here and there later on, he can easily wake up somewhere in Volume III with a shock of total surprise at Aragorn's approaching marriage to the lady. Not until the beautiful "Tale of Aragorn and Arwen" in Appendix A do we fully grasp her influence upon his life and see him whole.

No doubt Tolkien, making a literary virtue out of his unforeseen introduction of Strider, plays up for all they are worth the resulting sense of mystery and the excitement of gradual discovery of the truth about him. But Tolkien has not escaped the risks of puzzling readers into misconceptions that are hard to root out even on rereading the text several times. For instance, the travel-worn stranger with the "pale stern face" and "dark hair flecked with grey" sitting in the shadows in the common room of the inn at Bree may seem unduly secretive until we know his background. His father was killed by Sauron's orcs when he was a baby and he has been reared to manhood by Elrond in Rivendell under an assumed name to hide him from the Enemy, who would give much to trap the only remaining man with clear title to the thrones of both the North and the South Kingdoms. All his life he has been making arduous journeys far east and south to learn of those regions and peoples at first hand and to spy on Sauron. Under false names he has fought for both Rohan and Minas Tirith. Chief of the Dúnedain, he has quietly led them in patrols that have slipped along the borders of the Shire to guard it and the Ring it holds. They are homeless and solitary men, these Rangers, as their work demands, and he has become as grim and stern as any of them. Not the less so because as a young man he fell in love with the elfin princess Arwen, daughter of Elrond, whom by her father's command he cannot marry until he regains his throne. The long years pass without bringing him nearer to either goal, until the Ring reappears. Shortly before coming to Bree he has returned from a joint search with Gandalf for Gollum, whom he captured clear down near the borders of Mordor. And within the past week his Rangers have been routed by incursions of the nine Black Riders under the command of Angmar, the ancient enemy of his race.

This is the ambitious, weary and apprehensive prince who impatiently watches the foolish antics of the hobbits under the suspicious eyes of the crowd in the inn. To his mind the hobbits badly need taking in hand, as children who are playing games with the fate of Middle-earth. Having trailed them to Bree after overhearing their good-byes to Bombadil, he must now undertake to guide them to the safety of Rivendell. But how to persuade them to accept him — a complete stranger? He has asked the innkeeper Butterbur to take a message to the hobbits that he wants to talk to them, and has been ignominiously turned down. Like other folk in Bree, Butterbur is parochially contemptuous of mysterious Rangers. The incident has not decreased Aragorn's sense of anger and frustration, but it is typical of him that he manages to master them. After some mild but unsuccessful warnings to Frodo in the taproom to be more cautious, he quietly invites himself into the hobbits' private room and patiently sets out to win their confidence. He does not make the mistake of being ingratiating; on the contrary, he starts out with a shock tactic. Because of the debacle in the common room he treats them like the children they have shown themselves to be, and proposes to give them unspecified valuable information in exchange for the "reward" of being allowed to accompany them. The proposal is meant to be indignantly refused and when it is, Aragon applauds.

Step by step he arouses the hobbits to the dangers of their situation. He warms them to him by making fun of his own wayworn appearance which causes the innkeeper to scorn him: " 'Well, I have a rascally look, have I not?' " he asks Frodo "with a curl of his lip and a queer gleam of his eye." Aragorn is hiding here the very real hurt he feels. But when Butterbur enters the room again with a pointblank warning to the hobbits not to "take up with a Ranger," thereby disturbing Aragorn's efforts at conciliation, Aragorn strikes back acidly, asking whether Butterbur is prepared to guard them against the Black Riders. And the discovery that Butterbur is holding an important letter from Gandalf to Frodo, which he has totally forgotten to deliver for months, snaps Aragorn's patience with the "fat innkeeper who only remembers his own name because people shout at him all day." Aragorn is capable of lasting anger at laxity and stupidity and ingratitude. These are still in his mind weeks later at Elrond's Council when he says of his Rangers: "Travellers scowl at us and countrymen give us scornful names. 'Strider' I am to one fat man who lives within a day's march of foes that would freeze his heart, or lay his little town in ruin, if he were not guarded ceaselessly." Aragorn will have a long memory for injuries when he ascends the throne, but he will restrain it with a sense of justice, as at Rivendell he pulls himself up short with the reminder that his own policy has deliberately kept the Shire folk ignorant of their own danger: "Yet we would not have it otherwise. If simple folk are free from care and fear, simple they will be, and we must be secret to keep them so." The wisdom of such a policy may be debated, but certainly its intention is generous.

But back to Bree — Aragorn is deeply shaken with hatred and fear of the Black Riders while he tries to make the hobbits realize how terrible they are. His face is "drawn as if with pain, and his hands clenched the arms of his chair . . . while he sat with unseeing eyes as if walking in distant memory." He is reliving recent encounters with these living dead, whom he now proposes to face again, and is perhaps also remembering that his ancestors in the North Kingdom were obliterated ages ago by Angmar, their captain, his hereditary foe. Aragorn may resent slurs by others against his conviction of his own high worth, but he can be curiously humble about it himself when he offers his help to the hobbits on their journey. "I am older than I look. I might prove useful." Aragorn's problem with the hobbits is largely resolved for him by Gandalf's letter of identification. When Frodo asks him why he didn't reveal himself before as a friend of the wizard, Aragon gives several practical reasons but ends with the real one, which is emotional: " 'But I must admit,' he added with a queer laugh, 'that I hoped you would take me for my own sake. A hunted man sometimes wearies of distrust and longs for friendship. But there, I believe my looks are against me.' " He is weary of the pretenses imposed by his life of enforced disguise, and longs to be given the trust which he is finding out can only be won by first giving trust himself.

Throughout this scene Aragorn is holding powerful feelings under rein. Sometimes they escape for a moment, as with Butterbur. So also in the case of Pippin, whose well-meant but tactless remark that they would all look as disreputable as Strider "after lying for days in hedges and ditches" provokes him to a tart outburst, "It would take more than a few days, or weeks, or years, of wandering in the Wild to make you look like Strider . . . And you would die first, unless you are made of sterner stuff than you look to be." And Sam's persistent doubt that he is the real Strider draws a raw assertion of power: " 'If I had killed the real Strider, I could kill *you*. And I should have killed you already without so much talk. If I was after the Ring, I could have it — NOW!' " That he could easily take the Ring from the hobbits by force or fraud and use its magic to win his long-sought throne, and with it the maiden he loves, has not failed to cross his mind. Like every other leader of the West he is given one fateful chance to yield to its temptation. But he conquers it and is never bothered by it again. Taking his hand off his sword, he smiles suddenly. "I am Aragorn son of Arathorn; and if by life or death I can serve you, I will." By confiding to the hobbits his true identity he puts his life in their hands. And by his pledge of help he subordinates his own ambitions to their safety as bearers of the Ring.

All of the foregoing gives us some insight into the strong eruptions of rebellion and the hidden sensitiveness which Aragorn keeps under control by a yet stronger will. He is no Stoic. The apparently endless labors of his lifetime sometimes seem too much to bear. But in Tolkien's world as in ours it is not required of a man that he always love his burden or be patient under it — only that he continue to bear it. Aragorn bears his, usually with a rueful humor. As if purged by his former outbursts, he accepts with good grace Frodo's observation that if Aragorn were a spy of Sauron he would "seem fairer and feel fouler." He laughs as he replies, "I look foul and feel fair. Is that it?" Repeating the jingle that "all that is gold does not glitter," which warns the hobbits to look below the surface, and unsheathing to their gaze the broken sword mentioned in the same rhyme as belonging to the crownless one who shall be King, he smiles with gentle irony at the now silent Sam: "Well, with Sam's permission we will call that settled."

From then on he comes to respect and love the hobbits during the flight to Rivendell, and they finally to depend on his woodsmanship and courage and to like him, though they do not yet understand him well enough to love him. Frodo tells Gandalf at the end of the journey that "Strider saved us . . . I have become very fond of Strider. Well, *fond* is not the right word. I mean he is dear to me; though he is strange and grim at times. In fact, he reminds me often of you." Like pupils, like master, though Aragorn has sorrows and ambitions of a human kind that the wizard can never know. He can joke with the hobbits about the birds' nests behind the stone trolls' ears but he can also, as they near Rivendell where Arwen is, sing with a "strange, eager face" and shining eyes the haunting lay about the love of the man Beren and the elfin princess Lúthien, which so strangely forecasts his and Arwen's own love. None of the hobbits has the faintest glimmer of an idea why Aragorn chooses this particular legend to recite, and neither have we at first reading, thanks to Tolkien's failure to mention Arwen at all up to that point. But in the light of later revelations it can dawn on us that the longing for Arwen is a torment, a joy, a despair, a comfort to Aragorn in a time of little hope. Small wonder that he is "strange and grim at times," but he seldom speaks of the life of private emotion stirring within.

Whether, safely arrived at Rivendell with his charges, Aragorn has many opportunities for lovers' meetings Tolkien does not say. Presumably at least some. The indications, however, are that they are few. Frodo sees him with Arwen only once, and then they are only talking together in the presence of Elrond. Aragorn is gone much of the time with the sons of Elrond, scouting the country for Sauron's forces. He is not even present at the feast celebrating Frodo's recovery, though he manages to get away from his duties in time for the music afterward. Besides, things are rather awkward for Aragorn in the house of Elrond. He is still on probation, as it were, under the ban of Arwen's father against pressing his suit with her so long as he remains a homeless wanderer unable to offer her the rank she merits by birth and worth. This sort of parental restriction might mean little to what Treebeard would call more "hasty lovers," but it is one which Arwen and Aragorn both have felt bound to honor through years of separation. We can treat it as a mere fairy-tale prohibition, if we like, but if we accept the tradition of the genre we cannot interpret the lovers' acceptance of it as meaning that they do not deeply love each other.

We do not need to look upon the situation as merely traditional, however. Tolkien has so drawn the characters of the lovers as to make their obedience entirely in character, without detracting from the ardor of their love. Arwen is deeply devoted to her father and her kin, the noblest among the elves. Marrying Aragorn will mean that she must surrender her immortality as an elf and become a mortal being whose soul at death will be separated from the souls of her people while time endures, and perhaps eternally. She will do it, but she owes it to her father to fulfill his conditions before taking the hardly imaginable parting step.

On his side Aragorn has many reasons for respecting Elrond's wishes. He has been saved since infancy and trained by Elrond, incurring a heavy debt of gratitude and at the same time feeling for him something of the affection due to a father. Moreover, Aragorn is a man who, as later developments will show, has a strong sense of the importance of authority, propriety, law. It is by these principles that he governs when he himself becomes king in the end. He knows that if he expects his subjects to obey him freely out of respect for these principles he must first learn to obey them himself. It is unthinkable that he would urge Arwen to run off with him into the woods without her father's consent, or perhaps even with it. To ask Arwen to marry him under the best of conditions is to ask her to receive eventual old age and death, "the choice of Lúthien" as she herself calls it, an intolerable gift for any sensitive man to bestow on the woman he loves. The one thing he cannot do in that position is to press his suit hard upon her. Hence his apparent inactivity in wooing, and also the deep inner convulsions of his mind, the outward grimness, as he confronts the complex ironies of his lot.

When the members of Elrond's Council assemble to decide what to do with Sauron's Ring, Aragorn sits "in a corner alone . . . clad in his travel-worn clothes again" and takes no leading role in the final decision. This he leaves to Elrond and Gandalf, whose ideas about the Ring he knows from their years of mutual search for it, and which by his silence he approves. The task Aragorn sets himself is to win over Boromir, who as eldest son of the present Steward ruling in Gondor is a key factor in his hopes to ascend its throne. Nominally the Stewards still hold it in fealty to a rightful King who may return, but for centuries the southern branch of Elendil's heirs has been extinct, and nobody in Gondor dreams that any direct descendant of Isildur survives in the northern branch. Gondor's dire need for help against Sauron's armies and a recurring dream urging Boromir to seek it at Rivendell through "the Sword that was broken" give Aragorn his opportunity to reveal himself and assert his claim. As soon as Boromir has told his story, Aragorn dramatically casts on the table the two pieces of his sword and identifies it as the weapon of the dream. To a surprised Boromir Elrond then introduces Aragorn as "descended through many fathers from Isildur, Elendil's son of Minas Ithil" and hence by implication the legal heir to Gondor's throne, of which Elendil was first founder. Frodo exclaims that then Aragorn also must be rightful owner of the Ring, since his ancestor Isildur once owned and lost it. But Aragorn immediately renounces all ownership in it, and later in the scene says that he helped Gandalf search for it only because "it seemed fit that Isildur's heir should labour to repair Isildur's fault." He toiled only to undo an inherited wrong. As far as he is concerned the Ring belongs to nobody.

Instead, when Frodo displays the Ring, Aragorn relates an ancient prophecy among his people that when the Ring is found the sword, which Elendil broke while fighting with Sauron, will be reforged. Having thus reinforced the identification of the present sword as Elendil's, he presses Boromir directly with the question, "Now you have seen the sword that you have sought, what would you ask? Do you wish for

the House of Elendil to return to the Land of Gondor?"
The dynastic resonances of the question are obviously crucial. Boromir dodges them by admitting that the "sword" (not
the "House") of Elendil would be immensely helpful — if indeed it is the true sword of Elendil. Aragorn replies with a
courteous but firm kingliness: "I forgive your doubt." Little
does he resemble at the moment the figures of his great ancestors, he admits, because he has had "a hard life and a long," en-
during many journeys. But his home is in the North. He
stresses the fact, vital to his legal title, that the line of descent
in the northern kings has never been broken: " 'For here the
heirs of Valandil have ever dwelt in long line unbroken
from father unto son for many generations.' "

Boromir in his opening speech has boasted that his city of
Minas Tirith stands as the sole bulwark against Sauron, "and
thus alone are peace and freedom maintained in the lands behind us, bulwark of the West." Aragorn rebuffs that vaunt
by recounting the exploits of his Dúnedain: "You know little
of the lands beyond your bounds. Peace and freedom, do
you say? The North would have known them little but for
us. Fear would have destroyed them. But when dark things
come from the houseless hills, or creep from sunless woods,
they fly from us." And for this service the Rangers have not
had the glory and the thanks Gondor has. But now that the
Ring is found, the times are changing. Aragorn abandons his
earlier exploratory question to Boromir and concludes with a
decisive assertion: "I will come to Minas Tirith." Boromir
still avoids an answer by demanding proof that the Ring
Frodo has shown him is in fact Sauron's Ring of power. In
verification Frodo and Gandalf join in reconstructing the
movements of the Ring from the time when Isildur cut it off
Sauron's hand until it came through Gollum to Bilbo and
thence to Frodo. Seventeen years ago when he began to suspect that the ring Bilbo had was the ruling Ring, Gandalf says,

he called upon the Dúnedain to help guard the Shire, "and I opened my heart to Aragorn, the heir of Isildur." Significantly, by giving him this title Gandalf is adding to Elrond's his endorsement of Aragorn's legitimacy as claimant to Gondor.

Aragorn's successful capture and imprisonment of Gollum offers us a contrast with the behavior of Gandalf, Frodo, and Sam under comparable circumstances. Says Aragorn, describing the capture, "He will never love me, I fear; for he bit me, and I was not gentle. Nothing more did I ever get from his mouth than the marks of his teeth. I deemed it the worst part of all my journey, the road back, watching him day and night, making him walk before me with a halter on his neck, gagged, until he was tamed by lack of drink and food, driving him ever toward Mirkwood." There Aragorn left Gollum with the elves of the forest to be kept secure for later questioning by Gandalf.

Anyone who thinks that Aragorn, the future King, is or should be all sweetness and light should reflect on this passage. He is not gratuitously cruel to his prisoner but he feels no need to be gentle with the malevolent. Whatever measures of binding, gagging, and starving are necessary to his job of getting the slippery wretch into strong hands without danger of escape he takes. Not that he has no pity for Gollum. He recognizes that "he had suffered much. There is no doubt that he was tormented, and the fear of Sauron lies black on his heart." But such a one is far too dangerous to be on the loose. "His malice is great," and Aragorn is sure that he had just come from Mordor "on some evil errand." Under such circumstances there is a stern justice about Aragorn that weighs and rejects the risks of mercy. Consequently he does not get from Gollum the information which Gandalf later manages to charm out of him, but neither does he lose his prisoner to rescuing orcs as do the elves, through what Legolas admits was "overkindliness." Also he never comes close to winning Gollum's loyalty as Frodo does, but then he never suffers the concomitant betrayal, either. What Aragorn lacks is the conviction of Gandalf and Frodo that a free Gollum will perform ultimate good that Gollum himself does not intend. But this is an intuition beyond all reason. As King, Aragorn will later know how to temper justice with forgiveness. But we cannot expect a practical judge to act upon irrational intuitions that a criminal left at large intending to do evil will do good without meaning to.

The last stage of the skirmish between Aragorn and Boromir at the Council opens with the latter's proposal to its members that the Ring be not destroyed but wielded by one of their number against Sauron its maker. Already the thought of using it himself, which is implemented later in his attempt to snatch it from Frodo by force at Parth Galen, is stirring in his mind. Informed by Elrond of the Ring's deadly power for evil, he submits "doubtfully" for the time being and, in lieu, comes back to the possibility that for Gondor "the Sword-that-was-Broken may still stem the tide — if the hand that wields it has not inherited an heirloom only, but the sinews of the Kings of Men." Not a tactful doubt, but Boromir is a blunt man. Aragorn returns a soft answer, which is also soothingly indefinite as to time: "Who knows? We will put it to the test one day." Not wanting to return home empty-handed Boromir then moves on to the important step of issuing what is, in effect, as outright and immediate an invitation to Aragorn as his pride allows: "May the day not be too long delayed . . . For though I do not ask for aid, we need it."

By a combination of tact and boldness Aragorn has now won from Boromir everything he wants: recognition that the sword is Elendil's and that Aragorn is its rightful owner by unbroken succession, together with an invitation to accompany him back to Gondor without delay. Of course, Boromir is not yet yielding any specific admissions on the question of the succession. It is hard to visualize a man so dedicated to power eventually surrendering his position of advantage, as Faramir does afterward. What will happen when the two men reach Minas Tirith will happen. But Aragorn has already made a great stride toward his goal.

In keeping with his faith in individual freedom of choice is Elrond's refusal to exact an oath from any member of the Fellowship as to how far he will accompany Frodo. Each is to go only so far as he wills, and can turn back at any time. The general understanding at the outset is only that "they are willing to go at least to the passes of the Mountains, and maybe beyond." Aragorn clearly intends to go with Boromir to help defend Minas Tirith, not to accompany Frodo into Mordor. He says as much when he smilingly asks leave of Frodo once again to be his companion, and Frodo welcomes him with the delighted cry, "I would have begged you to come . . . only I thought you were going to Minas Tirith with Boromir." Aragorn answers, "I am . . . But your road and our road lie together for many hundreds of miles." To leave the options open as Elrond wishes, Aragorn and Gandalf make definite plans only as far as their stopover in Lothlórien, after which the members of the Company are to decide their several courses for the next stage. This vagueness of planning will throw Aragorn into an unexpected conflict of duties after Gandalf's disappearance in Moria and will thwart his desire to hasten on to Gondor.

On the night of their leaving Rivendell the Company wait silent and subdued. Aragorn, in particular, "sat with his head bowed to his knees; only Elrond knew fully what this hour meant to him." What it means is the beginning of the supreme trials which are to determine whether he dies defeated or lives to win Arwen and his crown. The odds against him are high, but he is girding up his will to overcome them. Once the Nine Walkers are on the trail southward he becomes again the excellent companion the hobbits have come to know when his cares do not press too heavily on him — dependable, approachable, and full of hope. Estel ("hope") he was named as a child, and his natural buoyancy asserts itself when it can.

Aside from the normal precautions against lurking dangers, Aragorn's main concern in the first part of the trip is to persuade Gandalf not to cross the Misty Mountains via the Moria caverns from which, as legends tell, Durin's dwarves were driven by a Balrog fleeing there from Morgoth's overthrow. Devoted as he is to his old mentor, Aragorn has a strong presentiment that Gandalf will never come out alive if he meets that dire spirit of the underworld. King Celeborn of Lórien evidently has the same thought later, for on hearing of Gandalf's death he exclaims against his "folly, going needlessly into the net of Moria." Galadriel comments more wisely, however, that none of Gandalf's actions was ever needless. She seems to mean that although Gandalf knew his peril he accepted even death if necessary as the only way to speed the Ring-bearer on his mission. There was no other pass over or around the mountains once cruel Caradhras hurled his blizzards at the travelers and Saruman blocked the Gap of Rohan against them.

After their escape from Moria, for all the survivors of the Company Lórien is a timeless land of rest, which yet harbors secret tests of purity of heart. One can find himself there, like Gimli, or lose himself, like Boromir. But Aragorn alone has passed that way before. There, years ago, he and Arwen plighted their troth, standing on the grave mound of King Amroth, who died for hopeless love, rejecting in favor of mortal life both the Shadow of Sauron in the East and the everlasting twilight of the elven lands in the West. Frodo sees Aragorn standing quietly, remembering her, "and he seemed clothed in white, a young lord tall and fair; and he spoke words in the Elvish tongue to one whom Frodo could not see. *Arwen vanimelda, namarië!* he said . . ." And to Frodo, smiling: ". . . here my heart dwells ever, unless there be a light beyond the dark roads that we must still tread, you and I."

The loss of Gandalf has left Aragorn as head of the Fellowship, but it is a tenuous headship that is limited by the free choices of its members and exercisable only by persuasion, if at all. He has acquitted himself well at the crisis caused by Gimli's absolute refusal to be blindfolded on entering the woods of Lórien. His statesmanlike solution of putting them all on an equal footing by asking that all be blindfolded has pacified the dwarf's stubborn pride. A man who can bring this off will make a fair and wise king. He is bound by Elrond's instructions, however, not to try to order what each person will do next for the future of the Quest. Boromir clearly is still going to Minas Tirith. But Aragorn himself can no longer say with his first happy assurance that he is going with Boromir, as at heart he still longs to do. Gandalf is not there to go with the Ring-bearer, as Aragorn suspects he would have done. Must Aragorn now take his place, or is his first duty still to his city of Minas Tirith? He rather inclines to interpret the prophecy of the dream to mean the latter. Of course, Frodo may decide to approach Mordor either directly from the north or indirectly through Minas Tirith from the west. If from the west, there is no problem until Frodo leaves the city, and meantime Aragorn can proceed there with a clear conscience. But Frodo has expressed no preference, and Aragorn cannot escape the feeling that the Ring-bearer must be left to make up his own mind. Should not Aragorn at least offer the best advice he can, though? And has he not some obligations now to the others who compose the Company? They also are undecided, and such indications as they give show that they are divided.

Accordingly, when asked by Celeborn during their farewells whether they are all going with Boromir, Aragorn can only answer, "We have not decided our course . . . I do not know what Gandalf intended to do." Boromir speaks up for the route to his city but "the others said nothing, and Aragorn looked doubtful and troubled." Celeborn carefully refrains from influencing them and instead gives them boats in which to float south downriver, a method of travel which Aragorn welcomes "not least because there would now be no need to decide his course for some days. The others, too, looked more hopeful." They leave with Celeborn's warning ringing in their ears that in the end they will have to face up to a choice, though Galadriel thinks perhaps the path of each one is already laid out for him without his seeing it yet.

They all live with the dilemma for many days during the voyage down Anduin, coming to no conclusions and hoping for outer events to give them a sign, until they reach the meadows at Parth Galen above the falls of Rauros. There Aragorn calls them together and, not voicing any preference of his own, puts the question to all: "What shall now become of our Company that has travelled so far in fellowship?" Shall all go to Mordor, all go to Minas Tirith, or some to one, some to the other? Nobody has a word to say. Aragorn then lays the burden on Frodo: "You are the Bearer appointed by the Council. Your own way you alone can choose. In this matter I cannot advise you." He thinks that even if Gandalf were present the decision would still be Frodo's. "Such is your fate."

While Frodo walks aside alone for an hour to make up his mind, his companions talk over the situation and make up theirs. They would all prefer to go to Minas Tirith, but if Frodo heads for Mordor now they all think they should go with him. Aragorn then argues that in so desperate a venture a smaller group has a better chance than a larger one, and suggests himself, Sam, and Gimli as companions for Frodo in Mordor. He thereby renounces his opportunity to fight for Gondor's capital, and all that goes with it — Arwen, the throne, the hope of leading an army cleanly against Sauron — for a share in what reason tells him is a hopeless enterprise. He has taken his stand. But he is dealing with a group of free agents who will have none of his proposal to leave them behind. Sam is sure that Frodo is screwing up his courage to go directly to Mordor as he knows he should. Pippin is all for stopping him. But Aragorn stands by a basically religious conviction that they not only should not but cannot force Frodo in either direction. "There are other powers at work far stronger."

In this he happens to be right, for at that moment Sauron and Gandalf are contending for Frodo's soul on the summit of Amon Hen. Frodo's resolve to steal away secretly from his companions to almost certain death in Mordor is his moral salvation, but his disappearance throws them into a confusion which Aragorn's best efforts cannot control. As they scatter in all directions he runs to the top of the mount to scan the surroundings, only to find that this move puts him too far away to help Boromir hold off the orcs who are carrying off Pippin and Merry, too late to save Boromir's life or share his death. Aragorn suffers a stab of self-blame even before Boromir dies: "Alas! An ill fate is on me this day, and all that I do goes amiss." When Boromir dies in his arms confessing failure and begging him to save Minas Tirith, this pain deepens into an anguish in which he holds himself responsible for what he considers the whole sorry collapse of his leadership: "This is a bitter end. Now the Company is all in ruin. It is I that have failed. Vain was Gandalf's trust in me. What shall I do now? Boromir has laid it on me to go to Minas Tirith, and my heart desires it; but where are the Ring and the Bearer? How shall I find them and save the Quest from disaster?"

Typically, Aragorn shifts none of the blame to Boromir, whose sincere repentence and heroic death in battle with the orcs completely redeem him in Aragorn's eyes. His grief for the fallen man is notably tender and generous, his funeral lament heavy with a sense of loss. It is much more than a conventional elegy for a brave stranger. Boromir was a subject of Aragorn's, and died on a mission to save the city they both love. The farewell song does not try to invest the dead man with virtues he never had but simply pictures the sorrow of the people of Minas Tirith as they wait in vain for the return of the captain they hold dear. After the burial, however, Aragorn does not let the pain of his self-reproach undo the mastery of his will over emotion or cloud the powers of observation and deduction by which he unravels the whereabouts of the other members of the expedition. Once these are known it is clear to him that his choice is either to take the remaining boat and follow Frodo into Mordor or else to pursue the orcs on foot. Aragorn does not ask the opinions of Legolas and Gimli but makes the decision for all: "Let me think! . . . And now may I make a right choice, and change the evil fate of this unhappy day! . . . I will follow the Orcs." He would have gone with Frodo and Sam into Mordor but the Ring-bearer has decided otherwise. He cannot abandon the other two hobbits to torment and death. "My heart speaks clearly at last." He does not even mention Minas Tirith, where his personal advantage calls him to go.

As the pursuit begins, Aragorn shows again his appreciation of the ties binding different intelligent species together that will make him a trusted King. He knows how to bind to him his companion elf and dwarf: "We will make such a chase as shall be accounted a marvel among the Three

Kindreds: Elves, Dwarves, and Men." This is the same breadth of understanding that will emerge in his statement to Éomer of the great moral imperative of Middle-earth: "Good and ill have not changed since yesteryear; nor are they one thing among Elves and Dwarves and another among Men." Aragorn seems to have risen from his crisis of self-confidence all the stronger on its account, for when Gimli and Legolas cannot agree on the advisability of resting at night during the pursuit they spontaneously leave the matter up to him. He settles it neatly. When across the plains of Rohan he catches sight of the White Mountains beckoning him south to Minas Tirith, he has no trouble turning his eyes away.

The meeting with Éomer and his troop just returning from wiping out the orcs Aragorn also handles with great skill. He understands the Rohirrim well, having ridden anonymously in their ranks many years before: "They are proud and wilful," he has told Gimli, "but they are true-hearted, generous in thought and deed; bold but not cruel; wise but unlearned . . ." The touchiness of his two companions at a slur against Galadriel's reputation almost precipitates a suicidal fight with the suspicious Riders of Rohan, but Aragorn springs between with a timely apology. Challenged to give his true name, he responds with one of those magnificent roll calls of his royal titles which sometimes blaze from him. He draws Andúril, shouting his battle cry: "Elendil! . . . I am Aragorn, son of Arathorn, and am called Elessar, the Elfstone, Dúnadan, the heir of Isildur Elendil's son of Gondor. Here is the Sword that was Broken and is forged again!" He takes the offensive, "Will you aid me or thwart me? Choose swiftly!" With the bold be bold. The stance he takes appeals perfectly to the warrior Rohirrim. Éomer is impressed, even awed enough to accept the identification claimed and thereafter to listen to Aragorn's inquiries and news with the respect due to a man of royal blood, the more so since he finds Aragorn condemning the neutralist policy that King Théoden has adopted toward Sauron and which he himself thinks wrong. Aragorn gives him a message to Théoden as from one king to another: "You may say this to Théoden son of Thengel: open war lies before him, with Sauron or against him . . . But of these great matters we will speak later. If chance allows, I myself will come to the king." After hearing about the alliance being formed against Sauron, and the loss sustained in the deaths of Boromir and Gandalf, Éomer begs him to come straight to Théoden as the present law of Rohan demands of all visitors. But Aragorn's insistence that he will fight the whole band if necessary to continue his search for the hobbits wins from Éomer permission to pass, together with a loan of prized horses, in exchange for a promise to come to court immediately afterward. Éomer risks his rank as Marshal, and perhaps his life, in going so far.

Éomer is moved by more than mere considerations of policy; he is moved by affection. He will tell Aragorn at the climax of events that he has loved him ever "since you rose up out of the grass before me." This love is reciprocated. Aragorn, looking after Éomer, Merry, and Théoden as they ride away from Helm's Deep some days afterward, tells his kinsman Halbarad, "There go three that I love." In this first encounter with Éomer Aragorn gains a close friend and ally who will become King of Rohan in the battle of the Pelennor Fields and will unhesitatingly support his title to the crown of Gondor. He also begins the realignment of Rohan against Mordor, which is soon to be completed by Gandalf in person.

It would be improper for Aragorn to thrust himself into the limelight in the scenes at Edoras and Helm's Deep, and he holds himself in the background with reserved power. The awakening of Théoden to Saruman's treachery belongs to

Gandalf, who has uncovered it. Aragorn does no more than make known to the Rohirrim almost casually that he is Elendil's heir wearing Elendil's sword. The defense of Helm's Deep against Saruman's armies belongs to Théoden and his thanes. Aragorn merely lends the weight of his arm to repelling attacks on the walls and to leading sorties with Éomer. He does not try to be more than a hard-fighting ally who knows his place. At only one point, on an errand of mercy, does he step out of that subordinate role to stand alone upon the battlements at dawn and warn the enemy, "Depart, or not one of you will be spared . . . You do not know your peril." He is giving the enemy, particularly the hillmen in their ranks, a last chance to escape. His senses as a Ranger tell him that Fangorn huorns, which will engulf them, are already arriving. At Isengard he takes no prominent part either. While the royal party goes off to survey the ruins he stays behind for a friendly chat with Merry and Pippin and, invited by Gandalf to broaden his experience by listening to the wiles of the captured Saruman, he listens without a word.

Aragorn begins to stir with the recovery of the *palantír* of Orthanc, which is his by right of inheritance from Elendil. When Gandalf offers it to him merely for safekeeping since it is a "dangerous charge," he asserts his title to it as the rightful owner: "Dangerous indeed, but not to all. There is one who may claim it by right . . . . Now my hour draws near. I will take it." Acknowledging the claim, Gandalf hands it to him with a bow and respectful caution: "Receive it, lord, in earnest of other things that will be given back. But if I may counsel you in the use of your own do not use it — yet! Be wary!" Gandalf distrusts his own strength to challenge Sauron by looking into the *palantír* which Sauron has warped to his own uses, and thinks its possession should be kept secret. Aragorn thinks otherwise. When he is joined that same night by his band of Dúnedain from the North bearing a hand-woven banner and message from Arwen, and by the two sons of Elrond reminding him of the prophecy that he must summon the faithless dead to his aid, he decides to disregard Gandalf's advice. After a struggle of wills he breaks Sauron's hold over the *palantír* and purposely reveals himself as Elendil's heir about to take the throne of Gondor. His aim of alarming Sauron is fulfilled. Remembering his defeat by Elendil, the enemy hurries to launch his attack on Gondor before it is quite ready. This anxiety and haste make possible his repulse. Most important, they keep Sauron from discovering that Frodo and Sam are slipping quietly into Mordor under his very eyes.

Through use of the *palantír* Aragorn grows to maturity. Hitherto he has been to a large extent the pupil of Gandalf. Now he is his own man. By his independent action he has set the basic stategy of the West, which is to seize and keep the military initiative at all costs in order to throw Sauron off balance and distract his attention from the real peril creeping unseen into his inner realm. Although, after the victory in the Pelennor Fields, Aragorn announces that he will obey Gandalf as supreme commander, the policy Gandalf adopts is really this same policy of Aragorn's. In pursuance of it a pitifully small army sets out to flaunt its banners at the very gates of Mordor. Aragorn can properly say then, "As I have begun so I will go on." His beginning is at Helm's Deep when he dared to match wills with Sauron over the *palantír*, with the throne of Gondor as the ultimate prize between them. Aragorn's real political rival is never Boromir or Denethor or Faramir but the Enemy whose thirst to rule Minas Tirith is personal and obsessive. The contest in the end is between the would-be tyrant and the lawful King.

Among these world issues the love of Éowyn for Aragorn blooms like a small and pathetic but lovely flower. Since Aragorn's manner of perceiving and rejecting her love reveals an intimate side of his nature that appears nowhere else, its right interpretation is vital. Tolkien himself makes it easy for us to go wrong by writing almost too well about Éowyn and not well enough about Arwen. Éowyn we see at some length in the flesh, living, loving, suffering; Arwen is like a beautiful legend in whom Aragorn believes but we hardly do, because we see her briefly only once, never hear her talk, never watch her act, until after the affair with Éowyn is all over. Consequently, out of sympathy for Éowyn, we may be tempted at the time to think Aragorn pretty much of a wooden fool, or a prude, or we may look for signs that he flirts with her at first meeting. Any of these attitudes would certainly be mistaken. Careful attention to the not always obvious clues Tolkien plants in the body of the epic (not to mention the full story in Appendix A) must convince us that Aragorn and Elrond's daughter remain constant lovers after their betrothal in spite of the separations imposed by circumstances and by Elrond's ban. This conclusion is not merely in keeping with the traditions of faithful love between hero and heroine in fairy tales but with an honest reading of the several meetings Éowyn has with Aragorn.

At first exchange of glances in Théoden's hall Aragorn sees her as "strong . . . and stern as steel, a daughter of kings" and "thought her fair, fair and cold, like a morning of pale spring that is not yet come to womanhood." He notes her cool pity for her besotted uncle. None of this suggests love-liking on his part, though it does imply admiration and perhaps compassion. Legolas, too, thinks her "cold," in the sense, I suppose, of interest in martial prowess at the expense of a gentler femininity. "And she now was suddenly aware of him: tall heir of Kings, wise with many winters, grey-cloaked, hiding a power that yet she felt." His kingliness and strength are the features that attract her, being precisely those which have been wanting in the aging uncle she has been forced to nurse in recent winters. As Éowyn offers the stirrup cup to the captains riding west to war, she looks at Aragorn with shining eyes and he returns her look with a smile. Their hands touch on the cup and he feels hers tremble. At that moment he knows where her thoughts are tending. They greet each other by name, "but his face was troubled and he did not smile." Had he returned her interest in him he would certainly not have been troubled by it. Rather, he finds himself now the object of an infatuation he never sought and, in honor, cannot encourage. Out of courtesy and fear of hurting her feelings he cannot even acknowledge openly that it exists. Her farewell words, "A year shall I endure for every day that passes until your return," are ostensibly for Théoden but actually are addressed to Aragorn, to whom her eyes turn as she speaks. He tries to keep the situation impersonal by pretending nevertheless that her words are for the king: "The king shall come again . . . Fear not! Not West but East does our doom await us." Whether he likes it or not, her love for him has created a special relationship between them, to which he must respond in some way. His words are a kindly signal of rejection.

That she has refused to read them as such becomes evident when he returns with his band of Dúnedain, with Gimli, Legolas, and the sons of Elrond, to Dunharrow to take the Paths of the Dead. She is "stricken." Having herself just found in her love a reason for living, she cannot understand why he seeks death, as she interprets his errand. She follows him to his lodging to ask him why. He explains that only by following those Paths can he do his part against Sauron, and adds as plain a discouragement to her affections as he can without referring to them direct: "Were I to go where my heart dwells, far in the North I would now be wandering in the fair valley of Rivendell." She ponders his words in silence and their probable allusion to his love for some other woman. Her resolve then is to die with him. Their colloquy in the dark proceeds on poignantly from his reminder of her duty to guard Dunharrow, to her rebellious cry that her duty is a cage from which she must break free to do noble deeds of arms, to her broken plea that she be allowed to go with the companions who "would not be parted from thee — because they love thee." She has spoken what is as close to an outright declaration of love as her maiden modesty allows before she turns away into the night.

Intolerable to both for different reasons is their farewell in the light of dawn. Acting as if they had never spoken of love, Aragorn drinks "to the fortune of your House, and of you, and of all your people." She weeps as she asks him, "Aragorn, wilt thou go?" Then, "wilt thou not let me ride with this company?" Finally, on her knees, "I beg thee!" To each plea Aragorn answers with merciful curtness, "I will"; "I will not, lady"; "nay, lady." Then he kisses her hand and rides away without looking back, "and only those who knew him well and were near him saw the pain that he bore." Her loss of Aragorn, capping the frustrations of her life as an unregarded girl in Théoden's house, drives Éowyn to ride in disguise with the host of Rohan looking for glory and death on the Pelennor Fields.

Her slaying of the Nazgûl chief brings her the one and would have brought her the other also had not Aragorn's powers of healing called her back to life. Standing with Éomer at his sister's bedside in the House of Healing, Aragorn tries delicately to diagnose for Éomer the origins of her malady without mentioning her passionate love for himself. But Éomer has been present when the two first met and has had eyes to see what happened. "I hold you blameless in this matter, as in all else," he says forthrightly. Gandalf adds the other element of the diagnosis, which Éomer has not noticed, the frenzied beating of the wings of Éowyn's spirit against the walls of Edoras, wanting freedom. Aragorn then takes the occasion to unburden his heart to his friend about the suffering he felt in having to act as he did: "Few other griefs amid the ill chances of this world have more bitterness and shame for a man's heart than to behold the love of a lady so fair and brave that cannot be returned." Sorrow and pity for her rode with him all through the days of his summoning the faithless dead, and he feared for what she might do in her despair. Yet, says Aragorn, she did not love him as she loves her brother Éomer. To her Aragorn was only "a shadow and a thought: a hope of glory and great deeds and lands far from the fields of Rohan" — in short, a method of escape from home. The truth of this insight is borne out by her sure and swift turning to Faramir as she comes to know his manliness and love for her during their long convalescence together. Her public troth-plighting to him closes the chapter between her and Aragorn. She looks at Aragorn, now King, and asks, "Wish me joy, my liege-lord and healer!" And he answers, "I have wished thee joy ever since first I saw thee. It heals my heart to see thee now in bliss." It is symptomatic of his ease that he now dares to use to her the familiar *thee* with which she addressed him in her wooing but which he avoided in addressing her. Never has Tolkien looked into the human heart to better purpose than in this inset tale of Éowyn and Aragorn.

But before all this can happen Aragorn must show the stuff of which he is made by winning Gondor. He grows in strength and sureness of touch with each passing test. His companions are drawn after him along the grim underground Paths of the Dead not only by the strength of his will but by their love for him, says Legolas. "For all who come to know him come to love him after their own fashion . . ." He is the heir of Isildur in action as well as name when he holds the unresting spirits of the oath-breakers to their pledge, and leads them on the wild ride that sends the Haradrim and the pirates of Umbar reeling in terror from Pelargir. There, and on the plains of Pelennor, he overcomes the enemies of Gondor by arms. But Gondor itself he overcomes by love. Éomer is already his loyal friend and supporter. Prince Imrahil and the city's other leaders in the field he wins as much by forbearing to press his title to the throne lest it rouse untimely divisions in the city as by its inherent validity and his own increasingly obvious ability to rule better than anyone else. He camps outside the walls on the night after the victory only as lord of the northern Rangers, and when called in by Gandalf to heal the sick enters heavily cloaked. His power over sickness, resembling that of medieval kings to cure the "king's evil," is taken by all as a divine gift, which can belong only to a sovereign. Under its virtue Faramir, recalled from the shadows, looks up at Aragorn with "a light of knowledge and love" and asks, "What does the king command?" His fealty is instant, complete, and lasting. And he occupies the crucial post of ruling Steward by reason of Denethor's death. The hearts of the citizens likewise turn to Aragorn while he labors all night among the wounded. They are looking for leadership anyway, and Aragorn comes to them with all the authentic marks of monarch and savior.

Much as been written, and justly, about the self-sacrificial courage of Frodo and Sam in the last stages of their journey through Mordor. But few or none have remarked on the equal if less solitary unselfish daring displayed by the mere seven thousand men whom Aragorn and his peers lead up to the Black Gate to challenge the ten times ten thousands inside. They come as a decoy knowing they are bound to be overwhelmed unless Frodo and Sam are still alive (they have not been heard from in weeks) and can first throw the Ring into Mount Doom. Destroying it even an hour too late will not save the little army outside. But meantime they are there

to give the Ring-bearer his maximum opportunity by distract-
ing Sauron's attention for the longest possible time. So desperate are the odds that some of the boldest have quailed
along the way and have been sent back by Aragorn to posts
of lesser terror where they can still be useful. Characteristic-
ally, he has done it with pity for weakness but without giving up the principle that duty requires those to go on who
can: "But keep what honour you may and do not run!" he
tells those he dismisses. The rest march on to face despair
in the final parley, when the Mouth of Sauron produces
Frodo's mithril coat and Sam's sword as proof that the two
are taken and that the seven thousand have acted as bait in
vain. Without hope they stand firm against Sauron's onsets
until suddenly the sounds of ruin inside Mordor tell them
that their gamble has actually worked. Frodo, or rather Gollum, has saved them at the last breath, but they no less have
saved the hobbits and so the West.

The ceremonies by which Aragorn ascends the throne are
just what they should be. Magnificent in themselves, they
reenact and refer back to the historical events from which he
derives his title, and they unite all the elements of the kingdom in a common consent which will assure its future political stability. On the morning of the coronation Aragorn, accompanied by Gandalf, Éomer, Imrahil, and the four hobbits,
steps out from the ranks of the returning army and walks up
to the city walls, where he is met by Faramir as Steward.
Faramir, calling himself "the last Steward of Gondor," holds
out in surrender the white rod of his office. Aragorn returns
it with the command to carry out his function. This proves
to be a full, stately recital of all the titles that identify Aragorn as the rightful King returned, ending with a question
called out to the assembled citizens of Gondor: "Shall he be
king and enter into the City and dwell there?" In answer "all
the host and all the people cried *yea* with one voice." If this

is not democracy by secret ballot it is certainly enthusiastic popular consent. The people as well as the chiefs have been consulted. Sauron would have done everything opposite.

Now comes the coronation itself. Faramir produces from the house of tombs the crown worn by Eärnur, the last king before the line of Stewards began. It bears the seabird wings and the seven gems surmounted by the great jewel star of Eärendil, worn by Elendil when he founded Gondor. Holding up the crown, Aragorn repeats in Elvish Elendil's promise when he landed from Númenor: "Out of the Great Sea to Middle-earth I am come. In this place will I abide, and my heirs, unto the ending of the world." Aragorn is making the promise his own. But he does not crown himself. He asks that the circlet be carried by the Ring-bearer to Gandalf, who is to set it on Aragorn's head. This is his modest and deeply felt recognition that "by the labour and valour of many I have come into my inheritance" and that Gandalf "has been the mover of all that has been accomplished, and this is his victory." Gandalf invokes religion as he crowns the kneeling Aragorn: "Now come the days of the King, and may they be blessed while the thrones of the Valar endure!" And with this, King Elessar enters the Citadel and unfurls the banner Arwen sewed for him.

Aragorn the man recedes from us into Aragorn the King. But there are still times when the regal robes are off. One such moment is the morning when Gandalf and he climb together on the slopes of Mount Mindolluin behind the city. Oppressed by the long prospects of responsibility stretching ahead and aware of Gandalf's imminent departure, Aragorn feels his loneliness: "I would still have your counsel," he confesses. It does not comfort him to know that Gandalf's work is done and his own only begun. He looks ahead, too, to the time of his own death and wonders who will rule after him if he has no children. Symbolically, the Tree in the courtyard at Minas Tirith still stands withered and barren. Gandalf then finds for him near the snowline the sapling of the White Tree, which, transplanted to the courtyard, will grow and bloom and bear other saplings in other years. As if to seal this promise of continuance, Arwen comes to be Aragorn's Queen, the future mother of sons and daughters.

Aragorn's first public acts justify confidence that he will be a strong, just, and far-sighted ruler. His foreign policy is designed to make friends of the Easterlings and Southrons, who have been traditional enemies of the West. He spares those captured in the War and sends them home free men. With their countries he signs equitable treaties of amity and commerce. Sauron's slaves he manumits and settles on fertile lands of which he makes them owners. To the primitive woses he gives in perpetuity the Druadan Forest in which they live. Ithilien is to be resettled by Faramir as Prince, and restored to loveliness. Mordor is razed. The ents are to reforest the rubble of Isengard. Aragorn himself will rebuild the former capital of the North Kingdom at Fornost. Roads will be cleared, communications restored, and the societies of hobbits, dwarves, men, ents, and other beings, which Sauron's policy estranged from one another, will be knit together again as they should be. In token of this reunion elves, dwarves, and men join to refurbish and expand the capital city of Minas Tirith. All is not joyful in the new dispensation, for the elves are going. Other Saurons, other wars, lie somewhere ahead. But Aragorn's friendship for all races of good will fit him well to inaugurate the Age of Men in a world still populous with many species of intelligent life.

CHAPTER VII

Seven Leaves

It is easy for the student to feel that with all his labour he is collecting only a few leaves, many of them now torn or decayed, from the countless foliage of the Tree of Tales, with which the Forest of Days is carpeted. It seems vain to add to the litter . . . But that is not true . . . Each leaf, of oak and ash and thorn, is a unique embodiment of the pattern, and for some this very year may be *the* embodiment, the first ever seen and recognized, though oaks have put forth leaves for countless generations of men.

"On Fairy-stories," p. 51

1. "Leaf by Niggle"

This short tale (written about 1939, published in 1945) [1] is an apparently simple but actually quite intricate vision of the struggles of an artist to create a fantasy world and of what happens to him and his work after death. The artist, in this case a painter named Niggle (he might equally well have been a writer), is racing against the summons of death to complete his one great canvas, a picture of a Tree with a background of forest and distant mountains. Because of outside distractions and his own weaknesses he dies leaving it unfinished. After death he goes through a period of discipline in Purgatory and thereafter finds himself inside the landscape depicted by his painting, which he is now able to complete with the aid of a neighbor, Parish, who was a prime hindrance to his work during life. He is then free to travel toward the mountains, which represent the next highest stage in his spiritual growth.

This little plot, so bald in summary, is in fact crowded with allegories, which give literary form to views about fantasy writing expounded by Tolkien in his lecture, "On Fairy-stories," delivered at the University of St. Andrews only a year before. The close connections between the tale and the lecture were pointed out by Tolkien himself when he printed them together under the newly devised joint title *Tree and Leaf* in 1964. "Though one is an 'essay' and the other a 'story,'" he wrote in the Introductory Note, "they are related: by the symbols of Tree and Leaf, and by both touching in different ways on what is called in the essay 'sub-creation.'" [2]

First as to the symbols. "Leaf" of course refers literally to any leaf in the foliage of Niggle's Tree, and also more specifically to the particular painted Leaf rescued from the destruction of the picture as a whole and hung in the Museum under the caption "Leaf: by Niggle." Figuratively, it stands for any single story taken out of a greater connected body of narratives; and also for this one story of Tolkien's, "Leaf by Niggle," seen in detachment from the whole body of his writing. The other symbol, "Tree," stands sometimes for that same whole body of Tolkien writing, but more often for the living, growing tradition of fairy stories in general, which the essay "On Fairy-stories" calls the "Tree of Tales." In the essay the collective literary productions of human wonder are centrally visualized as a tree with many branches having an "intricately knotted and ramified history." Some pages farther on Tolkien develops the image in great detail. The student of history, he writes, may feel that "he is collecting only a few leaves, many of them torn or decayed, from the countless foliage of the Tree of Tales, with which the Forest of Days is carpeted." It may seem impossible for anyone now to contribute a new Leaf, a new individual story, to this ancient marvel. But "the seed of the tree can be replanted in any soil," even that polluted by modern industrialism, and "each leaf, of oak and ash and thorn, is a unique embodiment of the pattern." In that final phrase, particularly, lies one germ of the story concerning Niggle's Tree, which Tolkien praises as "quite unique in its way," and of his Leaf, about which the Second Voice says, "a Leaf by Niggle has a charm of its own."

Another germ of the story was a large poplar tree outside Tolkien's window, which he often watched while lying in bed before it was first mutilated and later chopped down. He confides as much in the Introductory Note to *Tree and Leaf*.[3] But this is not the only, or the most significant, piece of autobiography he reveals in the Note. Both the essay and the story, he writes there, were composed during the same period (1938–1939) when he was writing the first nine chapters of *The Lord of the Rings*, which brought Frodo and his hobbit friends as far as the inn at Bree. There Tolkien's invention failed him: "I had then no more notion than they of what had become of Gandalf or who Strider was; and I had begun to despair of surviving to find out." The latter part of the sentence is eloquent of his state of mind at the time. Having barely survived the First World War, he feared that he would not survive the Second, which then loomed more and more ominously. He felt a sense of urgency and despair at the prospect of not living to complete not only *The Lord of the Rings* but the still vaster history of the early Ages of Middle-earth, which lay in fragments in his workshop. When we find Niggle in the same situation it is only natural to see a good deal of Tolkien in his story. In fact, allowing for artistic differences, the story may well be looked at as an effort on Tolkien's part to find some underlying meaning for all his labors, if not in this life then in the next.

Along this line of interpretation we notice that Niggle's world, like Tolkien's, is unmistakably Christian. It is governed by very strict laws (moral and religious in nature) requiring each man to help his needy neighbor, even at painful cost to himself and even in the absence of both gratitude and desert. These laws are enforced externally by an inspector. Internally their sanction lies in Niggle's own conscience and his imperfectly generous heart. He was "kind-hearted in a way. You know the sort of kind heart: it made him uncomfortable more often than it made him do anything; and even when he did anything it did not prevent him from grumbling, losing his temper, and swearing . . . All the same it did land him in a good many odd jobs for his neighbor, Mr. Parish, a man with a lame leg." Other interruptions to Niggle's painting, however, come from his own idleness, failure of concentration, and lack of firmness. Meantime he neglects to prepare for the long journey he has been told is imminent, and he is taken unawares by the coming of the Black Driver to take him through the dark tunnel. This situation inevitably recalls that in the medieval drama *Everyman*, to which Tolkien is giving a modern adaptation.

In the workhouse on the other side (an updated version of Dante's *Purgatorio*) Niggle is assigned hard labors aimed at correcting his sins and weaknesses. He learns to work at set intervals, to be prompt, to finish every task, to plan, to think in orderly fashion, to serve without grumbling. He is then ready to hear a dialogue between two voices, discussing what is to be done with him, one voice insisting on justice, the other pleading for mercy. Here the resemblance is to the debate between the four daughters of God — Righteousness and Truth against Mercy and Peace — at the judging of souls, a favorite theme in medieval drama and poetry. One prominent instance of it concludes the famous *Castle of Perseverance*. That Tolkien should employ techniques and ideas drawn from the literature of a period he knew so well is not surprising.[4] But his success in acclimatizing them to our times is remarkable. Again we are justified in stressing that they were, and still are, Catholic.

The other half of the connection between Niggle's story and the essay, mentioned in the Introductory Note to *Tree and Leaf*, is that they both touch "in different ways on what is called in the essay 'sub-creation.'" What different ways, and what is this thing called subcreation? The essay defines and analyzes subcreation as the process by which human imagination invents secondary worlds strange to the everyday primary world in which we live and move, but nevertheless possessed of an internal consistency of their own. Furthermore, and most significant for the Niggle story, the best of these imagined worlds reflect dimly a higher reality lying behind the appearances of the primary world: "Probably every writer making a secondary world . . . hopes that the peculiar qualities of this secondary world (if not all the details) are derived from reality or are flowing into it . . . The peculiar quality of the 'joy' in successful Fantasy can thus be explained as a sudden glimpse of the underlying reality or truth." [5]

Tolkien means Niggle's fate to be a literary embodiment of this doctrine. For, when the Voice of mercy wins its traditionally required victory he finds himself standing in the middle of the very landscape in his painting, left unfinished at his death, and looking right at the Tree, which was its main feature. The Tree is now finished, he sees. But its leaves are "as he imagined them rather than as he made them; and there were others that had only budded in his mind, and many that might have budded, if only he had time." In short, Niggle is now seeing clearly the reality of which he had only a partial vision while on earth. That this is Tolkien's meaning is made plain by a dialogue between a shepherd and Niggle's neighbor Parish, who joins him in the same landscape and is amazed that it should have been represented by the despised painting: "But it did not look like this then, not *real*," he exclaims in wonder. He is rebuked by the shepherd: "No, it was only a glimpse then . . . but you might have caught the glimpse, if ever you had thought it worth while to try." This key word *glimpse*, here twice written, is used several times in the essay in the same context to characterize the brief clouded insight into permanence which is all that a writer of tales can hope to catch.[6]

Such insight is never earned but is a power gratuitously bestowed. "It's a gift!" declares Niggle as he looks around him at the Tree and the woods. And Tolkien comments, "He was referring to his art, and also to the result, but he was using the word quite literally." Translate painting into verbal narrative. Broaden the reference from the single story about Niggle (Leaf) to the full panorama of Tolkien's legendary history of Middle-earth (Tree), which was in his thoughts when he wrote both story and essay. Then emerges Tolkien's faith that his own incomplete life's work images in some sense ultimate truths that are not bounded by the particular details it narrates. Even if he never survives to finish it, it will always have the eternal validity of shadowing forth in human words a portion of the great Tree of Tales, which soars always just at the edge of man's vision.

There is more. The Tree itself may be finished but Niggle discovers that other scenes of the forest landscape, only roughly sketched in his painting, are likewise still shadowy in the reality he now inhabits: ". . . in the Forest there were a number of inconclusive regions that still needed work and thought." He sees what needs doing, but to his surprise is unable to accomplish it without the aid of his neighbor Parish, whom he had always considered the worst of pests and the bane of his art. Looking more precisely at the Tree, he has also become aware that its best leaves have been painted "in collaboration with Mr. Parish." When Parish is sent to help him it is the combined work and thought of the two men that gives the forest its final elaboration of substance.

This episode of recognition and reconciliation has its Purgatorial function, of course, but it also introduces two associated literary meanings previously presented by Tolkien in the essay. One of these is Tolkien's belief that a subcreator of tales, besides "glimpsing" existing reality, is allowed by God's grace to contribute to the ongoing process of divine creation. In Tolkien's words, the quality of a writer's secondary worlds is "derived from Reality *or flowing into it*" (italics mine). More explicitly, Tolkien continues, "So great is the bounty with which he has been treated that he may now, perhaps, fairly dare to guess that in Fantasy he may actually assist in the affoliation and multiple enrichment of creation." Niggle begins by painting as well as he can a dimly discerned ideal world existing in the mind of God (the notion verges on the Platonic). He ends by bringing into being aspects of that world that were inchoate when he arrived. So, when he departs for the mountains, he leaves behind "the house . . . the garden, the grass, the forest, the lake, and all the country," each complete "in its own proper fashion." Not that Niggle or Parish or any other subcreator can scheme such completions helter-skelter out of his own head. They have a "proper fashion," a law of their own, which must be observed. Nevertheless, the human contribution is genuine and original. Niggle's and Parish's contributions are so vital that the country they have helped to create is forever after known to the Two Voices as "Niggle's Parish." They find it "very useful indeed" in rehabilitating newcomers to the afterlife. It is not only "splendid for convalescence" but "for many it is the best introduction to the Mountains." This sounds like an application of the doctrine, defended in Tolkien's essay, that one prime function of fantasy is Recovery from physical and spiritual blindness to the astounding world we live in: "Recovery (which includes return and renewal of health) is a re-gaining — re-gaining of a clear view." [7]

Niggle's astounded perception that his best painting has been done in collaboration with Parish exemplifies a further doctrine of Tolkien's, that no writer can subcreate a secondary world successfully without first having a clear-eyed knowledge of life in our primary world. The only contribution which could possibly have been made to Niggle's painting by this lame, whining neighbor with his endless demands on Niggle's time and energy must consist in these very demands. Without them Niggle would not have been forced daily to grapple so closely with the hard facts of actual existence. Morally, this is his salvation. Artistically, it gives him a strong sense of fact essential to fantasy. Over and over the essay "On Fairy-stories," insists: "Fantasy does not blur the sharp outlines of the real world; for it depends on them." Tolkien's very definition of a fairy story requires it to construct an imaginary world that is recognizably different in content and tone from the workaday one. It must contain "images of things that are not only 'not actually present' but which are indeed not to be found in our primary world at all." A firm knowledge of the difference is the *sine qua non* of sanity. It is also necessary to the craft of writing a tale (or painting a picture) which allows us Escape from the humdrum in order that we may return to it with fresh eyes, able to see that it is not really humdrum at all. Parish's gift to Niggle, then, was to provide the frustrating dreariness that pricked his imagination to frame ("glimpse") a greener, more spacious world for the refreshment of himself and others.

Perhaps mirroring his pessimism in 1939 as to the reception of his own work, Tolkien ends the story by showing how few people have the slightest appreciation of Niggle's painting. Typically, Parish and the Inspector value it only as a bit of canvas handy for patching leaks in the roof. After Niggle's death it is in fact used for that purpose. Only the mild little schoolmaster, Atkins, troubles to rescue a scrap bearing a single leaf, which is hung in the town Museum and seen by "a few eyes" before it is destroyed when the building burns down. At a meeting of the Town Council, which drifts into a discussion of whether Niggle's painting was of any "use" at all, the few words Atkins speaks in defense are loudly overborne by Tompkins, a gross man who says all the stupid things Tolkien's enemies were to parade later on. He considers Niggle's world "old-fashioned stuff" and "private daydreaming." Tompkins' idea of useful art is "a telling poster" and he is one of those reductionists for whom flowers are "digestive and genital organs of plants." This bitter little scene closes aptly with the remark of Perkins, another councilor: "Never knew he painted." Tolkien cannot long remain bitter or despairing, however. The last words spoken are those of the Two Voices, whose idea of the "use" of Niggle's labors is not that of careless or wrong-headed humanity.

Tolkien has fought through to a meaning for his work. Unheeded except by a few it may be, perish in the end with all man's other artifacts it certainly will, but it is a glimpse of ultimate reality, and there is a safe and continuing usefulness for it somewhere beyond "the walls of the world."

2. *"The Lay of Aotrou and Itroun"*

Published in December 1945,[8] this fairy-tale tragedy in octosyllabic couplets was the second of Tolkien's short pieces to reach print, "Leaf by Niggle" having appeared earlier in the same year. Tolkien is predominantly a prose writer, but every reader of *The Hobbit* and *The Lord of the Rings* is aware from their many inset poems that his prose easily spills

over into verse. It was predictable that he would one day ex-
periment with independent, longer narrative poems like "The
Lay of Aotrou and Itroun" and "The Homecoming of
Beorhtnoth." And, given Tolkien's interest in ancient
genres, it is also natural that the one should have a medieval
model, the other an Anglo-Saxon. The "Lay" looks back to
the Breton lays of the twelfth to fourteenth centuries, sung
by minstrels mainly to audiences in northern France but
based on old Celtic tales from Britain.[9] True to type, it tells a
story of love and magic. But Tolkien has chosen to give his
poem an unusually strong religious cast, which transforms the
customary series of knightly exploits and amours into a story
of temptation and fall. He has also built into it image patterns and variant refrains of more than medieval sophistication to deepen and darken the grim flow of its tragedy.

Tolkien loves to wrap a past inside a past. The minstrel
who is reciting the "Lay" says at the outset that the story he
is about to tell happened in Britain long before his time. He
has picked it up from "Briton harpers." The ruined castle by
the sea described in the opening stanzas was once populous
and prosperous. He will relate how the "dark doom" of its
lord caused it to fall into its present decay. The cause began
in the lord's own discontent. Failing to count the blessings of
a loving wife and a rich demesne, he brooded on his wife's
childlessness until he disprized what he had: "his pride was
empty, vain his hoard." In a medieval setting the word *pride*
immediately evokes the idea of selfish arrogance bordering on
sin. And the word *hoard*, in Tolkien's vocabulary, sounds
the alarm against "possessiveness," the greed of ownership
which lusts to make everything its own. The poet carries forward stress on this trait of the knight's by speaking of his
repugnant visions of strangers taking over his property after
his death if he has no heirs. He forgets prayer, abandons
the "hope" he should repose in God, and falls into the mortal
sin of despair. In consequence, without telling his wife or

anybody else, he all alone adopts the "counsel cold" (later termed by the minstrel "evil rede") to seek the aid of a witch. This resolve is summed up in the minstrel's comment, "his hope from light to darkness passed." The significance of such a course would be immediately apparent to a medieval audience. To lose hope is to turn away from the second of the three cardinal theological virtues proclaimed by the Church: faith, hope, and charity — no one of which can long endure without the other two. The knight's faith and charity are as imperiled as his hope. By this comment the minstrel has begun in the mind of his audience an association of the words *cold* and *darkness* with evil despair, *hope* and *light* with good. He proceeds to build upon them.

The witch whom the knight visits lives in a "cave" in the "homeless hills," a cunning weaver of spells to entangle heart and wits. The sunlight striking the upper edge of her "hollow dale" is "pale," but darkness fills the bottom of the bowl, where she sits waiting on her "seat of stone." At this strategic point the minstrel suddenly stops to insert his second four-line refrain. It is strategic because this refrain immediately strikes the hearer as being slightly different from the first four-line refrain which stands at the head of the "Lay," and moves him to think back to isolate the difference as well as the sameness. This comparison leads to the discovery that whereas the first refrain alluded only to wind ("blowing ever through the trees") and caves ("stony shores and stony caves"), the second keeps these but adds other features:

> In Britain's land beyond the waves
> are stony hills and stony caves;
> the wind blows ever over hills
> and hollow caves with wailing fills.

The additions are the witch's "stony hills" over which the wind is now blowing, and her "hollow cave" in which it is

wailing ominously. By association through her stony hills
and stony seat, "stone" has been sucked into the imaginative
connection with evil, as have "cave," "pale," "hollow," and
"hills," which are not only stony but "homeless" as distinguished from the warm home which the knight has left behind. Indeed this insight into the poet's method of establish-
ing mood associations tends to hark back to the first refrain
and to give to its "stony caves and stony shores" a retroactive
quality of warning.

The knight arrives at sunset "alone between the dark and
light" and rides "into the mouth of night." The "alone" begins to take on a sinister urgency, which increases as the
poem proceeds. The other references are literally to times of
day, but they are also signs of the spiritual darkness into
which the light of the knight's "hope" was earlier said by the
poet to have passed. The knight advances "halting to the
stony seat" of the witch and meets her eyes, "dark and pierc-
ing, filled with lies," as the eyes of the minions of the Father
of Lies always are. He need not tell her his errand. She
knows "the hunger that thither him had brought," because it
is what gives her power over him. From her "darkening
cave" she brings him

> a phial of glass so fairly made
> 'twas a wonder in that houseless place
> to see its cold and gleaming grace;
> and therewithin a philter lay
> as pale as water thin and grey
> that spills from stony fountains frore
> in hollow pools in caverns hoar.

In powerful combination here they all are again, the things
and sensations already attached by the poet to evil: the
"houseless," homeless place, the barren "stone" of seat and
cave and fountain, the "cold" of phial and "fountains frore"
(cognate with the "counsel cold" that drove the knight

there), the "hollowness" of the pools from which the accursed potion comes, its liquid as "pale" and "grey" as the sun setting on the lip of the witch's dale, or the light of his hope fading into the night of despair. Additionally, the harper is preparing an antagonism between the accursed water of the witch and the "waters blest of Christendom," which are to redeem the knight later in the tale. An extra touch of irony enters with the use of the word *grace* to denote the phial's lovely outward shape and at the same time connote the fatal absence of divine grace as a spiritual component of its contents.

Acceptance of such a potion is a mortal sin, which the knight tries to slough away by offering to pay for it in gold, the stuff that his greed considers irresistible. But the witch wants him to commit himself more deeply before she sets her price by actually using the phial on his wife, which will further endanger his soul. In good fairy-tale fashion she postpones naming the payment until after it has worked, on the sufficiently sardonic pretext that she, the mistress of lies, will have no "lies" told about the efficacy of her product. Another major milestone in the story having passed with the knight's agreement to the bargain, the minstrel sings the third refrain. This keeps up the same unbroken roar of seas pounding and winds blowing, but adds suggestively that in Britain "woods are dark with danger strong," in reference to the knight's growing peril.

The polarity of dark-death as against light-life appears again when the knight emerges from these woods to see the "living light" in his castle windows where his wife waits. Sleeping beside her, he dreams that night of children playing in the "gardens fair" of his home. The audience will have opportunity to watch the minstrel's art make these gardens alive with children, the symbol of the "heart's desire" of the childless pair. A sunny morning greets the lord at his awakening, but it cannot win him back from his purpose.

Deceitfully he proposes to his lady that on their coming wedding anniversary they hold a merry feast to pray for the birth of children:

> we'll pray that this year we may see
> our heart's desire more quick draw nigh
> than yet we have seen it, thou and I;
> for virtue is in hope and prayer.
> So spake he gravely seeming fair.

That virtue lies in hope and prayer is indeed the Christian burden of the entire story. The minstrel's putting it into the mouth of a man who has abandoned both is another master stroke of irony to show up the knight for the hypocrite he is. The more so because his intent at the time is to win his wife's confidence so that he may slip the potion into her festive wine. And what is this "heart's desire" of which he speaks but the flawed "hunger" which drew him to the witch's den? The lady agrees happily to the feast. Superficially gay but plangently sad with inner meaning, the fourth refrain now pictures the innocent pairings of birds in Britain's springtime woods, against which the unnatural guilt that the knight is about to smuggle into his union stands out all the more grievously.

Very different from the malicious laughter of the witch is the loving laughter with which his wife pledges him happiness and long life as she drains the enchanted cup. By his own fault he will be dead within a year. But before the scene darkens again a bright interlude intervenes during which the lady becomes pregnant and the lord dreams once more of those unborn children playing "on lawns of sunlight without hedge/save a dark shadow at their edge." The poet never lets that limiting shadow quite go away. When lovely twins are born the people of the castle rejoice, thinking them the

answer to "prayer," and even envying their master and mistress, whose prayer they think has been "answered twice."
The wrongness of their interpretation is meant to stab the
audience with reminder of the knight's deceit. The storyteller now proceeds to intensify this deceit as the knight,
standing at his wife's bedside still gay in manner, still hypo-
critical, assures her, "Now full . . . is granted me/both hope
and prayer," and asks her whether the fulfillment of "heart's
desire" is not sweet. In all purity she answers gaily that it is
sweet indeed

> at last the heart's desire to meet,
> thus after waiting, after prayer,
> thus after hope and nigh despair.

She has meant and practiced the virtues to which he only
pretends, though doing so has cost her struggle. The difference between the genuine and the false is starkly drawn.

But the potion has not yet ceased its appointed work. It
causes the knight to promise fatuously to get for his wife anything at all she may desire, even water from a well "in any secret fount or dell," without thinking of the danger of meeting
the witch again. Indeed his mention of a secret fount suggests
a compulsion to seek her out. In his lady, too, the potion has
implanted a sharp longing for "water cool and clear" and for
"deer no earthly forests hold." To find these for her the lord
rides into what the fifth refrain now sinisterly calls "the forests pale," where he pursues a white doe, heedless of "dim
laughter" ringing through the trees. He lusts feverishly for
the impossible beast

> whereon no mortal hunt shall feast,
> for waters crystal-clear and cold
> that never in holy fountain rolled.

By his past surrenders he has acquired a positive taste for waters that are unholy in preference to waters blest — the waters of baptism and the holy water commonly used in churches to ward off evil.

Being a cunning trapper of light and life, the witch (now called by Tolkien a "Corrigan") [10] has woven the sun "into a snare." Around her dell "the trees like shadows waiting stood/for night to come upon the wood," as a shadow always edged the gardens of the knight's desire. When the knight arrives at the cavern where she sits, "all green is grey." He sees her hair as "pale" and hears her voice as "cold/as echo from the world of old." Asking him how he intends to repay her "here after waiting, after pain," she echoes mockingly his wife's greeting to him after childbirth, "thus after waiting, after prayer." The payment the witch finally demands is sexual "love," putting aside his lady and wedding her instead. Up to this point the knight has trifled far with evil, but giving it his "love" entails an irreversible transfer of allegiance which would be the end of him.

Here on the brink what saves him is a surge of real love for his wife. "My love is wed," he cries. It gives him strength to refuse the witch's demand, and to deny her power to turn him to "stone/and wither lifeless and alone," as she angrily threatens to do. And he is right, as the harper's medieval audience would well know. With the symbolic religious meanings which *stone*, *lifeless*, and *alone* have acquired in the course of the story, the witch's menace is to impose on the knight the barrenness and solitude of spiritual death. She is bluffing. In the Catholicism of the Middle Ages, spiritual choices lie only in the power of the human will, aided by divine grace. Consequently the knight is able to ride off homeward toward his wife and toward "the waters blest of Christendom" to which their love has reconciled him. When the witch prophesies that she will kill him in three days if he leaves, he retorts that he will die when God pleases, in old age or in the Crusades.

It pleases God, however, to let the witch's lethal spell work on his body, though not on his soul. He has saved his soul; mercy will go so far. But he has sinned severely, and justice must have its due. To allow him to live on to enjoy life with the children he has begotten by the aid of black magic would be to reward sin. So, as the knight rides home, the minstrel brings into his sixth refrain the sound of a bell blown by the wind over the countryside. The bell turns out to be the "sacring bell," rung when the priest elevates the host in saying mass, heard by the dying knight next morning as he nears his castle from "the hoar and houseless hills" of the witch's cave. His last thoughts as he dies three days later are for the welfare of his wife.

The knight has won the essential, but at terrible cost. The minstrel dwells on the growing suspense and grief of his lady, which results in her death soon after she discovers his body lying on its bier in the church. Returning to the early line about the knight, "his pride was empty, vain his hoard," describing the discontent with which the lack of children poisons all his other real happiness, the singer repeats it with a single trenchant change: "his pride was ended, vain his hoard." The *empty*, which reflected the knight's wrongful and needless despair, turns into the *ended*, which puts a period not only to pride but to all earthly passion and possession. And what of the children left orphans, the children for whose sake the knight put himself and his lady through the whole sordid ordeal? If they grew up to play in that castle garden, adds the poet doubtfully, the dead father and mother "saw it not, nor found it sweet/their heart's desire at last to meet." Alas for the "heart's desire," he seems to say, it may lead men along strange byways, and betray them in the end.

The seventh and last refrain returns to virtually the same

form as the first. In Britain's land beyond the waves the elemental powers of sea and wind outlast the petty spans of human life and desire. Sad is my tale, concludes the minstrel by way of apology, but then so is life. Our consolation must come from religious hope. Praying for the dead knight and lady of his song, for himself, and for all who have listened to him, he skillfully picks up and repeats from earlier parts of the narrative familiar phrases which carry its central lessons:

> God help us all in hope and prayer
> from evil rede and from despair,
> by waters blest of Christendom
> to dwell, until at last we come
> to joy of Heaven where is queen
> the maiden Mary pure and clean.

A prayer ending is conventional for most Breton lays [11] and for many another genre of medieval literature, but few writers of the period use it with the artistic skill and weight of summary meaning with which Tolkien endows his minstrel surrogate. In fact, Tolkien's craft in handling image and symbol has been learned from modern poets and is not medieval at all. His successful marriage of medieval religious theme to present verse techniques in "The Lay of Aotrou and Itroun" has a pre-Raphaelite flavor, but it produces a poem with which it is hard to find any other of like kind to compare anywhere.

3. *"Farmer Giles of Ham"*

The publication year, 1949, of this joyously mock-heroic tale gives us a clue to why it was written. The prewar clouds which oppressed Tolkien in "Leaf by Niggle" had passed away with victory in 1945, bringing "days less dark" but "no less laborious" by reason of his final drive to complete *The Lord of the Rings*. Though much revision was still in order, the epic was finished at last in 1949 after eleven years of more or less steady toil. Only an artist, scientist, or scholar who has suffered the happy bondage of such years can imagine the relief of the shackles dropping away. There seems to follow a need to celebrate the new freedom, which can take the form of poking fun at the type of materials just mastered. Chaucer, caught in the mazes of *The Canterbury Tales*, parodied the high chivalric ideals of his "Knight's Tale" with their humorous opposite in the Sir Thopas caricature in later years. Similarly in "Farmer Giles" Tolkien laughs good-humoredly at much that is taken most seriously by his epic, and not only there but also by his previous scholarship and literary criticism.

Few readers, save professional editors of ancient manuscripts at least as old as the Middle Ages who have wrestled in prefaces with problems of authorship, date, sources and analogues, linguistics, and so on, know enough about such things to enjoy fully the nonsense of Tolkien's Foreword to "Farmer Giles." [12] Tolkien pretends to be editor and translator (from "very insular Latin") of an ancient manuscript recounting the origin of the Little Kingdom in pre-Arthurian Britain. Solemnly he discusses the nature of the document (a late compilation derived from popular lays contemporaneous with the events), the author (an inhabitant of the Little Kingdom at a time when the events were already long past, as shown by his intimate knowledge of the geography of that region) and the boundaries of the Little Kingdom in time and place. The latter, from internal evidence, is somewhere in the valley of the Thames. But the date of its existence requires profounder analysis. Tolkien is obliged to call upon the aid, though not by name, of Geoffrey of Monmouth's popular and quite fictitious *Historia regum Britanniae* (published in 1139) for a chronology of the many divisions within the island after Brutus, of which "the partition under Locrin, Camber, and Albanac was only the first . . ." [13] Somewhere between then and Arthur's time, "after the days of King Coel maybe . . ." [14] occurred the rise to the kingship of Farmer Giles of Ham, whose unabridged titles in the original Latin march over most of the manuscript's first page, matching in resonance those of Queen Victoria, or Aragorn at his proudest in *The Lord of the Rings*. Tolkien as translator voices the usual pious hope of the scholar that the document will throw light on a dark period of British history, as well as the origin of "some difficult place names." Of this philological jest more anon.

The compiler of the manuscript under translation is evidently already, in some vague post-Arthurian age, nostalgic about the greater simplicity of life in the old days of which he writes. In a supiciously Tolkienish vein he looks back to the happier past when "there was more time . . . and folk were fewer, so that most men were distinguished"; "villages were proud and independent still in those days." One hopes that Tolkien is smiling here at his penchant for a pre-preindustrial society. He is certainly smiling at the talking animals of fairy stories in describing the Farmer's dog, Garm, who "could not even talk dog-latin; but . . . could use the vulgar tongue (as could most dogs of his day) either to bully or to brag or to wheedle in." And he is certainly smiling as he begins the portrayal of his mock-hero "who could bully and brag better" than his dog could. Giles says he is busy keeping the wolf from the door, "that is, keeping himself as fat and comfortable as his father before him." He was "a slow sort of fellow . . . taken up with his own affairs," giving little thought to the Wide World outside his village. In this he recalls the hobbits of the Shire. And somewhat like them he is intruded upon by a giant from Wales, "larger and more stupid than his fellows," who is no distant relative of Tolkien's trolls.

Cowardly master, roused by quaking dog, seizes his blunderbuss, runs out, pulls the trigger in a spasm of terror when he sees the giant, and "by chance and by no choice of the farmer's" spatters him in the face with scrap iron. Tolkien's shameless introduction of a seventeenth-century blunderbuss into pre-Arthurian England is funny enough in itself but he has another card to play with it. In case anyone asks what a blunderbuss is, the compiler of the manuscript refers him to the answer given by "the Four Wise Clerks of Oxenford," who reply: "A blunderbuss is a short gun with a large bore firing many balls or slugs, and capable of doing execution within a limited range without exact aim. (Now superseded in civilized countries by other firearms.)" This quotation corresponds word for word with the definition of *blunderbuss* given in the *Oxford English Dictionary*. Of course "the Four Wise Clerks of Oxenford" must then be the four editors of the Dictionary: James A. H. Murray, Henry Bradley, W. A. Craigie, and C. T. Onions. Since Tolkien was Rawlinson Professor of Anglo-Saxon at Pembroke College, Oxford, when the Dictionary was first printed in 1933, and helped in its preparation, the blunderbuss incident takes on the aspect of a private joke with his colleagues, along the lines of his *Songs for the Philologists*, privately printed for the Department of English at University College in 1936. Not exclusively so, however, for Tolkien catches up the parenthetical remark about supersession of the blunderbuss by other firearms "in civilized countries" to remark ironically that this village of Ham was not yet civilized enough to use any other weapons more lethal than bows and arrows — which rather turns the joke against the Dictionary editors. One would like to know exactly who composed that definition of *blunderbuss* for the *Oxford Dictionary*.

Giles duly becomes "the Hero of the Countryside," gets drunk, and comes home "singing old heroic songs." He receives a testimonial and an ancient sword from the reigning monarch of the Middle Kingdom, who rejoices in the appellation "*Augustus Bonifacius Ambrosius Aurelianus Antoninus Pius et Magnificus, dux, rex, tyrannus, et basileus Mediterranearum Partium.*" The "Ambrosius Aurelianus" may derive from "Aurelius Ambrosius," chronicled by Geoffrey of Monmouth [15] as Arthur's predecessor and uncle. And if Tolkien wishes to aggrandize him further by adding the name of a pope and a Roman emperor or two, so much the richer the jest when the king in question is a petty miser and ineffectual fool.

It is left to the village parson to read the runes on Giles' sword and so to identify it as "Caudiomordax, the famous sword that in popular romances is more vulgarly called Tailbiter," particularly renowned for slaying dragons. This busy blade outdoes all the greatest blades of fable from Arthur's Excalibur and Roland's Durendal to Aragorn's Andúril. Those others are merely wielded by heroes, but Tailbiter makes a hero of any man who wields it. Whenever a dragon is within five miles, it leaps from the sheath of its own accord, and during combat it wisely delivers all the strokes at the dragon's most vulnerable spots by forcing its owner's arm into the right maneuvers. Obviously this is an embarrassing sort of weapon to own when a dragon named Chrysophylax Dives, "cunning, inquisitive, greedy, well-armoured but not over bold," invades the kingdom after a hard winter, particularly for Giles who is not overbold himself.

Tolkien now turns his parody against the institution of knighthood.[16] In the brave days of old, the King's knights efficiently kept down the population of dragons, and when Augustus Bonifacius, etc., formerly held feast at Christmastide (as Arthur did in *Sir Gawain and the Green Knight* and other romances) he could always count on being served Dragon's Tail (as Arthur never ate until he heard or saw some noble exploit). But that glory is fled. Now the high table is reduced to eating an imitation tail made of cake baked by the royal cook. The situation is so bad that in a delightful reversal of human skepticism about dragons, the younger dragons never having met a knight, conclude, "So knights are mythical! . . . We always thought so." The knights are engaged in gossiping about the latest fashion in hats when Chrysophylax descends on the kingdom, devouring "two persons of tender age" and one very tough, stringy priest. Their information about these ravages being still quite unofficial, the knights do nothing until officially notified, and then bethink themselves of several remarkable reasons for postponing action — of which Tolkien remarks wryly that "the excuses of the knights were undoubtedly sound."

How the adventure of killing the Worm is thrust upon Giles' unwilling shoulders, how the slow village smith named Fabricius Cunctator (no doubt after Hannibal's Roman adversary Fabius the Delayer) makes for him a ridiculous suit of armor surely descended from that worn by Plautus' Braggart Soldier, and how Chrysophylax refuses to fight because he was not challenged first according to the rules of chivalry are narrated with fine zest. But to my mind the high points of comedy come in the talk that ensues between Giles and the dragon, and other later talks of the same kind. "Conversations with a Dragon" would be as good a subtitle for the story as any. Chrysophylax the Rich finally buys his release from the people of Ham by promising them incredible sums from his hoard in the mountains. But the village folk have forgotten that dragons, once freed, have "alas! no conscience at all" about keeping promises. "The parson with his booklearning might have guessed it . . . He was a grammarian, and could doubtless see further into the future than others." Even admitting that in the Dark Ages grammarians were often suspected of magic, we should no doubt also see in the word here a pun on philologists and a consequent laugh at their pretensions. Tolkien is hitting out at every target in sight, not excluding himself.

But he is not yet finished with the knights. Enraged by the perfidy of Chrysophylax in not keeping his word to bring back his treasure, the King orders all the knights out in pursuit, and Giles too, though he is too "plain and honest" to want to be "dubbed." As soon as the knights approach the mountains of Wales and find ominous footprints, they bring Giles up to the head of the line to examine them and tell him to go first. "Lead on!" they say. Then, like Arthur's knights before the founding of the Round Table, they fall to "discussing points of precedence" as they ride, but whereas Arthur's champions dispute who shall be first, these paladins dispute who shall have the post of safety in the rear. Chrysophylax's sudden attack kills several knights "before they could even issue their formal challenge of battle" and panics the others' horses, which flee, "carrying their masters off whether they wished it or no. Most of them wished it indeed." The baggage ponies and servants also run away at once. "They had no doubt as to the order of precedence." Since his old gray mare (the Rosinante of the story) for her own reasons refuses to budge, Giles is left to face the dragon alone. After another long bargaining session, in which Tailbiter is very persuasive, Chrysophylax agrees to carry his treasure back to the village then and there if Giles will let him keep a part in his cave. Giles accepts, "showing a laudable discretion. A knight would have stood out for the whole hoard and got a curse laid upon it," as happened to Fafnir's hoard.

The tale of Giles' founding his own Little Kingdom with the help of the dragon has its climax in the Battle of the

Bridge, wherein the forces of the Middle Kingdom are dispersed by a single snort of steam from Chrysophylax, and Giles refuses to meet the King in single combat for fear of hurting him. Many lays are sung to celebrate Giles' deeds. "The favourite one dealt with the meeting on the bridge in a hundred mock-heroic couplets." Tolkien is leaving no doubt of the literary genre to which this tale belongs. In the same vein he has Giles get the jump on the future King Arthur by inaugurating "an entirely new order of knighthood" called the Wormwardens, headed by the twelve village lads who guard the dragon. Besides, if Arthur has his Guinevere Giles has his Agatha, who "made a queen of great size and majesty . . . There was no getting round Queen Agatha — at least it was a long walk."

Before the end Tolkien has one shaft more to aim at philologists. The Foreword had promised to throw light "on the origin of some difficult place-names." Take, for instance, the name of the river Thames. One of Giles' titles was "Dominus de Domito Serpente, which is in the vulgar Lord of the Tame Worm, or shortly of Tame." But he was also known as "Lord of Ham." Out of "a natural confusion" between "Ham" and "Tame" arose *Thame*, "for Thame with an *h* is a folly without warrant." Tolkien says he gets this etymology from "the learned in such matters." He may be laughing merely at bad philology, but more probably his target is the speculative tricks played by philology as generally practiced. Similarly, Worminghall, the great hall of the Wormwardens, has sunk today to *Wunnle*, "for villages have fallen from their pride."

"Farmer Giles of Ham" is an outburst of pure good humor. The fact that it mocks the heroic does not mean that in 1949 Tolkien embraced the fashionable cult of the antihero, any more than his fun with his beloved philology meant that he renounced his devotion to it in the past or its charms for the future. After that date he gave years of revision to readying *The Lord of the Rings* for publication, and he has never stopped work on *The Silmarillion.* "Farmer Giles" is simply a vacation from the "things higher . . . deeper . . . darker" which these epics treat. That a writer can laugh at what is dearest to him does not signify that it has grown less dear. It signifies only that he is able to laugh at himself.

4. *"The Homecoming of Beorhtnoth, Beorhthelm's Son"*

Having lived through two World Wars, in one of which he was severely wounded, Tolkien had most of a lifetime in which to think long thoughts about war. And having cut his philological baby teeth on the great Anglo-Saxon war poem *The Battle of Maldon,* along with its companion pieces in the Old English literary canon, he had the same length of time in which to decide that it was being generally misinterpreted. At some date not long after the Second World War these two streams of thought ran together to prompt him to write a sequel to *Maldon* in the form of a dramatic dialogue in alliterative verse between two of Beorhtnoth's retainers searching the battlefield by night for the corpse of the English leader after his defeat. Tolkien published it in *Essays and Studies of the English Association* [17] in 1953, together with an explanation and defense of his new reading of the Maldon poem on which his sequel is based.

Briefly, as Tolkien summarizes it, the more orthodox interpretation saw the poem merely as a celebration of the heroic deaths of Beorhtnoth and all his hearth companions while resisting a Danish onslaught on the English coast in A.D. 991. Tolkien proposed instead that the hinge of *Maldon* was the poet's censure of Beorhtnoth's *ofermod* in letting the Danes freely cross an otherwise impassable causeway and hurl their overwhelmingly superior numbers at the English host. *Ofermod*, Tolkien suggested, was not the mere "overboldness" it was usually construed to mean, but "overmastering pride," a criminal lust for personal fame. Hence, *Maldon* was predominantly the account of the unnecessary deaths of many brave men caused by the selfish folly of one.

Tolkien properly points out in the essay "Ofermod," which follows his poem, that *Maldon*, understood in this way, has a "sharpness and tragic quality" not present in an interpretation of it as purely heroic throughout, because "by it the loyalty of the retinue is greatly enhanced." [18] Loving their chief and honoring their pledges of allegiance to him, Beorhtnoth's *heorðwerod* fight to the death in spite of his besotted judgment, which is betraying them all. "The Homecoming" takes its point of departure from this view of the events of the fight. By putting the reader right among the corpses on the battlefield after nightfall it drives home with utter immediacy the horror of a carnage that need never have taken place. Its method of doing so is to present the words and actions of two of Beorhtnoth's servants, sent by the Monks of Ely to bring back their master's body for burial. The searching, the finding, the carrying — these make up the whole action of Tolkien's short (under 400 lines) narrative poem.

The two searchers are cunningly chosen for maximum spread and contrast of outlook. Both are members of the earl's household, warmly devoted to him. Torhthelm is the young son of a minstrel, being trained in his father's profession to sing of Finn, Froda, Beowulf, and other heroes of northern saga. The old lays have captured him so powerfully that he lives more in the past than in the present. Though nominally a Christian, he is constantly seeing Christian England of A.D. 991 from the point of view of pagan beliefs and customs four centuries gone. Especially, since he has never been in any battle, he romanticizes war. Sharply set off against him is old Tídwald, who has had all too much experience over the years, fighting in the militia bands, and has seen too many stricken fields to have any illusions about this one. Harpers' songs mean little to him. As a farmer his mind is on the ravages to land and people by the Danes. As a committed Christian he looks to Heaven to give consolation for the sorrows he sees all around him in this life and due recompense in the next. Tolkien's artistry lies in devising a series of encounters between the outlooks of these two very different men so as to bring out the themes in which he is interested.

At the start of "The Homecoming" the long night search among the tangle of bodies, which death has robbed of identity as Englishman or Dane, has unnerved Torhthelm. Stimulated by pagan legends that ghosts of the unburied dead must walk the night, his imagination hears them gibbering in every gust of wind. For this he is mocked by Tídwald and told to "forget your gleeman's stuff." The old farmer is matter-of-factly unheaping corpses distinguishable only as "long ones and short ones,/the thick and the thin." Not unkindly he reminds the boy that England is Christian now and "ghosts are under ground or else God has/them . . ." But to Torhthelm the mirk seems "the dim/shadow of heathen hell, in the hopeless/kingdom where search is vain." It is no accident that Tolkien chooses a hell image here to describe the aftermath of battle.

Among the many of Beorhtnoth's household thanes whose deaths are sung in *Maldon* the author calls only two specifically *young:* Wulfmaer, son of Wulfstan, and Aelfwine, son of Aelfric. These are the two whose bodies the searchers discover first and identify by the light of their lantern. Tolkien has the point to make that promising young men are the most numerous and most lamentable victims of war. In order to make it, he goes far beyond the single adjective of *Maldon*, giving both Torhthelm and Tídwald repeated laments on the youth and worth of the slain men. Tídwald, particularly,

thinks it ", . . a wicked business/to gather them ungrown."
Wulfmaer was "a gallant boy" with "the makings of a man,"
Aelfwine "a brave lordling, and we need his like."
Torhthelm likewise is moved to indignation against the
bearded sons of Offa who fled while the Danes beat down
"boys" younger than himself. Yet with an inconsistency
born of his minstrel training he wishes he himself had been in
the fight, to show that he loved Beorhtnoth as well as any of
his titled lords and would never have run away as some of
them did. Tídwald's sad retort is that Torhthelm's time for
battle will come all too soon and, when it does, he will not
find it as easy as the songs say to choose between shame and
death. This part of "The Homecoming" accentuates the
most wasteful side of the wide waste of war, that it cuts off
the young. And Tolkien piles waste upon waste by putting it
into a setting in which the deaths are all needless, all sacrifices
to the pride of Beorhtnoth, whom even Tídwald still loves.

When the two searchers finally uncover Beorhtnoth's body
they say a Christian prayer for him, but Torhthelm also feels
the need to burst into a chant in praise of the hero dead, traditional in ancient heathen lays (in *Beowulf*, for instance) and
incorporated by Tolkien into *The Lord of the Rings* for the
funerals of Boromir and Théoden. Torhthelm's song blends
the pagan with the Christian, praising Beorhtnoth on the one
hand for his brave heart and generosity in gift-giving, on the
other for "his soul clearer than swords of heroes," and culmi-
nating in the cry: "He has gone to God glory seeking."
Unknowing as yet that the earl's folly in pursuing "glory" is
the cause of the entire tragedy, the young singer later again
raises a burial chant for him as

> to his hearth-comrades help unfailing,
> to his folk the fairest father of peoples.
> Glory loved he; now glory earning . . .

But the reader, instructed by Tolkien's own analysis of the battle, is meant to know and catch the full irony of lauding the dead leader for that very quality that destroyed the people he was supposed to guard and guide.

One subtheme of "The Homecoming" is Torhthelm's gradual and by no means uninterrupted discovery that the heroic grandeur he sees in his sagas is not compatible with the unheroic reality he is finding on the Essex battlefield. In consequence, from time to time he wavers uncomfortably between the two. He has just seen that youth can die. Now he is horrified by the revelation that Beorhtnoth's mangled body, when it is found, is headless. "What a murder it is,/this bloody fighting!" is the exclamation wrung from him. Tídwald seizes the chance to educate him further by reminding him that war and death were just as unglamorous in the times of Froda and Finn, which he delights to sing about: "The world wept then, as it weeps today." But in the next moment Torhthelm is again envisioning for Beorhtnoth a magnificent funeral pyre and burial in a high barrow surrounded by his weapons and jewels in the antique fashion. He has to be brought back by Tídwald's impatient recall that since these are Christian days the earl will be laid simply in the grave after a Requiem mass by the Monks of Ely, and that the two of them had better get on with the job of transporting the corpse.

Just then, however, Torhthelm, startled by stealthy movements in the dark, is sure that they are made by the "troll-shapes . . . or hell-walkers" of Norse folklore. He attacks them with Beorhtnoth's blade, which he has picked up, and kills one of them. Sardonically Tídwald hails him as "my bogey-slayer!" He shows the youth that he has killed nothing but a miserable English corpse stripper, who could easily have been put to flight by a boot in the pants. This, too, has been a needless death, in its own small way not unlike the

earl's greater slaughter, since both result from imaginations un-
balanced by emulation of the mighty past. And the fact that
the killing has been done by Beorhtnoth's own sword is another of art's little perfidies.

Up to this point Torhthelm has not known that the English
chief gave the Danes the advantage of crossing the causeway.
Now Tídwald tells him with a mixture of sorrow, anger, and
love. In so doing he tries to open his young companion's eyes
to the part played in Beorhtnoth's decision by the seduction
of bardic fame: he was too "keen . . . to give minstrels matter for mighty songs./Needlessly noble." But, to judge from
Torhthelm's failure to comment, the lesson does not sink in.
Instead, he ruminates on the vagaries of historical change
that have pulled down the last living descendant of the Saxon
earls who conquered England, while bringing on the scene a
new race of conquering Danes. To him Beorhtnoth's chivalry was too much in accord with that of many of the noblest
heroes of old to seem "needless." So missing what Tídwald
(and through him Tolkien) considers the key to a proper understanding of the meaning of the battle — the initial guilt of
Beorhtnoth — Torhthelm never does comprehend the true
nature of the horror and pity hanging over that battleground.
His historical analogies are true enough, and well worth
drawing, but they go off at a tangent from the immediate
tragedy of the battle itself. Also, what is to Torhthelm only
an interesting historical configuration translates itself for Tídwald into concrete facts of farmers robbed and killed, wives
and children carried off into serfdom. "Let the poets/babble,
but perish all pirates!"

Though Tídwald seems to have done most of the methodi-
cal physical work of getting Beorhtnoth's corpse to the
wagon that is to bear it to Ely, Torhthelm's wilder emotions
have wearied him to the point of needing rest. But Tídwald's
suggestion that he lie in the wagon with the corpse, using it

as a pillow, strikes the younger man as revoltingly brutal. Not at all, replies the old farmer; Torhthelm has misused his songs so long for dressing up ugly facts in the fancy language of poetry that he has never learned to accept them bare. To demonstrate, Tídwald by way of parody extemporizes a sentimental poem relating in high-flown style how a faithful servant, weary with weeping for the master he loves, bows his head on the beloved breast as they journey together toward the grave. Decked out like that, he says, his suggestion about lying in the cart with Beorhtnoth would appeal to Torhthelm as noble. The latter accepts the rebuke, gets into the wagon, falls asleep, and dreams.

Speaking out of his dream Torhthelm is no longer the callow romantic youth but a mouthpiece for something greater and more impersonal than himself, the spirit of heroic paganism. He foresees Beorhtnoth's burial and the slow oblivion of time that overtakes him as his tomb crumbles and all his kin die out. Then his prophecy broadens into a vision of the doom awaiting the whole human race when its candles flicker out and everlasting night rushes in. Is there nothing men can do to vanquish the darkness and the cold? No, for the doom is that of Ragnarok, when gods and men will be swept away by the forces of chaos. But meantime manhood demands that they gather together in lighted halls to defy with undaunted spirits the defeat that is bound to come. Torhthelm, still dreaming, hears and repeats what they chant:

> Heart shall be bolder, harder be
> purpose, more proud the spirit as our power
> lessens! Mind shall not falter nor mood waver,
> though doom should come and dark conquer.

Tolkien is paraphrasing here the famous lines spoken by a member of Beorhtnoth's war band in the *Maldon* poem as they await the last onslaught, lines praised by Tolkien in his accompanying essay as "a summing up of the heroic code" of the north. Likewise in his celebrated lecture delivered to the British Academy in 1936, "Beowulf: the Monsters and the Critics," Tolkien had singled out this same defiance of fated doom, without fear and without hope, as the core of that poem. He had used there, too, the same image of man at bay in his lighted halls besieged by the darkness outside. In short, he is giving us in Torhthelm's assertion of the will's inner victory what seems to him the finest that Norse paganism has to offer. It is very fine indeed. Tolkien admires it. He has said so repeatedly elsewhere, and by implication he says so again in "The Homecoming." But for him personally as a Catholic it is not enough, for it stops with life on earth.

As Torhthelm has spoken for more than himself, so also Tídwald speaks for the new age of Christianity (and for Tolkien, too, it seems) in his reply to the gleeman's apprentice:

> . . . your words were
> queer, Torhthelm my lad, with your talk of
> wind and doom conquering and a dark ending.
> It sounded fey and fell-hearted,
> and heathenish, too: I don't hold with that.

So far as this world goes, Tídwald's view of the propects are hardly more cheerful than Torhthelm's. The coming morning, like others before it, will bring only more labor and loss till England is ruined. Wars will go on, "ever work and war till the world passes," and roads will be rough for Englishmen in Æthelred's or any other time. But the world will pass, and what lies beyond is foreshadowed by the Requiem mass being sung by the Monks of Ely as "The Homecoming" ends: "*Dirige, Domine, in conspectu tuo viam meam.*" Here at last after courage shines hope.

Looking back over Tolkien's poem from its beginning, we may well be impressed by the crusading spirit with which he has Tídwald knock down every attempt by Torhthelm to idealize war. On the other hand he never hints that a fight with a determined enemy can or should be avoided. It would be nice if the Danes would stay home and stop ruining England, but since they will not they must be resisted by arms. Tídwald hates the invaders, has often fought them in the past, and will continue to fight them in days to come. His anguish after the Maldon fray is not that there has been a fray but that bad leadership has lost so many precious English lives without stopping enemy destruction of the land. If men must die in battle, let their deaths at least buy safety for their people. Tolkien, of course, writes here only about a specifically defensive war fought on English soil. The situation is essentially the same in *The Lord of the Rings* where the war against Sauron is again a war of defense waged in the home territories of the West against a foe implacably bent on invasion and enslavement. About other sorts of wars fought elsewhere for other reasons it is safe to deduce from the two works only that Tolkien's deep hatred of waste and death would make him insist that they be plainly necessary to the defense of freedom at home. He does not seem to be optimistic that wars will ever cease.

Finally, we should be clear that Tídwald's impatience with Torhthelm's saga-quoting and saga-living is less with the sagas themselves than with the young man's misreading and misapplication of them. Tídwald objects to their use as a substitute for life — and so does Tolkien through him. The writer or reader of fantasy, he prescribes in his essay "On Fairy-stories," must start from a strong grasp of the primary world of experience, and must always return to it from his adventures in the secondary worlds of fancy, refreshed and reawakened to present realities. Young Torhthelm, lacking such a grasp, is constantly confusing the two worlds, with the result that he understands neither. This is not the fault of the sagas. Properly seen, they reveal the *lacrimae rerum* in the battles, loyalties, treacheries they relate. "You can hear the tears through the harp's/twanging . . ." says Tídwald. And he concedes that they have comfort to offer today's suffering: "The woven staves have yet worth in them/for woeful hearts . . ." "The Homecoming" is certainly a warning against disproportion in the uses of fantasy. But it is very far from being a repudiation either of the heroic northern lays, which have been a lasting enthusiasm of Tolkien's life, or, almost needless to say, of his own works of the imagination whose forefathers they are.

5. *"Smith of Wootton Major"*

This, the last (in 1967) of Tolkien's minor works to be published to date, has the same major theme as "Leaf by Niggle," his earliest. Both are short prose narrative meditations on the gift of fantasy, what it is, whence it comes, and what it does to the life and character of the man who receives it. But since the earlier story is deeply Christian, whereas "Smith of Wootton Major" is not overtly religious at all, they formulate and resolve in quite different terms the range of problems they have in common. As against "Leaf by Niggle's" setting in modern England, followed by an afterlife in Purgatory, the present story unfolds in a landscape of no recognizable time or place, in which the village of Wootton Major lies only a few miles away from the country of Faery, and those who know how may easily walk across the boundary between them. Not that signs of date and nationality are completely lacking. The villagers' English names, guild system, Great Hall, and pregunpowder weapons hint at medieval England, but where are the knights, castles, villeins, priests, and other features of the feudal Middle Ages, and who ever heard of a medieval village with an independent Council electing a Master Cook as key official?

No, though the villagers are human beings, Tolkien skews them slightly hobbitward, and consequently out of historical time and space. Their perpetual feasting all year round, their insistence on "full and rich fare" at every feast, and their exaltation of cooking into the supreme art, especially in the Great Cake at the Twenty-four Feast for children (given once every twenty-four years) are all marks of hobbitlike gusto for food.[19] This skewing is just enough to make Wootton Major a compatible neighbor to a region of Faery inhabited by elves and alien in its many marvels. Tolkien needs some continuity of strangeness to prevent the journeys back and forth between village and Faery from jarring the imagination.

The story opens with the incursion of Faery into the village by the agency of the then Master Cook, who brings back with him from a visit to that land a small "fay-star" looking like tarnished silver and an apprentice named Alf, in appearance only a boy "barely in his teens" but actually the King of the "Fairies" (a name here used interchangeably for "elves").[20] The King's immediate purpose is to see that the star, perennial symbol of the elves, is given at the next Twenty-four Feast to a child fitted to wear it on voyages of exploration into Faery, and, long range, to stir up in all the children of the village their aptitudes for wonder. His efforts are opposed and derided by his master, Nokes, the newly appointed Master Cook, a sly ignoramus who holds the common view that a delight in fairies, and what they stand for, is not for adults but only for the very young: "Fairies he thought one grew out of." In this way Tolkien broaches one of his favorite themes, the incessant war waged against fantasy and all its works by the dullard and the skeptic who understand them superficially or not at all.

Fairies and childhood candy are forever associated in

Nokes' mind. So he covers with sugar-icing the Great Cake he bakes for the Feast because "that will make it pretty and fairylike." And he trivializes the whole concept of what a fairy is by perching on top of the cake to represent the Fairy Queen "a little doll . . . dressed all in white, with a little wand in her hand ending in a tinsel star, and *Fairy Queen* written in pink icing round her feet." Naturally such a man snickers at Alf's solemn assurance that the fay-star truly comes from Faery. Nokes will pop it into the cake batter with other gift "trinkets" to be found by the children when they eat their slices of cake. At the Feast he makes a hoary joke about the trickiness often attributed to fairies in folklore, telling the youngsters that the cake contains one present for each of them "if the Fairy Queen plays fair. But she doesn't always do so: she's a tricky little creature. You ask Mr. Prentice." When no child finds the fay-star in his slice, Nokes laughingly suggests that the Queen has magically taken it back to Fairyland, "Not a nice trick to play, I don't think." As elsewhere noted, against all such vulgar errors — that elves are tiny, toylike, mischievous, busy with magic tricks credible only in the nursery — Tolkien protests long and earnestly in "On Fairy-stories." [21] These are the misconceptions, he says, that blind adult minds to the great range and power of their proper heritage of creative fantasy.

Despite Nokes, the King contrives to have the fay-star swallowed by the son of the village blacksmith. It begins its transforming work on him six months later on his tenth birthday, when for the first time in his life he really hears the dawn song of the birds sweeping westward as the sun rises. Tolkien portrays this experience as not merely an awaking to something new but as a sudden remembering of something once known but since forgotten. Young Smith exclaims, "It reminds me of Faery . . . but in Faery the people sing too," although he has never been there. He then sings "in strange words that he seemed to know by heart." Years later, when he brings back three flowers that chime like bells as a gift from Faery, his son, Ned, who has never been there either (and has no star to admit him), finds he remembers them: "there is a scent in the bells: a scent that reminds me of, reminds me, well, of something I've forgotten." And the Fairy Queen herself implies to Smith, when he at last meets her, that the sight of her image on the cake has given all who saw it a "glimpse," which is a memory, of her country — and theirs. Tolkien seems Wordsworthian in his belief that recollections of Faery are among those clouds of glory which the newborn human soul trails into the world, only too often to be erased or stunted in later life.

As Smith matures his voice grows "ever more beautiful" until passersby stop to listen to him sing as he works in the village smithy. This music he has learned from the elves during the excursions he is beginning to make into their country. His products at the forge also come to bear their stamp, for as he hammers out all the usual articles of iron needed by the villagers for daily life they "had a grace about them, being shapely in their kinds, good to handle and look at." The traveler in the realms of fantasy, as Tolkien insists in his doctrine of Recovery, is no mere dreamer but brings back a freshness of vision, which brightens and beautifies everything he sets his hand to. This beauty is even more apparent in the ironwork which Smith shapes for pure delight "into wonderful forms that looked as light and delicate as a spray of leaves and blossom," yet stern with the strength of iron. The allusion here to leaf and blossom immediately connects Smith with the Tree that runs through many of Tolkien's writings, his prime symbol for the subcreative art of fantasy. Smith is adapting that art to his own particular mediums of song and metalwork, as Niggle did to painting and as writers do in telling fairy stories.

How he learns the art in Faery becomes clear in the description of the visits he often spends there "looking only at one tree or one flower" in its outer marches. At a later stage, nearer the heart of the kingdom, he is allowed to discover "the King's Tree springing up, tower upon tower, into the sky, and its light was like the sun at noon; and it bore at once leaves and flowers and fruits uncounted, and not one was the same as any other that grew on the Tree." Surely this is the Tree of Tales, whose interwoven branches and foliage represent all story, which Tolkien depicts in "On Fairy-stories" and which Niggle tries to paint. Smith's quest for it is the journey of the spirit that precedes art. His success in finding it is the final vision that validates the art itself.

But Faery in the present story is more than just a vague terrain from which to derive allegories about art. Tolkien asks us to accept it as a solidly physical area closely adjacent to Wootton Major, though the villagers never go there and few of them are even willing to be told that it exists. It has a life of its own into which even Smith, with his star glowing brightly on his forehead, ventures at his peril. Far from being the toyland which Nokes dismisses, it is, he finds, a region of beauty and terror not altogether hospitable to mortals. Trying to get around its Outer Mountains, he comes to the Sea of Windless Storm where elven warriors disembark singing on their return from battles in the Dead Marshes against the armies of Unlight.[22] They pass over his prostrate body as if he were not there. Evidently a mysterious struggle against nameless evils is taking place inside Faery itself, but among these evils Smith "was as safe as a mortal can be in that perilous country. The Lesser Evils avoided the star, and from the Greater Evils he was guarded." Guarded by whom against what exactly? Tolkien prefers not to say. He intimates only that the issues at stake are moral, aligning the forces of good against evil. He has always believed that fairy stories should be inherently moral (though not didactic), and his own versions of Faery are always governed by moral laws.[23]

The lesson Smith learns from observing these wars going on is peculiarly personal. He sees that "many of the Evils cannot be challenged without weapons of power too great for any mortal to wield." So impressed is he by the magnitude of the contending hosts and their weapons and by his own impotence to take any share in the struggle that he resolves never to make any weapon of war in the village smithy: ". . . among all the things that he made it is not remembered that he ever forged a sword or a spear or an arrow-head." Since the elves continue to make and use such weapons, though more potently, the logic of Smith's resolve is not altogether clear. Weapons can still be needed in defense of justice in the world of Wootton Major. Psychologically, Smith seems to have concluded that all struggles are basically moral and cannot be settled by swords and spears. Consequently he will make none as a matter of principle. In any case a powerful aversion to physical combat is obscurely at work here. One is reminded of Frodo throwing away his war gear on the plains of Mordor, never to resume it again.

Because of Tolkien's unvarying idea that the paths of elves and men are sundered, in none of his fairy lands or elven homes can a mortal man be more than a temporary guest. Smith is broken-hearted to learn that Faery cannot be his permanent home. He realizes this when he saves himself from a Wild Wind hunting him by clinging to a birch tree, which weeps when stripped of its leaves and which begs him to go back to his own land: "You do not belong here. Go away and never return!" Presuming to penetrate the Inner Mountains without invitation to the lucid Vale of Evermorn, he is informed by one of the maidens dancing there that his star is not "a passport to go wherever he wished." Much is concealed from him by mists, much is wiped out of his memory after he has seen it. But Smith is not at home in Wootton

Major either, although he has wife and children there. Only to them and a few others can he confide those excursions across the border which make up so great a part of his life. He is cut off from most of the population, since "too many had become like Nokes" and would have ridiculed him. Such, then, Tolkien seems to say, is the tragic homelessness of the man who lives and creates fantasy in a rationalistic age.

Smith meets the Fairy Queen only twice, but these encounters provide the supreme moments of his life. On the first occasion he dances with her, not knowing who she is, in the Vale of Evermorn, and is lifted up to live above himself, as is the subcreator of secondary worlds of fantasy at the height of his inspiration. Smith sees her for the second and last time by her express summons on a peak in Faery by night, surrounded by a host of elven spearmen but herself taller than their spears. Recognizing the awesome being he faces and comparing her in his mind with the tawdry image mounted by Nokes on his cake, he is ashamed for mankind. The Queen laughs and tells him not to be: "Better a little doll, maybe, than no memory of Faery at all. For some only the glimpse. For some the awaking." This "glimpse," which is all that most people (as also in "Leaf by Niggle") ever remember of the enchanted lands, is at least better than no memory at all. Tasteless vulgarizations of Faery, in spite of the damage they do in driving away discriminating minds, have their uses for those who sleep most of their lives away. But in those who can wake up, memory may be set ablaze by even the most wrong-headed, most unpromising imitations.

The Queen has given Smith his heart's desire, which is to see her, dance with her, and learn her thoughts, "some of which gave him joy, and others filled him with grief," for the greatest of the elves have sorrows and joys, and Faery has its dark places as well as its light. Now by an inexorable law, which she has no power to change, he must leave Faery forever. "The time has come. Let him choose" is the message she gives him to deliver to the unknown King. Since he must give up the star anyway, it may not strike us as much of a choice to let him decide whether to surrender it voluntarily. But in any moral choice — and this is moral — the assent of the chooser's will is all-important. Often we do what we must, but it makes all the difference whether we agree to do it or have to be dragged by the heels. Tolkien regards the option offered to Smith as conferring real freedom, in keeping with his ruling principle that all moral decisions must be free. When Smith, with dizziness and pain, tears the star from his brow and returns it to Alf, the King, he is rewarded by being allowed to name his "heir," the child who is to be fed the star at the next approaching Twenty-four Feast.

Smith returns to his house sadly enough but strengthened by the gift given him by the Queen on parting. This is a comprehensive vision of the primary world of the village side by side with the secondary world of Faery, and of himself in relation to both: ". . . he seemed to be both in the World and in Faery, and also outside them and surveying them, so that at once he was in bereavement, and in ownership, and in peace." Standing outside the two worlds, he is able to see that he belongs partly in each and wholly in neither, and to feel for them taken together a sense both of owning and not owning, which resolves itself finally into peace. Smith comes back to Wootton Major "a giant" in spiritual growth, accepting the loss of Faery and ready to take up his domestic duties and his work at the smithy, which he has neglected of late during his long journeys away. His bereavement of past wonders is to be compensated for, especially, by teaching his son the secrets of his art at the forge and much else he has learned, not "only the working of iron." Yet a residue of sadness persists. The child who is to get his star will not know that Smith once owned it, he remarks ruefully. "That's the way with such gifts . . . I have handed it on and come back to hammer and tongs."

By what law was Smith obliged to leave Faery, never to return? And why? By the law of time, it seems: "The time has come." The time referred to is Smith's age. Tolkien very precisely keeps count of the passage of the years during the story. The boy of nine who first eats the star in his cake at the Twenty-four Feast that opens the narrative is fifty-seven years old at the second return of the Feast that closes the story forty-eight years later. Tolkien apparently is saying that a man can become too old for wanderings in Faery. His powers of apprehending its marvels and translating them into art decay with age. Younger people of talent wait to take his place. Not that literally only one writer of fantasy can hold the field at any given time, of course. But it is fitting for an established master of the genre as he feels his genius dying to accept an obligation to withdraw in favor of fresh pens.

Reading "Smith of Wootton Major" as Tolkien's personal farewell to his art is tempting, and has at least as good an argument to support it as reading Shakespeare's *The Tempest* in the same autobiographical light. Is it mere chance that Tolkien was fifty-seven years old in 1949, when he completed *The Lord of the Rings?* At that age, and after so arduous an effort, he would have been only human in concluding, either then or at some time in the years soon after, that his career as a writer of fiction was substantially over. He was not to know that he would live on for many years longer and resume work on the still unfinished *Silmarillion.* This is not to say, either, that he necessarily wrote the Smith story in 1949. He may have, or he may have waited some years until the autumnal mood was on him again. We do not yet know its date of composition. As for its late publication in 1967, when Tolkien was seventy-five, an autobiographical threnodic interpretation would help to explain why he wanted to keep it private until his closing years.

Such, at least in outline, is the case for holding that in "Smith of Wootton Major" Tolkien broke his wand and drowned his magic books. We are not required to go all the way toward autobiography, however. Smith can be any practitioner of the White Art who travels far "from Daybreak to Evening" and in his old age comes home, tired, to hand on his passport to his successors. There is no denying the elegiac tone of the ending, with its falling leaves and sunset, its pain, its attempt to find in homely things comfort for a youthful intensity of life never to be reached again. This melancholy is enchanced by the departure of the Fairy King from the village, sneered at by Nokes and unregretted by all save a few of its inhabitants: "Most people . . . were content. They had had him for a very long time and were not sorry to have a change." The indirect reference to us of the twentieth century is clear enough. Tolkien is not hopeful about our age. The elves have left us, and we have not mourned to see them go.

6. "Imram" [24]

By this title (Celtic for "voyage") Tolkien purposely associates his poem with that group of tales of early Irish seafaring into the western Atlantic which were popular throughout Europe from about the eighth century on and are now called *imrama* by modern scholars. By selecting Saint Brendan's voyage as his subject he also almost inevitably turns our eyes to that example of the type much more widely circulated than any other, the Latin prose *Navigatio Sancti Brendani Abbatis*, surviving today in at least 120 manuscripts and translated during the Middle Ages into nearly every European vernacular. [25] Since "Imram" is a short poem of 132 lines and the *Navigatio* is 35 pages long in its most recent English translation, Tolkien obviously has to select what he regards as a few central incidents from the welter of marvelous events which the Latin prose narrates with so much gusto. On the other hand, it is fair to say that almost everything in the poem exists in some form or other in the *Navigatio*. Watching how Tolkien selects, omits, and alters gives an unparalleled view of the artist at work.

Both the poem and the prose tale begin at Brendan's monastery of Clonfert in Galway, his "Meadow of miracles," whose Celtic name is *Cluain-ferta*. Tolkien uses the Celtic form, which modern translations of the Latin prose likewise call attention to.[26] Both versions describe the voyage as taking seven years. In both, the Saint and his crew of monks sail westward for a very long time (forty days in the *Navigatio*, over a year in "Imram") [27] before they see anything but ocean. A divergence between the poem and the prose begins, however, in the account of the first unusual phenomenon the travelers meet with. In the *Navigatio* it is an island where they are fed by unseen hands and one monk succumbs to demonic possession. In "Imram" their currach sails under a dark cloud covering the sky overhead, which they find is being spewed out by a volcano in eruption. Now the cloud and the volcano are both in the *Navigatio*, but there Brendan encounters them at different times and only near the end of his quest. There the cloud, in fact, is not volcanic smoke but a supernatural barrier across the surface of the sea protecting the Land of Promise of the Saints, so thickly that the monks can scarcely see one another while in it.

Tolkien's combining the two episodes and bringing them forward early into the voyage have the effect of giving the cloud a physical cause and a more inclusive function in "Imram." It is no longer a screen around the single island of the saints but a boundary between the normal Atlantic and that paranormal area of it in which the ensuing strangeness of the poem occurs. The *Navigatio* needs no such boundary. There the entire Atlantic from Ireland westward is dotted with islands no one of which is ordinary. Its marvels have no geographical beginning. At least to the modern mind, Tolkien's repositioning of the cloud and his giving it a natural volcanic origin enhance the voyage's credibility, as well as its orderly structure.

The volcanoes in "Imram" and the *Navigatio* are unmistakably the same volcano. As the poem pictures it,

> Upreared from sea to cloud then sheer
>   a shoreless mountain stood;
> its sides were black from the sullen tide
>   up to its smoking hood,
> but its spire was lit by a living fire
>   that ever rose and fell:
> tall as a column in High Heaven's hall,
>   its roots were deep as Hell.

In the *Navigatio*, too, the peak is towering, steep, and black: "The cliffs at the water's edge were so high that the summit was obscured; they were as black as coal and wonderfully sheer, like a wall." Besides, the monks see the flames rising and subsiding periodically just as in the poem: "they saw the mountain . . . vomiting forth flames sky-high and then sucking them back upon itself." One of their number is trapped by demons there. Tolkien prefers to suppress the demons, but their presence may have contributed to his phrase about the roots of the volcano being "deep as Hell." For his additional idea that the peak rises from drowned lands "where the kings of kings lie low" there are suggestions in the *Navigatio* of transparent waters through which Brendan and his companions discern undersea landscapes,[28] but more probably Tolkien is thinking of kingdoms overrun by the ocean in *The Lord of the Rings*, specifically Númenor.

The second landfall of the monks in "Imram" corresponds basically to the *Navigatio*'s "Paradise of Birds," but with

many significant changes. Most obvious of these is in the topography of the island. In the prose it is green and pleasant,
easy of access, sunlit. To make Brendan's landing excitingly
hazardous Tolkien surrounds it with "cliffs no man could
climb." Nor can any boat find harbor except in one very
narrow rockbound inlet, which his crew does not discover
until they have almost despaired of their lives. This is precisely the monks' experience at a rocky island in the *Navigatio*, which does not connect with the Paradise of Birds at all.
Moreover, Tolkien transfers to the latter's beaches gems
which in the *Navigatio* belong to the Land of Promise. But
the monks in "Imram" show no interest in taking home a
boatload of precious stones, as they do in the prose account.
In this way Tolkien keeps their monastic vows of poverty
unbroken and preserves the ascetic tone of his poem.

This care is in keeping with his effort in the poem to present the island as a holy place, both explicitly and by use of
Grail imagery. On landing, Brendan's party senses an atmosphere of sanctity "and holy it seemed to be" — even before it
arrives at the White Tree standing in a dale, which is "like a
silver grail/with carven hills for rim." The Tree itself, "more
fair than ever I deemed/in Paradise might grow," is as thick
as a tower and immeasurably tall, and is covered with white
"leaves" growing "more close than swan-wing plumes."
When the monks chant their prayers a sound of trumpets
rings out overhead:

> The Tree then shook, and flying free
> from its limbs the leaves in air
> as white birds rose in wheeling flight
> and the lifting boughs were bare.

By twice calling the white objects covering the boughs
"leaves" Tolkien is plainly saying that, although they look

like plumes of swans and wheel in the air like birds, they are in fact not birds but birdlike leaves of a mysteriously responsive kind. This point explains why he never calls the island the Paradise of Birds as does the *Navigatio*. There are no birds on Tolkien's island. For him it is, if anything, the island of the Tree.

Nevertheless, a comparison of Tolkien's passages with those in the *Navigatio*'s description of the Paradise of Birds shows that he took many elements from it, while rejecting others. Thus the Paradise of Birds, too, is holy but for different reasons. It is blessed because it is the sanctuary of fallen angels, not allied to Lucifer, who are permitted to come there on holy days in the form of white birds to sing the praises of God.[29] During the whole stay of the monks on the island from Easter to Pentecost these expiatory spirits join them daily in chanting the divine offices. They perch so thickly on "an exceptionally tall tree . . . with a trunk of colossal girth" as almost to cover it: "This tree was full of pure white birds; so thickly had they settled on it that there was hardly a branch, or even a leaf, to be seen." They never fly off from the tree like Tolkien's leaves but, unlike them, they are definitely birds, not leaves. Why has Tolkien changed the identity of the white objects covering the Tree in his poem? Because he wants to summon up once more one of the master images of all his work, the Tree of Tales, which is the symbol of Faery. As noticed often before,[30] every leaf on that Tree is a tale organically linked to all other tales of secondary worlds to form the Tree which symbolizes the whole. Neither birds nor fallen angels fit in with that well-established symbolism. Yet the beauty and airiness of birds in flight, suggested by the *Navigatio*, have moved Tolkien in "Imram" to incorporate them into his Tree metaphorically for this occasion.

But Tolkien has still another meaning to add to the Tree

and its island. In the poem he specifies that after the leaves have whirled up from the Tree, the song which the monks hear coming down from the "star-lit sky" is "not of bird:/neither noise of man nor angel's voice . . ." Rather, he says, it may be sung "by a third fair kindred in the world" yet lingering "beyond the foundered land." Remembering Tolkien's predilection for elves, we are driven to conclude that the singers here are indeed elves, whose delight is always in singing. This conclusion is reinforced by Tolkein's repeated description of the island as lit by stars or "moonlight dim," never by the sun. In *The Lord of the Rings* Tolkien called elves "the People of the stars" and assigned to them in the Undying Lands of the far West the island of Eressëa, also known as Evereve, where no sun shone. Things begin to fall into place. The island to which the monks have come is this homeland of the elves. And the Tree, besides being the Tree of Tales, is also a seedling of Telperion, the White Tree of the Valar, transplanted to grow in Eressëa before being taken on to Númenor and thence to Middle-earth to grow in the courtyard of the kings of Gondor.

The cluster of associations around the image of the Tree in "Imram" is therefore very rich. Nor do they jar with the religious theme of Brendan's search for salvation. The White Tree of the Guardian Valar has a religious penumbra in *The Lord of the Rings*. And in his essay "On Fairy-stories" Tolkien invests the Tree of Tales with an aura of holiness as an emblem of man's cooperation with God in the work of continuing creation. As for elves, their adoption by the half-divine Valar as neighbors and disciples endows them with many attributes not granted to men. Compared with his first stop at the volcano of raw fire, Brendan's experience of the sacred Tree and the elves ethereally singing marks a stage forward in his spiritual odyssey.

In "Imram" what happens to the little band after they leave

the island of the Tree is veiled in indistinct allusion. Brendan speaks of seeing a single great Star,

> a light on the edge of the Outer Night
> > beyond the Door of Days,
> where the round world plunges steeply down,
> > but on the old road goes,
> as an unseen bridge that on arches runs
> > to coasts that no man knows.

At this edge of the created universe he has smelled, he says, the sweet odor of flowers "as keen as death" and heard "words beyond this world," both, it would seem, coming from the Land of Promise he set out to seek. The implication is that Brendan has been allowed to reach it somehow and to disembark there, but he refuses to tell his questioning disciple anything more about it. Let the disciple go labor on the sea and find out the answers for himself. Of that kind of knowledge each man must earn his own.

Here again the "Imram" account both resembles and differs from that in the *Navigatio*. In the latter, two landings on the Land of Promise, an earlier one by the monk Barinthus and a later by Brendan, are explicitly related, and many details about the features of the Land itself are supplied. Among them, according to Barinthus, "All the plants we saw were flowering plants . . ." so that he was able to ask his brethren on his return home: "Can you not smell by our garments that we have been in Paradise?" This is the odor the poem refers to. Both voyagers on landing are greeted by a shining man (called an "angel" by Barinthus) who informs them that they are indeed walking on the island God "intended for His saints," which "will be revealed to your successors at the time when Christians will be undergoing persecution." These presumably are among the "words beyond the world" heard by Brendan in "Imram," but Tolkien refuses to come out and say so. Tolkien also omits the angel's direction to Brendan to "return to the land of your birth" because his time has come to die and he is to be buried with his predecessors: ". . . you shall soon be laid to rest with your fathers." However, the poem shows Brendan carrying out the command by returning to Galway and dying in his own monastery of *Chuainferta.* And what of the Star, which in "Imram" Brendan sees "high and far . . . a light on the edge of the Outer Night"? It stems, apparently, from the light which everlastingly brightens the Land of Promise in the *Navigatio,* its source being Christ Himself: "for Christ Himself is our light." Tolkien lifts it into the sky and concentrates it symbolically in a Star, in which, however, any Christian reference is left covert. We are reminded of the one star seen by Sam shining high above Mordor as the sign of a transcendent beauty that its shadows can never darken.

In both "Imram" and the Latin prose tale Brendan's pilgrimage is to a place of ultimate holiness, but the two conceptions of its location differ radically. The Land of Promise in the *Navigatio* is geographically an island in the uttermost western Atlantic, hidden from sailors by a miraculous dense cloud yet anchored physically in the same salt sea as all the other islands Brendan visits. The prose narrator quietly assumes a flat earth at the western extremity of which lies the Saint's goal. He accepts popular Irish thought of the period about the shape of the world. Once Tolkien imports into his poem the idea of a "round world" plunging "steeply down," the Atlantic can have no western limit except continental America. He is thereby forced to take the Land of Promise out of the physical universe altogether. He does so by inserting a "parting of the seas" at which the visible Atlantic continues on westward while the road to the Land of Promise separates from it "as an unseen bridge that on arches runs" invisibly. This solution, if it can be called that, may owe something to the Bifrost [31] of old Norse mythology, the bridge across which the hosts of Muspell will ride to attack the gods in heaven at the end of the world. At any rate, Tolkien purposely keeps it misty and semimetaphorical.

Having removed the Land of Promise from the Atlantic, he is also free of the need to think of it as an island, and indeed to think of it in any particular terms whatever. He can transform it from a future haven from persecution for the saints into a region outside time, "beyond the Door of Days," and mysteriously evocative of a less literal Heaven. He can and does drop the very name of Land of Promise of the Saints. And he further guards his mystery by the literary device of Brendan's refusal to talk circumstantially about it. A medieval audience, with its capacity to absorb all Brendan's adventures as "wonders God had deigned to show him," would have begrudged the loss of every detail Tolkien left out, but no doubt he well understood our less transmutative modern imagination in deciding to draw the veil.

"Imram" opens grimly enough with the tolling of Brendan's death bell as he begins his tale to his eager questioner. Tolkien, however, has so selected and rewritten the three episodes from the *Navigatio* as to make of his poem a successful, and therefore essentially happy, pilgrim's progress toward salvation. Surviving the demonic volcano under the cloud, Brendan toils on to a difficult anchorage on the holy island of the Tree and hears the song of the "third fair kindred," who are neither men nor angels but seemingly somewhere between these two. He is then ready for admission briefly to some Paradise-like place "beyond this world" where he sees "things out of mind." Death becomes the only fitting climax to the poem, and the tolling bell loses the grimness with which the poem began.

7. *The Adventures of Tom Bombadil*

In publishing this little miscellany of mainly light verse in 1962, Tolkien falls back on the same scholarly pretense which served him well in *The Lord of the Rings* — that he is merely the editor of material taken from hobbit records in the Red Book of Westmarch. This disguise enables him in the Preface to say of the collection as a whole that it reveals hobbit preferences for poetic forms which are full of "rhyming and metrical tricks," and for subject matter "on the surface, light-hearted or frivolous, though sometimes one may uneasily suspect that more is meant than meets the ear." [32] The description is accurate. Most of the sixteen poems included are experimental in versification and most are, inwardly as well as outwardly, frankly only playful trifles. Some half-dozen, however, invite a search for deeper meanings, and one or two are downright cryptic. Tolkien uses his editorial role to discuss in the Preface who the authors of individual poems are (usually Bilbo, Sam, or Frodo), the genre of hobbit poetry to which they belong, possible origins of some pieces in the lore of southern Gondor, comparative dates of composition, and other matters traditionally within the province of the editor.

Since only the first two poems in the book have anything to do with Bombadil, its title can mislead, but it has the larger truthfulness of telling the reader that most of the pieces are connected in some degree with persons, events, or places familiar to him in *The Lord of the Rings*. Indeed, three are repeated verbatim from the epic: "The Man in the Moon Stayed Up Too Late," sung by Frodo in the inn at Bree; Sam's "The Stone Troll," sung to cheer up his companions on the long road to Rivendell; and Sam's "Oliphaunt," recited when he first sees the beast in battle in the Vale of Ithilien. Why did Tolkien choose these particular songs for republication here seven years after their appearance in the epic? Probably because as sheer, gay nonsense rhymes they fit in well with the general tone of his new collection. Also, each of the three is paired with one or more fresh poems which serve as parallels or contrasts.

Thus "Oliphaunt" is only the first of a group of three comic verse versions of bestiary lore, the other animals treated being Fastitocalon, the giant sea turtle, and the domestic cat. All of these creatures are presented with the same kind of intimately affectionate wonder that runs through the medieval bestiaries. Beneath the comic they all show a tinge of the formidable, too. Oliphaunt is terrible in battle. Fastitocalon, like the bestiary whale, will sink the unwary sailor who lands on him and kindles a fire, thinking him an island. From the hobbit point of view, better never to land on uncharted land; better still never to go to sea at all. The cat seems all innocence in slumber, but its dreams are of hunting and slaughter, like those of its savage kindred in the jungle.

Similarly Frodo's nursery jingle about the Man in the Moon carousing in the inn is followed by a poem titled "The Man in the Moon Came Down Too Soon," which barely avoids a tragic tone. In it the Moon Man grows lonely in his pale, jeweled domain and pines for the spinning earth below, the warmth of its fire, the vivid colors of its land and sea, the "sanguine blood" of men, their food, their wine, above all their companionship. What saves the tale for comedy is that its hero is the sort of bumbler who trips by accident on his own stairs and falls into the Bay of Belfalas. Netted up and set on land by fishermen, he is a bedraggled figure who allows himself to be tricked out of his rich garments, jewels, and silver by a surly innkeeper in exchange for a bowl of cold porridge by a smoky fire:

> An unwary guest on a lunatic quest
> from the mountains of the Moon.

This is only one of a series of puns and comic touches by which Tolkien keeps the poem light. But he is almost of two minds about it, for he is treating a subject habitually sad with him, the gulf fixed between men and dwellers in Faery, which is institutionalized, so to speak, by the Ban of the Valar in *The Lord of the Rings*. For a change, his approach here is from the side of the monarch of Faery who tries to share the life of Earth in vain. The final two poems in the collection will take up the theme again, but from the side of mortal men, tragically.

The grisly slapstick of "The Stone Troll" finds no parallels in its companion piece, "Perry-the-Winkle." Whereas the first relates with relish the encounter of a man with a troll who is gnawing his uncle's shinbone, the second has some elements of pathos in picturing a lonely troll searching through the Shire for a hobbit who will dare to be his friend. Its dominant mood, however, is that of fun. His appearance scares the mayor and creates panic in the marketplace until a brave hobbit rides off on his back to have tea with him in his cave. The ensuing popularity of the troll because of his "cramsome bread" and the fame as a baker, which comes to his hobbit friend from learning the recipe, are pure Shire food-worship with a happy ending.

In none of the poems so far discussed does Tolkien reach very high. Writing for amusement, he purposely pulls back from the heights he sometimes attempts to scale in many of the other poems embedded in his great prose epic. This intent to stay on a comfortably gay level is particularly clear in the two Bombadil poems that open the collection. Almost totally absent from them is the mysterious aura of primal strength which sets Tom outside the spell of the one Ring and snatches the hobbits from the tomb of the barrow-wights. So much so that Tolkien feels it necessary to explain in the Preface that the two poems were written by Buckland hobbits who "had . . . little understanding of his powers." They regarded Bombadil "with amusement (tinged with fear)."

Accordingly, the adventures Tom goes through in the poem which gives the collection its title consist of his escapes from traps set for him by friends and enemies in the Old Forest, but since none is made to seem really dangerous the tone is mainly one of delight in woodland escapades. "No one has ever caught Tom walking in the forest," says Goldberry in *The Lord of the Rings*. The present verses show how he cannot be caught, and end by telling how he instead catches Goldberry to be his bride. The events related, then, occur before Frodo and his friends are rescued by Bombadil. The same is true of the boating trip in the second poem, which he takes downriver to visit Farmer Maggot. The visit serves an important function in the epic because it is by the Farmer that Tom is warned that the four hobbits are traveling unprotected and will need his help. This gravity of purpose, however, is smothered by episodes of converse with woodland creatures as well as hobbits, and by the merry meeting of feast, dance, and song with which the Farmer's family celebrate his coming. Both poems employ the same couplet form — replete with feminine endings — which marks Tom's every song in the epic, but fare all the better for the absence of intervening "poetic" prose passages with the same rhythms, which make his talk in the epic somewhat monotonous and too highly mannered.

"Errantry," the third poem in the book, has a quite different sort of connection with *The Lord of the Rings*. Tolkien himself calls attention in the Preface to the identity of its verse form with that used by Bilbo in the lay of Eärendil, which he sang to Frodo in Rivendell. The two poems are utterly incongruous in content, however. The Eärendil lay narrates the apotheosis of a hero, whereas "Errantry" details the aimless wanderings of a messenger knight so ridiculous as to forget the very message he is charged to deliver. In his pose as editor Tolkien explains that Bilbo first wrote the piece as a specimen of hobbit "nonsense rhyme" and then later transformed it "somewhat incongruously" into the legend of Eärendil. We can believe, if we like, that under this editorial disguise Tolkien is telling us the order in which he himself composed the two poems, but this would be to identify Bilbo with Tolkien and to make a playful editorial mystification a serious assertion of chronological fact. It seems far more likely that Tolkien wrote the Eärendil lay first, about 1939 or 1940, while inditing the Rivendell episode in Part I of the epic, and parodied it in "Errantry" much later, at the time when he composed all or most of the verses in the present miscellany. Besides, psychologically it is much more normal to break down heroic into mock-heroic than to build up heroic out of sportive "nonsense rhyme." Tolkien devised "Farmer Giles" as a spoof of knighthood not before but after the knightly adventures of *The Lord of the Rings*.

Be that as it may, "Errantry" and the saga of Eärendil as sung by Bilbo are obviously designed for contrast. It is as if Tolkien challenged himself to see whether, using a theme of endless wandering common to both poems, the same metrical shapes and rhyme patterns, parallel descriptions of ships and armor, and even some identical lines and phrases, he could produce in the one case a tragedy and in the other an airy jest. Looking at the passages picturing the armor of the two heroes we can see both the similarity in structure and the polarity in tone:

> "Eärendil"
> In panoply of ancient kings,
> in chainéd rings he armoured him;
> his shining shield was scored with runes
> to ward all wounds and harm from him;
> his bow was made of dragon-horn,

his arrows shorn of ebony,
of silver was his habergeon,
his scabbard of chalcedony;
his sword of steel was valiant,
of adamant his helmet tall,
an eagle-plume upon his crest,
upon his breast an emerald.

"Errantry"
He made a shield and morion
of coral and of ivory,
a sword he made of emerald,

. . . .

Of crystal was his habergeon,
his scabbard of chalcedony;
with silver tipped at plenilune
his spear was hewn in ebony.
His javelins were of malachite
and stalactite — he brandished them,

. . . .

Knight Errant's sword of emerald, his javelins of copper and cavern stalactites are no more outrageously impractical than his "gondola" sprinkled with three separate perfumes, his proposal of marriage to a butterfly "that fluttered by," his battles with "the dragon-flies of Paradise," and so on. While Eärendil's ship is being readied by the Valar to sail the skies forever as the Evening Star, Errant's gondola "of leaves and gossamer" is performing a kind of "Imram" voyage among mysterious ocean isles, meeting with adventure after adventure until, remembering that he started out with a message, he goes home to discover what it is in order that he may set forth again, only to forget it again, *ad infinitum*.

The two poems do not destroy each other. Each is good in

its own kind. In aid of the distinction between kinds Tolkien keeps the verse form sober for "Eärendil" but pushes it to baroque excesses in "Errantry" by often rhyming the middle of one line with the end of its predecessor:

> There was a merry passenger,
> a messenger, a mariner:
> . . . .
>
> He called the winds of argosies
> with cargoes in to carry him
> . . . .

The "Errantry" rhymes are often so far-fetched, as above, that it is hard to tell when Tolkien intends a rhyme.

"Princess Mee" falls in the category of poems of which the Preface remarks that "sometimes one may easily suspect more than meets the ear." Since the Preface does not discuss it at all, and it is not related in any way to *The Lord of the Rings* or to any other poem in the compilation, we are free to make of it what we can. On its face it simply tells the story of the little (young?) elfin Princess Mee who, dancing one starry night on the surface of a pool in the woods, looks down to see for the first time Princess Shee dancing upside down toe to toe with her and returning her wondering gaze. Since none of her fellow elves can tell her the way to the land where Shee lives, Mee meets her nightly on the pool, where they dance together alone:

> So still on her own
> An elf alone
> Dancing as before
> With pearls in hair
> And kirtle fair
> And slippers frail

Of fishes' mail went Mee:
Of fishes' mail
And slippers frail
And kirtle fair
With pearls in hair went Shee!

For the meaning of the poem the first two lines of this final stanza are decisive. Of all the elves Tolkien ever writes about, Mee is the only one who dances constantly alone — with her reflection. We are to understand that the poor Princess has fallen in love with herself, and that Tolkien is giving us a transcription of the Narcissus legend. With this realization the poem, heretofore merely quiet and charming, becomes suddenly deadly.

Tolkien also is proving himself master of the short line. He has done very well with the four-foot line of "Errantry" and now does even better with the two-foot line of "Princess Mee." In the stanza quoted the descending description of Mee from hair down to toe, ascending from toe to hair in identical detail for Shee, admirably evokes the picture of the elf Princess dancing above her own image.

"Shadow Bride" and "The Mewlips" are the two poems of the collection which lend themselves to definitive interpretation least readily, and perhaps not at all. One is never quite sure whether they are more than surface. "Shadow Bride" may be no more than what it seems, an abrupt little tale of a bewitched man without a shadow who, when a lady strays near, pounces upon her and "wraps her shadow round him." Whereupon she must dwell underground perpetually except for one night a year when the two of them dance together till dawn "and a single shadow make." Without invoking modern psychological theories about the shadow selves we are all supposed to have — theories which do not seem characteristic of Tolkien's thought — we may take note of resemblances to the Proserpina legend. But since discrepancies between the poem and the legend are as numerous as the likenesses, dogmatism would be unwise.

"Shadow Bride" remains puzzling partly because it cannot be related to any person or episode in Tolkien's other writings or, indeed, to any other poem in the miscellany in which it appears. The same can almost be said about "The Mewlips," mysterious creatures whom the poem warns the reader directly not to visit lest they devour him. The "Merlock Mountains" and "the marsh of Tode," which must be traversed before the visitor arrives at their underground dwellings "by a dark pool's borders" beside a "rotting river-strand," are not recognizable as known places in Middle-earth.[33] The temptation is to see these Mewlips as just one more marvelous birth from Tolkien's imagination, like orcs, shelobs, and woses. There are tantalizing hints of something more, however. These beings lurk in cellars where they count their gold by the light of a single candle. The cellars have doors with entrance bells to be rung, and their walls drip with moisture. These details bring to mind an urban slum, and the dangers of being swallowed up by its gray and greedy swampiness. Every reader of Tolkien knows his hatred of modern industrialism and its cities. Is he conjuring up here an allegory of its ultimate horrors? This is quite possible. No more can safely be said.

The poems have been growing increasingly somber toward the end of the collection. Now the final three pieces take leave of the comic altogether. Nor is their meaning in doubt. For all of them Tolkien in the Preface forges bonds with *The Lord of the Rings* or its backgrounds, but the bonds are not always close. "The Hoard," for instance, is said to contain "echoes" of a Númenorean tale of the First Age concerning the man Túrin and the dwarf Mim. Since nowhere are we told the story between them and they are never named in the poem itself, the nature of these "echoes" cannot be defined. The poem stands on its own as a grimly marching ac-

count of the power of a hoard of treasure to rot the characters of its successive possessors. Singing elves, the original
artisans, are slain or chained by an avaricious dwarf, who
thereafter spends his days doing nothing but work in order to
add to the hoard. In his old age, too feeble even to see his
precious stones or hear the approach of an enemy, he in turn
is killed by a young dragon. After a lifetime of being "to his
gold chained" the dragon, now old in his turn, is easily dis-
patched by a young knight. Many years later, "his glory
fallen, his rule unjust," the old knight is easily surprised by
the slayers who come to burn his hall and seize his kingdom.
The murderers do not uncover the hoard, however, which
remains lost underground in the care of its final owner,
Night. It has been lethal, not merely physically but morally.
A hoard of treasure is, as we know, Tolkien's perennial object of the cardinal sin of "possessiveness."

"The Sea-Bell" is associated by Tolkien in the Preface with
a body of hobbit poems describing the "wandering-madness"
which afflicts some of their race and leaves them "queer" if
they ever return home. More particularly, he says, someone
in the Red Book has subtitled it "Frodos Dreme," meaning
one of those despairing dreams which tormented Frodo after
his return to the Shire·from Mordor. This ascription may account for its being written in the first person singular, the
only poem in the book so written. Again, however, the
poem needs no such connection to give it value. It is in fact a
superb expression of a favorite theme of Tolkien's, the loneliness of the human being who can live neither with his own
kind nor with those creatures of the imagination who inhabit
Faery, the enchanted land to which he is irresistibly called.

Walking alone by the shore the narrator (or dreamer) is
summoned across the seas by the clang of a buoy heard in a
shell that he picks up. But he does not belong in the lovely
country of "ever-eve," as he discovers when its invisible peo-

ple whom he can hear singing and dancing flee him with "never a greeting." In a moment of high poignancy the wanderer shouts angrily that he is "king of this land" and demands, "Speak to me words! Show me a face!" In swift punishment he is isolated until he is old in a wood where he can hear insects and birds but no human voices. Even after he has crawled back defeated to his own country, his seashell dead and silent, he walks the sad lanes and blind alleys, not belonging there either: "To myself I talk;/for still they speak not, men that meet." Tolkien is saying something vital here about the homelessness of the creative artist.

The coming departure from Middle-earth of all the elves (save those content to lose the high heritage of their race) shadows the whole ending of *The Lord of the Rings*. "The Last Ship," also the last poem in the book, envisions the final boatload leaving Gondor. The elves in it call to Fíriel, a mortal woman on the shore, to come with them in the one seat still empty. She would like to go, for she is "elven-fair" and her youthful beauty, inexorably fading on Earth, will not fade in Elvenhome, "where the White Tree is growing,/and the Star shines upon the foam." But as she steps forward, "deep in clay her feet sank," and she cries out that she cannot come, for "I was born Earth's daughter!" She has to return home, don her smock of russet brown, and "step down" to her daily labors, as did Smith at Wootton Major. In one way or another the Ban of the Valar still holds, Tolkien seems to say. Mortal clay may visit Faery but can establish no lasting citizenship. To claim kingship there as does the nameless narrator of "The Sea-Bell" is to reenact the sacrilege of the Númenoreans trying to conquer Valinor, and to be punished by a death of body and spirit. The theme of limits to man's access to Faery haunts Tolkien's works, and never more tellingly than in the two poems that conclude this collection.

Bibliographical Note

Notes

Index

Bibliographical Note

Richard C. West, *Tolkien Criticism: An Annotated Checklist* (Bibliographies and Checklists, no. 11. Kent, Ohio: Kent State University Press, 1970) gives full information about all of Tolkien's writings, their various editions, and places and dates of publication both in England and in America. Only a few highlights need be mentioned here as a help to the general reader.

The first edition of *The Hobbit* (London: Allen and Unwin, 1937) has achieved rare-book status, and the 1938 edition (Boston: Houghton Mifflin Company) scarcely less so. Subsequent printings by these two publishers in London (1951) and Boston (1958) are available in large libraries and many bookstores, either in hardbound or paperbound editions.

The three volumes of *The Lord of the Rings* were first published in London by Allen and Unwin, 1954–55. This first edition was issued in the United States the following year (Boston: Houghton Mifflin Company, 1955–56). Tolkien's own subsequent revisions, however, appear in a second, three-volume hardbound edition (London: Allen and Unwin, 1966). This is considered the standard edition and it is the one I have used in preparing this book. A one-volume paperbound edition, also published by Allen and Unwin, omits all but one of the useful appendices.

Most illuminating for Tolkien's theory of fantasy writing is his essay "On Fairy-stories," originally composed as a lecture for delivery at the University of St. Andrews in 1938. He has since

revised and enlarged it several times. In its final form it appears
in *Tree and Leaf* (London: Allen and Unwin, Unwin Books, 1964)
as well as in the paperback collection *The Tolkien Reader* (New
York: Ballantine Books, Inc., 1965). The texts are the same. *The
Tolkien Reader* has the unique value of also including several of
Tolkien's shorter pieces: "The Homecoming of Beorhtnoth
Beorhthelm's Son"; "Leaf by Niggle"; "Farmer Giles of Ham";
The Adventures of Tom Bombadil. In 1969, Ballantine Books
issued the one-volume paperback *Smith of Wootton Major and
Farmer Giles of Ham.* They are also available in separate volumes
from Allen and Unwin.

Unfortunately two of Tolkien's narrative poems, "The Lay of
Aotrou and Itroun" (*Welsh Review*, IV:4 [December 1945]) and
"Imram" (*Time and Tide*, 36 [December 3, 1955]), still can be
read only in the periodicals in which they first appeared.

Notes

CHAPTER I *Middle-earth: An Imaginary World?*

1. Revised and enlarged, the lecture was published in essay form in *Essays Presented to Charles Williams* (London: Oxford University Press, 1947). The essay, further revised, is reprinted in *Tree and Leaf* (London: Allen and Unwin, Unwin Books, 1964).

2. See *The Lord of the Rings*, 2nd edition (London: Allen and Unwin, 1966), Prologue, I, 23–24. All references to the epic will be to the three volumes of this edition.

3. Compare similar statements in I, 17; III, 313, 385, and especially 411.

4. *Tree and Leaf*, pp. 27–28.

5. Ransacking the Pleistocene for niches into which to fit the Ages of Middle-earth is a pleasant pastime, which one hopes the players of the game are not taking seriously. See Margaret Howes' delightful article, "The Elder Ages and the Later Glaciations of the Pleistocene Epoch," *Tolkien Journal*, IV: 2 (1967), which picks a span from 95,000 years to 65,000 years ago.

6. Compare Sam's bestiary poem entitled "Oliphaunt" in *The Adventures of Tom Bombadil* (London: Allen and Unwin, 1962).

7. "On Fairy-stories" considers communication with the animal world a basic human need. See Chapter V.

8. The description I give of the Valar and their country in this and subsequent paragraphs is a blending of information from *The Lord of the Rings* (chiefly Appendices A and B) with elaborations later published by Tolkien in *The Road Goes Ever On* (London: Allen and Unwin, 1968), pp. 65–66.

9. The *Navigatio Sancti Brendani Abbatis* is discussed in detail in my analysis of Tolkien's "Imram." See Chapter VII.

10. *The Road Goes Ever On*, p. 66.

11. These examples come mainly from Appendices A and B, but most of them are alluded to also in the course of the three volumes of the epic.

12. Detailed readings of each of these shorter pieces of fiction appear under appropriate headings in Chapter VII.

CHAPTER II *The Hobbit*

1. All references are to *The Hobbit* (London: Allen and Unwin, 1966).

2. Only in the very last paragraph does Tolkien attach this limited framework to a wider cosmic order, foreshadowing the ideas discussed in the next chapter, as Gandalf asks Bilbo laughingly: "Surely you don't disbelieve the prophecies, because you had a hand in bringing them about yourself? You don't really suppose, do you, that all your adventures and escapes were managed by mere luck, just for your sole benefit?" This reference is too fleeting to affect the atmosphere of the tale as a whole and would not, I suppose, mean much to children.

3. On one or two occasions Tolkien's choice of similes is obviously dictated by children's interests: Bilbo laughs at the dwarf Fili wrapped around with spider webs "jerking his stiff arms and legs as he danced on the spider-string under his armpits, just like one of those funny toys bobbing on a wire." But his atrocious punning in describing the origins of the game of golf seems destined for the unlucky ears of adults.

4. See *The Hobbit*, all of Chapter V.

5. Introductory Note to *Tree and Leaf*, p. 5: "At about that time we had reached Bree and I had then no more notion than they [Frodo and his companions] had of what had become of Gandalf

or who Strider was; and I had begun to despair of surviving to find out."
6. *The Hobbit*, p. 297; *Lord of the Rings*, III, 226.

CHAPTER III *Cosmic Order*
1. As discussed in Chapter V, the section on the elves.
2. *The Road Goes Ever On*, p. 60.
3. *The Road Goes Ever On*, p. 65.
4. Compare Gandalf's answer to Frodo's resentment that he is born in times troubled by Sauron (I, 60).
5. In *The Road Goes Ever On* Tolkien remarks that the prayers to Elbereth "and other references to religion in *The Lord of the Rings* are frequently overlooked." Despite the absence of churches, priests, formal liturgies, and the like, Tolkien is not drawing a purely secular Middle-earth, as many critics prefer to believe. His cosmos in the epic may not be exactly Christian but it contains many of the transcendent elements of a more than pantheistic religion.

CHAPTER IV *Sauron and the Nature of Evil*
1. W. H. Auden, "The Quest Hero" in *Tolkien and the Critics*, edited by N. Isaacs and Rose Zimbardo (Notre Dame, Indiana: University of Notre Dame Press, 1969), pp. 40–61.
2. *Tree and Leaf*, p. 52.
3. *Tree and Leaf*, p. 53. In *The Hobbit* (p. 229) Tolkien satirically describes the rage of Smaug the dragon on discovering a theft from his hoard as "the sort of rage that is only seen when rich folk that have more than they can enjoy suddenly lose something that they have long had but have never before used or wanted." His condemnation of the compulsive lust of the dwarves in that tale, and throughout *The Lord of the Rings*, for treasure for its own sake aims at the same target.
4. W. H. Auden, "Good and Evil in *The Lord of the Rings*," *Tolkien Journal*, III: 1 (1967), pp. 5–8.
5. Auden, "The Quest Hero," p. 57.
6. *Tree and Leaf*, p. 52.
7. Auden, "Good and Evil in *The Lord of the Rings*," p. 5.

CHAPTER V *The Free Peoples*

1. Edmund Wilson, "Oo, Those Awful Orcs," *Nation*, 182: 15 (April 14, 1956).
2. Mark Roberts, "Adventure in English," *Essays in Criticism*, VI (1956), see especially p. 454.
3. *Tree and Leaf*, pp. 18, 20, 58, 68–69.
4. Rose Zimbardo, "Moral Vision in *The Lord of the Rings*" in *Tolkien and the Critics*, pp. 100–8, tries to rank them according to the degree of "essence" possessed by each, not very convincingly.
5. It is this distinct uniqueness of racial character that makes it impossible for me to agree with the view, for instance, that the members of Frodo's Company all represent Man in his several aspects. See Gunnar Urang, *Shadows of Heaven* (Philadelphia: Pilgrim Press, 1971), p. 107.
6. *The Hobbit*, p. 178.
7. "They were valiant, but the history of those that returned to Middle-earth in exile was grievous . . ." (III, Appendix F, p. 416.)
8. *Tree and Leaf*, p. 16: ". . . elves are not primarily concerned with us, nor we with them. Our fates are sundered, and our paths seldom meet."
9. Auden, "Good and Evil in *The Lord of the Rings*," p. 5, takes what I think is the erroneous view that elves are sinless, unfallen. Fëanor's theft of the light of the Two Trees was surely a fall, as was the departure of the Noldor from Valinor against the command of the Valar.
10. Auden, "The Quest Hero," p. 57: ". . . while Good can imagine what it would like to be Evil, Evil cannot imagine what it is like to be Good."
11. *The Road Goes Ever On*, p. 60.
12. *Tree and Leaf*, p. 12: Because elves are not supernatural like men, "the road to fairyland is not the road to Heaven; nor even to Hell, I believe." This seems to mean that elves have no immortal souls in the same sense that men do.
13. Appendix F (III, 415): The dwarves' name for their race is

"the Khazad . . . and has been so since Aule gave it to them at their making in the deeps of time." Those living in the Third Age "are the descendants of the Naugrim of the Elder Days, in whose hearts still burns the ancient fire of Aule the Smith . . ." Aule seems to be a Vala who created the first dwarves as the Norse gods created dwarves out of the dead body of Ymir. See note 14 below.

14. *The Elder Eddas and the Younger Eddas*, trans. B. Thorpe and I. A. Blackwell, 1906, p. 270.

15. *The Hobbit*, p. 24.

16. *Tree and Leaf*, p. 39.

17. *Tree and Leaf*, p. 20.

18. *Tree and Leaf*, p. 5.

19. Wilson, "Oo, Those Awful Orcs," pp. 312–14.

20. In *The Adventures of Tom Bombadil*, Tolkien includes a poem subtitled "Frodos Dreme," which is a nightmare of rejection both in the Undying Lands and on Middle-earth. See my discussion in Chapter VII.

CHAPTER VI *Aragorn*

1. Roger Sale, "Tolkien and Frodo Baggins" in *Tolkien and the Critics*, pp. 287–88.

2. William Ready, *The Tolkien Relation* (Chicago: Henry Regnery Co., 1968), p. 101. Reprinted in paperback under the title *Understanding Tolkien* (New York: Coronet Communications, 1969).

CHAPTER VII *Seven Leaves*

1. "Leaf by Niggle" was originally published in *Dublin Review*, 216 (January 1945) and then reprinted in *Tree and Leaf*. Tolkien's Introductory Note to the reprint states that it was "written in the . . . period 1938–39."

2. *Tree and Leaf*, p. 5.

3. "One of its sources was a great-limbed poplar tree which I could see even lying in bed. It was suddenly lopped and mutilated by its owner, I do not know why."

4. Kenneth Sisam's anthology, *Fourteenth Century Verse and Prose* (London: Oxford University Press, 1921) for which Tolkien prepared the Glossary, includes the *Harrowing of Hell* from the York cycle of religious plays and *Noah* from the Towneley cycle. Tolkien obviously knew medieval drama well.

5. *Tree and Leaf*, pp. 61–62.

6. *Tree and Leaf*, p. 62: ". . . a sudden glimpse of the underlying reality or truth." And on p. 60: ". . . a fleeting glimpse of Joy, Joy beyond the walls of the world, poignant as grief."

7. *Tree and Leaf*, p. 52.

8. In *Welsh Review*, IV: 4 (December 1945).

9. Eight English Breton lays are collected in *The Breton Lays in Middle English*, ed. Thomas C. Rumble (Detroit: Wayne State University Press, 1965). And Mortimer J. Donovan analyzes both French and English examples of the type in *The Breton Lay: A Guide to Varieties*, (Notre Dame, Indiana: University of Notre Dame Press, 1969).

10. *Corrigan* does not appear in the *Oxford English Dictionary* or *English Dialect Dictionary*. Both works, however, list *corrie* as a Scottish word meaning "a circular hollow on a mountain side," which in effect is the witch's "hollow dale" in the hills, also referred to as a "bowl" (p. 255). A Corrigan would seem to be a dweller in a corrie.

11. For example, six of the eight lays in Rumble's collection have such endings. The prayer which concludes "Sir Orfew" is especially close to Tolkien's in part of its wording.

12. See *Farmer Giles of Ham* (London: Allen and Unwin, 1949).

13. *Farmer Giles*, p. 7. Geoffrey of Monmouth, *Historia regum Britanniae*, Book II, Chapter 1.

14. Geoffrey of Monmouth, Book V, Chapter 6.

15. Tolkien mentions this king in the notes to line 26 of his edition of *Sir Gawain and the Green Knight* (coedited by E. V. Gordon, London: Oxford University Press, 1925, 1960), as a British leader who fought against the Saxons.

16. In *The Adventures of Tom Bombadil*, the third poem, entitled "Errantry," puts its knightly hero through a series of adven-

tures so ridiculous as to become a parody of the chivalric romance, in the same general class as *Farmer Giles*.

17. "The Homecoming of Beorhtnoth Beorhthelm's Son," *Essays and Studies of the English Association*, New Series 6 (1953), 1–18. Reprinted in *The Tolkien Reader*.

18. See *The Tolkien Reader* (New York: Ballantine Books, 1966).

19. Also indicative of hobbit tastes and ambitions is the widespread fame won by the hobbit hero of "Perry-the-Winkle," in *The Adventures of Tom Bombadil*, by learning from a lonely troll the recipe for "cramsome bread." He becomes "a Baker great" celebrated in song "from the Sea to Bree."

20. See *Smith of Wootton Major* (London: Allen and Unwin, 1967).

21. See *Tree and Leaf*, pp. 12 ff., 33 ff., 49–50. Tolkien repeats the same protests often in *The Lord of the Rings*, e.g., III, 415–16.

22. Very like the Dead Marshes outside Mordor in *The Lord of the Rings*.

23. *Tree and Leaf*, p. 20.

24. The poem was first published in *Time and Tide*, 3 December 1955, and was accompanied by two illustrations from Helen Waddell's *Beasts and Saints* (London: Constable & Co., Ltd., 1934), which excerpts brief episodes of Brendan's voyage from the *Navigatio* Latin mentioned in note 27 below.

25. Foreword to *Navigatio Sancti Brendani Abbatis* in *University of Notre Dame Publications in Medieval Science*, edited by Carl Selmer (Notre Dame, Indiana: University of Notre Dame Press, 1959), XVI, pp. xxi–xxii. Also Geoffrey Ashe, *Land to the West* (New York: Viking Press, 1962), pp. 53–63.

26. Selmer, VII, pp. xxxi–ii.

27. All my references to the *Navigatio* are to J. F. Webb's English translation appearing in *Lives of the Saints* (Baltimore: Penguin Books, 1965). This is based on Selmer's edition of the Latin text mentioned in note 25 above. Webb's footnote, p. 33, reads " 'Meadow of Miracles' (*saltus virtutum*) = 'Cluain Ferta,' Clonfert in Galway."

28. In another early *imram*, *The Voyage of Maildun*, which

Tolkien may or may not have known, the "lovely country beneath the waves" is more fully described than in the *Navigatio*.
See the translation of the Maildun text in Patrick W. Joyce, *Old
Celtic Romances* (New York: Longmans Green and Co., 1914).
29. This passage describing the tree and fallen angels perched on
it in the form of white birds is translated from the Latin in substantially the same words by Helen Waddell in the book from
which the illustrations for Tolkien's poem were taken. (See note
25.) I do not know whether Tolkien knew this little popular miscellany before writing the poem or had anything to do with selecting the illustrations.
30. See "Leaf by Niggle" and *Smith of Wootton Major* in ad-
dition to "On Fairy-stories," where the chief expositions of the
symbol of the Tree are to be found.
31. *The Elder Eddas and the Younger Eddas*, p. 323.
32. See *The Adventures of Tom Bombadil* (London: Allen and
Unwin, 1962).
33. Unless the "marsh of Tode" recalls the Dead Marshes just
north of the boundary of Mordor, where mining pits have been
filled with water and men killed in battle lie on the bottom. Is it
possible, too, that the "Merlock Mountains" are reminiscent of
"the Morlockian horror of factories" alluded to by Tolkien in
"On Fairy-stories," *Tree and Leaf*, p. 57?

Index